Introduction to Anthropology of Integration

Introduction to Anthropology of Integration

A handbook for teachers, educators, and parents

Foreword by
Christine de Marcellus Vollmer

Mark Georges

GRACEWING

First published in England in 2024
by
Gracewing
2 Southern Avenue
Leominster
Herefordshire HR6 0QF
United Kingdom
www.gracewing.co.uk

No part of this publication may be reproduced, stored in a retrieval system, or transmitted in any form or by any means, electronic, mechanical, photocopying, recording or otherwise, without the written permission of the publisher.

The right of Mark Georges to be identified as the author of this work has been asserted in accordance with the Copyright, Designs and Patents Act 1988.

© 2024 Mark Georges

ISBN 978 085244 988 2

Typeset by Gracewing

Cover design by Kevin Reis

To parents, teachers, and educators around the world who love the children entrusted to their care

CONTENTS

Foreword xiii

Acknowledgements xv

Introduction. xvii

Part I: The unity of the human person and the goal of human life 1

1 Levels of being and the existence of the human soul 7
    1.1 The development of the intellect 7
    1.2 The natural apprehension of levels of being in nature 8
    1.3 Levels of being in St. Thomas Aquinas 10
    1.4 The existence of a spiritual principle in the human person 13

2 Man as a unity of body and soul 15
    2.1 Manifestations and implications of body/soul unity 17
    2.2 The three levels of action of the human person .. 18

3 The goal of human life: true happiness 25
    3.1 St. Thomas Aquinas 30
    3.2. Happiness as harmony 32

4 Personal fulfilment through knowledge and action 39
    4.1 Knowledge and human perfection 39

4.2 Personal growth through action 42
4.3. Habits and virtue 44
4.4 Classical notions of virtue 51
4.5 A new approach to virtue in anthropology of integration 57
4.6. The role of example and family life 60
    4.6.1 The perennial value of the traditional family structure ... 63

Part II: The three dimensions of the human person ... 67

5 The biological dimension of the human person ... 75

5.1 Human morphology 75
5.2 Bodily integrity 76
5.3 Natural inclinations on the biological level 80
5.4 Biological inclinations in action: Sense perception and appetites 81
    5.4.1 Sense perception of concrete objects 81
    5.4.2 The duality of sensitive reactions—the sense appetites 84
    5.4.3 The passions 85
    5.4.4 Conditioning 89

6 The emotional-psychological dimension of the human person 93

6.1 Feeling safe or independent "I" 95
6.2 A sense of belonging or "I" valued by another ... 96
6.3 Sense of significance or the "I" valued for a role in a community 97
6.4 Educating emotions 100
    6.4.1 Genetic bias or temperament 100
    6.4.2 Emotional affirmation and regulation in early childhood 104
    6.4.3 Family life, good example, and guidance 106

Contents

    6.4.4 Impact of traumatic experiences on emotional development 109
    6.4.5 Psychological conditions.. 111
  6.5 Emotional/Psychological inclinations in action: Cognition and response 112
    6.5.1 Emotional regulation... 115

7 The spiritual dimension of the human person 123
  7.1 Human intelligence...124
    7.1.1 The practical reason and the principle of *synderesis* 129
  7.2 From inclinations to fundamental values through cognitive integration 132
    7.2.1 Self-preservation and the value of life.................... 139
    7.2.2 The sexual inclination and the value of the family 141
      a. The complementarity of the sexes................................. 143
      b. The integrity of the sexual act 149
    7.2.3 The inclination to truth and society 153
    7.2.4 Conclusion 156
  7.3 The will 157
    7.3.1 True and apparent goods 159
  7.4 The spiritual dimension in action: cognition and response 160
  7.5 The moral conscience 160
    7.5.1 Using and improving conscience............................. 173

Part III: Formative integration 181

8 The virtues for integration related to life 189

9 The virtues for integration related to relationships 195
  9.1 Chastity 195
    9.1.1 Chastity at different stages of development 203

9.2 The virtue of loyalty 228
9.3 The virtue of charity 230
   9.3.1 Charity and human dignity 234
   9.3.2 Cultivating true love 237

10 The virtues for integration related to society 243
10.1 The social dimension of the human person 243
10.2 Justice 249
   10.2.1 Commutative justice 251
   10.2.2 Legal justice 252
   10.2.3 Social justice 253
10.3 Social love 258

11 Character formation as integral development 263
11.1 The Pedagogy of the integration of the human person (PIHP) 270
11.2 *Alive to the World*. A model PIHP programme 272

12 Evil, sin, and disintegration 283

13 Integration and identity 293
13.1 Identity 296

Conclusion 305

FOREWORD

In this wonderful handbook, Father Mark Georges has done a remarkable job of explaining, in easy-to-understand terms, some of the anthropological, philosophical, and pedagogical truths about human learning which have been known for centuries, but which in recent generations of educators had become disconnected.

Education, the passing-on from one generation to the next of cultural, moral, and practical understanding and behaviour—the basis of civilization—has tended, with massification and professionalization, to become distanced from the truly human sciences. Professional and occupational concerns have overtaken the space, and competition, with its examinations and tests, has reduced education to a race for position, and encouraged rote learning and group-thinking.

Our world requires a return to integration, both of education and of the individual. And, like Father Mark, Carlos Beltramo and I considered this our call and challenge, creating a complete K-12 curriculum for classroom use, while developing the *Pedagogy of the Integration of the Human Person (PIHP)* to address these, and many other issues. Since 2000, *Alive to the World* has been a project to help teachers to accompany and encourage children and adolescents to encounter the sterling foundations of human flourishing in their discovery of values and virtues, through original and critical thinking. This K-12 programme, although delivered as a continual story of a group of children as they grow up, has been an effort to reunite for the modern day those anthropological, philosophical, and pedagogical truths described by Father Mark, in a medium efficacious to help fulfil the longing of children and adolescents to find significance and belonging.

Mark Georges has met the challenge of demonstrating a "metaphysical framework for understanding the human person that builds on what is time tested and proven but at the same time giving a new perspective". Indeed, an excellent practical explanation and guide for bringing a universe of wisdom to today's students.

This book will be of great use to all who are occupied with, or interested in, education.

Christine de Marcellus de Vollmer
Founder
Alive to the World International
(www.alivetotheworld.org)
June 2024

ACKNOWLEDGEMENTS

The handbook that you have in your hands was originally conceived as a supplement for teachers and parents to the *Alive to the World* programme developed by Christine Marcellus de Vollmer and her associates. I wish to acknowledge the wonderful work they have done and are doing all over the world in transmitting values and virtues to the next generation.

In addition, I would like to thank the many people who have given their time and support to make this work possible.

INTRODUCTION

This text provides an overview of what is called Anthropology of Integration. The text draws on data from the social sciences and uses many concrete examples, but it is mainly a philosophical work. It builds on a long tradition that places confidence in the natural ability of the human person to know and discover what is good for his or her true happiness and what is contrary to it. In common language this is akin to common sense.[1] This is the proper starting point for philosophical reflection. Philosophical ideas, however, need to be articulated and presented in a coherent system so that they may be properly assimilated, communicated, discussed, and refined. The philosophical tradition of Aristotle and St Thomas Aquinas is rooted in common sense and is a time tested and proven framework for metaphysical reflection. The ideas developed in this book are grounded in the conceptual foundations that are elaborated in this tradition. Philosophy, however, also needs the input of research in science and the humanities to better express the metaphysical principles at work and to connect with the prevailing culture. This work aims to present a metaphysical framework for understanding the human person that builds on what is time-tested and proven but at the same time giving a new perspective. In that sense it articulates a novel vision called Anthropology of Integration which brings to bear the advances in science and psychology. It also draws on the peculiar sensibility of our age to be in harmony with self, things, nature, others, and the transcendent as well.

In its essence, Anthropology of Integration seeks to unpack in a new way, the richness of the simple proposition that the human person is a unity of body and soul. It suggests that there are different dimensions of the human person that need to be carefully differentiated and articulated, and at the same time, there is a unity that must be understood and fostered for our behaviour to be truly human. This perspective, where differences and unity are affirmed at the same time, is what is meant in general by the notion of integration. In this text, this concept is developed in the context of an important metaphysical principle which states that living beings naturally tend to what is good for attaining their full development and purpose. In the human person this tendency is not only in the soul, but in every dimension of his or her being.

Men and women are endowed with freedom. The natural tendencies within his or her being require education and deliberate orientation towards his or her true good. This is the task of Integration. When proper integration is lacking, the tendencies give way to disordered desires for apparent goods that undermine human dignity.

The reader of this introductory book, up to now, may have heard of this new approach to Anthropology only in passing. That is not a surprise because it is not easy to find a systematic presentation entitled Anthropology of Integration. The author of this text was introduced to it through books and articles by Antonio Malo and training material authored by Christine Vollmer, Carlos Beltramo and others for the *Alive to the World* series for teaching values and virtues from Kindergarten to the last year of High School.[2] This programme is being implemented in many countries and has had a phenomenal reception by over a million children worldwide. The appeal of a programme like this, along with its excellent pedagogy, is the underlying anthropology that sustains it, which this book aims to make more easily accessible.

Anthropology of Integration addresses deep gaps in the formation of young people today which is the reason for its importance and for its attractiveness when expounded or incorporated in programmes such as the *Alive to the World* series. A deficiency identified by many authors is the fact that ethics is often perceived by the youth as an external imposition of rules by a body or person invested with authority. While these guidelines may be seen as needed for order and efficiency, the rules and procedures established can seem cold, harsh, and imposing, at odds with something we feel as being natural and liberating.[3] A deeper understanding of the unity of body of soul overcomes this dichotomy by connecting natural impulses and moral judgement in an integrated way.

On a yet deeper level, the perspective adopted in this text centres around human dignity. The goal of integration that is sought incorporates the traditional classification of virtues around the cardinal virtues of prudence, justice, fortitude, and temperance. It also breaks from this model to elaborate on, and to place in the forefront, those virtues that safeguard and promote the dignity of the human person. These are habits such as diligence, loyalty, charity, and generosity, which, in this perspective, are considered as centrepieces of moral life, rather than derivatives of the cardinal virtues.

Introduction to Anthropology of Integration

Considering the challenges facing society today, this approach is particularly relevant. Contemporary society expounds ideals of freedom and opportunities for all, but the harsh reality is that there are persistent issues in many countries, and also on the world scale, which privilege certain classes, races and nations. The moral norms and customs espoused as mainstream may seem to perpetuate an unacceptable status quo for many people. When systemic inequality persists, it becomes paramount to transmit an anthropology that centres on the dignity of the human person. On the side of those who feel marginalized, this focus helps to build the self-confidence and inner strength that is needed to believe in one's natural rights and one's ability to rise above the current situation through dialogue, hard work, and inner conviction, taking advantage of the opportunities that exist. On the side of those who are privileged, effectively linking genuine happiness to its true core in human dignity, will help to create an awareness of the need to reach out to remedy the injustice, treating all with the same respect and consideration.

This handbook is comprised of three parts. After the introduction, the first part discusses the core metaphysical insight of Aristotle at the heart of Anthropology of Integration, which is the understanding of man as a unity of body and soul. The soul is inseparable from the body and at the same time is spiritual in nature. The soul of every human being is created individually and uniquely by God, with the same loving design, nature, and destiny. Along with this foundation we will look at the aim or goal of human life as authentic happiness considered as the harmonious integration of the different dimensions of the human person. The first part ends with an explanation of how the actual attainment of true happiness or fulfilment takes place in concrete action.

In the second part, the body/soul composite in man is looked at in its three dimensions: biological, emotional and spiritual. This part of the book aims to introduce important concepts such as natural inclinations, emotions, values, and virtues from a philosophical perspective, taking into account modern research in medicine, psychology and neuroscience. Integration will be considered in its upward aspect where biological and emotional tendencies lead to the comprehension and acceptance of fundamental goods of human nature in the spiritual faculties. We can call this upward or *cognitive* integration.

Building on the concepts of the previous section, the third part of the book shows how the different dimensions of the human person can be articulated in decision making and concrete action in a way that leads to genuine happiness. Here integration seeks to harmonize human behaviour with fundamental values in a way that is not forced or clumsy, but free and natural. Values imbue and shape the emotional and corporeal dimensions of the human person. In this sense, it can be called downward or *formative* integration. The key virtues that emerge as centrepieces of anthropology of integration are discussed.

The final chapters take up the topic of character formation in the light of the anthropology articulated. Evil and sin are discussed from the perspective of the disintegration of the individual at the core of his or her dignity. Moral evil is revealed as anti-natural as it dehumanizes the human person. The discussion looks at how disordered actions leads to disintegration through vice and brings unhappiness. The practice of virtue, on the other hand, brings integration and leads to happiness. The notion of identity is considered in the last chapter as a consequence of the unity of body and soul that characterizes human nature and, at the same time, fruit of an integrated life.

By way of introduction, it may be useful to consider a scenario in a make-believe universe where aliens are coming to planet earth. They arrive with their spacecrafts and, hovering above the earth in space, they begin to gather information about our planet and the humans that inhabit it. Naturally their technology is eons ahead of ours and so they tap into our servers, cameras, and devices to obtain vast amounts of information about every aspect of human activity all over the world and throughout the centuries of human existence. Seeing the constant violence, strife, corruption, and divisions on all levels and in every place and age, they conclude that humans do not know what is good for their own selves. They resolve that the best option for dealing with humans would be to invade and impose order. Given their advanced technology, their plan is to implant a device in each individual so that in the moment a person sets about to do harm, he or she will be incapacitated to do so and necessarily will have to choose a different permitted course of action. Invasion follows, the plan is executed, and the world is purged of chaos. It becomes safe and ordered with a high standard of living for all using the advanced alien technology. Given this scenario we can ask the following:

1. Are the aliens correct in their judgement that humans do not know what is good for them?

2. Is the world a better place after the imposition of order?

3. Would you welcome an invasion of this sort, or would you resist it? Why?

In answer to the first question, C. S. Lewis wrote:

> Anyone studying Man from the outside as we study electricity or cabbages, not knowing our language and consequently not able to get any inside knowledge from us, but merely observing what we did, would never get the slightest evidence that we had a moral law. How could he? For his observations would only show what we did, and the moral law is about what we ought to do.[4]

Despite their advanced technology, it seems that the aliens fell short in limiting their study to the question of whether or not humans did what may be considered scientifically beneficial to them. When we penetrate into the inner dimension of the human person, we discover that he is free. This freedom is expressed in the action of the intelligence that is able to deliberate over possible ways to act in a given context, and the power of the will to execute one of these. A boy, for example, might be afraid to tell his parents that he failed an exam, because he feels sure that he would be scolded. He knows that he should tell them the truth. He can also consider other options, such as lying about his grade, making up false excuses for why he failed or saying that the exam was postponed. Because he is free, he can choose to act out one of these other options. This does not mean, however, that he did not know what was the right thing to do. If he told the truth, even though he may be punished, the boy would be acting in accord with justice and showing that he trusts his parents. By overcoming his fear of being punished, he becomes a more courageous person, and he reinforces the good habit of being just. The bond of trust between him and his parents is also affirmed. All this makes him a better person. Knowing what is good, the human person can freely choose it and grow as a person. He or she can also reject what is good in favour of an "apparent good" at the service of selfish pursuits and pleasures that are destructive and degrading.

Turning to the second question, one may have the impression that a safe, well-organized world with high living standards for all is much better than the present state of affairs on the planet. But are we better off if there is no freedom? When I choose to do good because I want to, isn't that much more human than doing good because I am forced to? You may say perhaps: "I freely choose that restriction, so I don't feel forced", but are we justified in having it imposed on everyone?

The third question is left for each lector to consider on his or her own.

The anthropology outlined in this booklet centres on self-realization as the fruit of free choice. It shows that the discovery and discernment of the way to true happiness is born of an interior impulse that involves the whole person. The moral law is not something that is imposed but rather something every person has access to and is drawn towards in the natural unfolding of human behaviour. St. Thomas Aquinas defined the natural moral law as *participatio legis aeternae in rationali creatura*, a participation of the rational creature in the divine law.[5]

Introduction

He uses the term *natural*, which highlights that the impulse to know and the grasping of the moral law is the result of a natural process that needs to be cultivated and matured. In the end, one does not have the sense of following an imposed rule, but rather of self-realization in love for God and others. Jutta Burgraff makes this observation in her book *Made for Freedom*, referring to St Thomas Aquinas: "It's impossible," she writes, "to do things one considers absurd or harmful, at least for an extended period of time, without encountering difficulty. This principle also applies to the practice of religion. St. Thomas prudently notes: 'One who avoids doing evil, not because it is evil, but because it is a command of the Lord, is not free. On the contrary, he who avoids the evil because it is evil, he is free … He is not free in the sense that he is not subject to God's law, but because his interior dynamism leads him to do what the divine law prescribes'".[6]

A second core feature of the anthropology outlined here is the aspect of integration. A simple analogy can help to illustrate its importance. A vessel such as a boat, for example, needs a good engine if it is to go anywhere. In anthropology, this would be the emotions. Without desire or drive, a person can hardly "get going" to accomplish anything. They may get a push from the outside and manage on inertia for a while but then their activity quickly grinds to a halt if there is no desire. A well-tuned engine, however, is not enough for a vessel to be useful. There needs to be a braking system and a navigation system. Without this, the boat will just head in the direction it happens to be pointing in or where the wind and waves happen to nudge it[7]. The outcome would be to get lost or crash. The engine, the braking system and the navigation system, when they all properly function, enables an integrated action that makes the vessel useful. In our anthropology, if the engine is the emotions, the braking system and navigation system refer to the intelligence and will which give direction to our actions. As with the boat, the emotions together with the powers of intelligence and will, when they work together properly, enables an integrated action that makes self-realization possible.

It was affirmed earlier that the philosophy of man that this document outlines is rooted in what can be called implicit philosophy. During his pontificate, John Paul II wrote an important document for our times entitled *Fides et Ratio* where he took up the theme of the relationship between faith and reason. He acknowledged the important contribution that philosophy has for shaping culture, and in that discussion points towards an *implicit philosophy*. This expression is used in this text in the sense that it was outlined there. The Holy Father wrote:

> Although times change and knowledge increases, it is possible to discern a core of philosophical insight within the history of thought as a whole. Consider, for example, the principles of non-contradiction, finality, and causality, as well as the concept of the person as a free and intelligent subject, with the capacity to know God, truth, and goodness. Consider as well, certain fundamental moral norms which are shared by all. These are among the indications that, beyond different schools of thought, there exists a body of knowledge that may be judged a kind of spiritual heritage of humanity. It is as if we had come upon an

implicit philosophy, as a result of which all feel that they possess these principles, albeit in a general and unreflective way. Precisely because they are shared in some measure by all, this knowledge should serve as a kind of reference-point for the different philosophical schools. Once reason successfully intuits and formulates the first universal principles of being and correctly draws from them conclusions which are coherent both logically and ethically, then it may be called right reason or, as the ancients called it, *orthós logos, recta ratio*.[8]

In this work we have connected implicit philosophy with the Aristotelian-Thomistic tradition. The text above shows that there is a broader understanding of the term as well, which is important to Anthropology of Integration. This broader understanding refers to what is popularly called "common sense". It is a knowledge that does not have to do with any particular brilliance but simply the proper functioning of the intellect in grasping universal truths accessible to all. Even though profound metaphysical concepts will be used in elaborating on an integrative approach to man, this anthropology is proposed as a rational development of what is intuitive, natural, and accessible to all when there is a minimum of interior freedom and proper education in values and virtues. In one of his writings Chesterton considers the question of whether jury duty should be taken away from the common man and given to experts. He convincingly shows how western civilization stands on implicit philosophy in entrusting serious crime cases to a selection of common men. "Our civilization has decided, and very justly decided," he writes, "that determining the guilt or innocence of men is a thing too important to be trusted to trained men." Better that this "awful matter" be left to those "who know no more law than I know, but who can feel the things that I felt in the jury box."⁹

We all have the experience of how simple and "uneducated" people can be wise and mature in their decision-making and choices, perhaps without arriving at them from a rigorous process of reasoning. Anthropology of Integration aims to give a metaphysical grounding to this reality, providing a tool to safeguard and affirm the broad sense of implicit philosophy in our age.

Notes

1. Mariano Artigas, *Introduction to Philosophy* (Manila: Sinag-Tala Publishers, Inc., 1990), 31.
2. "Alive to the World," Alive to the World, accessed November 15, 2023, https://alivetotheworld.org/en/.
3. Gertrude E. M. Anscombe, *Human Life, Action and Ethics*, ed. Mary Geach and Luke Gormally (Exeter: Imprint Academic, 2005), 169; Alasdair MacIntyre, *After Virtue: A Study in Moral Theory*, 3rd ed (Notre Dame, IN: University of Notre Dame Press, 2007), 10; Servais Pinckaers, *The Sources of Christian Ethics* (Washington, D.C: Catholic University of America Press, 1995), 327.
4. Clive S. Lewis, *Mere Christianity*, ed. Kathleen Norris (San Francisco: HarperOne, 2015), 23.
5. Thomas Aquinas, *The Summa Theologica of St. Thomas Aquinas*, English Dominican Province Translation edition (New York: Christian Classics, 1981) I-II, q. 91 a. 2.
6. Jutta Burggraf, *Made for Freedom* (New York: Scepter Publishers, 2012), 67.
7. Later it will be shown that this example falls short because the

emotions include the natural inclinations which do not point in an arbitrary direction. They are powerful tendencies that lead to the comprehension of what is good for the human person, the direction to which the vessel should go.

8. John Paul II, *Fides et Ratio*, 4.
9. G. K. Chesterton, *Tremendous Trifles* (California: CreateSpace Independent Publishing Platform, 2018), 42.

Part I
The unity of the human person and the goal of human life

Before launching into our exposition, it is useful to state anew, that while this text draws on data from the social sciences and uses many concrete examples, it is mainly a philosophical work. The term "anthropology" that is used in the title of the book, when used in the social sciences, refers to the study of man, what all persons are like and what they have in common. In this context, anthropology looks at the physical characteristics of human beings, their origin, their environment, their social relations and culture and other aspects of human experience. In this book, the term "anthropology" refers principally to philosophical anthropology. Like the science of anthropology, its object is the study of man. As a philosophical discipline, however, the approach is quite different. Man is considered from the perspective of metaphysics, that is, the ultimate causes of his being and nature.[1] In this work we will focus on deeper questions about the human person, such as his or her body/soul unity, the nature of freedom and what is the goal of human life. A new perspective is presented, taking into account the concepts and advances in the natural sciences of anthropology, psychology and neuroscience.

Among the many developments in the human sciences, the notion of integration, in particular, that is present in recent research in these fields, will be developed from a philosophical perspective. Daniel Siegel, for example, places the notion of integration at the centre of his interdisciplinary research on human behaviour. He explains the importance of neural integration—the linkages among differentiated aspects of the brain—for enhancing human relationships.[2] Kenneth Burrett and Timothy Rusnak with other researchers developed a model for character education in the 90's which they defined as an "integrated approach". They upheld that the goals of Integrated Character Education are to fulfil personal development goals such as physical and psychological health, positive self-concept, interpersonal skills, and responsibility and caring, and social goals such as upholding the social system, belief systems, and intellectual traditions and preserving the physical environment.[3] Along these lines, Carlos Beltramo from the University of Navarra has proposed a pedagogy for character formation centred on the concept of integration. It is called Pedagogy of the Integration of the Human Person. In a document published by the Instituto Cultura y Sociedad (ICS) of the University of Navarra, he explains: "it proposes the practical conditions so that learners, through specific actions, attain an increase in their own integration. Every pedagogical activity that the student manages to perform satisfactorily reveals a certain degree of integration and leads to a growth of that integration, this being the properly pedagogical and operational function of integration".[4] The teaching methodology proposed by Carlos Beltramo has been implemented in a programme for character building called Alive to the World which was mentioned before. The founder, Christine de Marcellus Vollmer, was kind enough to write the foreword for this book. It is now in eight languages, 24 countries and reaches over 1 million children worldwide. The programme has proven effectiveness and shows that the focus on integration is well aimed.[5]

In the introduction we used the analogy of an operations centre for navigation and control to explain the intelligence and will. While this analogy is useful, it applies only in a limited way. The spiritual faculties and the emotions are conceived in this analogy as disjointed and separate. In fact, they form a single unitary reality. This section looks at the unity in the human person, leaning on important philosophical insights from the Aristotelian/Thomistic tradition.

Notes

1. Artigas, *Introduction to Philosophy*, 41.
2. Daniel J. Siegel, *Mindsight* (New York: Bantam, 2010), xii.
3. Kenneth Burrett and Timothy Rusnak, *Integrated Character Education* (Arlington, VA: Phi Delta Kappa Educational Foundation, 1993), 8.
4. Carlos Beltramo, "Marco Teórico Del Proyecto Educación de La Afectividad y La Sexualidad Humana" (Instituto Cultura y Sociedad (ICS), Universidad de Navarra, Pamplona, 2018), 58, https://www.unav.edu/documents/2832169/19134947/modelo-pedagogico.pdf.
5. "Alive to the World."

1 LEVELS OF BEING AND THE EXISTENCE OF THE HUMAN SOUL

1.1 The development of the intellect

When a child comes into the world, the external senses are developed along with the basic human instincts. The intelligence however, as St. Thomas Aquinas affirms, is *tamquam tabula rasa*, like a clean writing surface.[1] We are all aware that curiosity is a basic drive that characterizes a healthy human being. It begins in infancy when a child begins to play with objects in its environment and to exhibit more and more sophisticated mental operations regarding those objects. It never fails to catch our attention how a small child, hardly three years old, is captivated with a bird or squirrel or lizard. Playing freely in a field, they see it as a place of discovery, adventure, and fantasy—a huge amusement park given to them by a powerful father.

How a child's mental operations develop has been extensively studied by the psychologist Jean Piaget. Initially a child performs operations that are focused on the concrete, specific or here and now. With the help of a nurturing adult, the capacity for objectivity in thought grows and the mind naturally begins to understand the conservation of things beyond changes in their attributes.[2] In philosophy, this power is called simple apprehension, and with it the intellect begins to develop. It is called apprehension because it takes hold of or grasps things mentally. The word "simple" is used because the intellect takes things in simply, without affirming or denying anything about it.

1.2 The natural apprehension of levels of being in nature

Through simple apprehension, a child knows that there are different levels of being in the universe. There is the world of non-living things—rocks, minerals, artefacts and so forth—and the world of living things. In the world of living things there are creatures who are special—Mom and Dad in the first place and then other human beings. The apprehension of this distinction is not immediate. At two years old, a child is already aware of self and is able to choose based on cognition on the sense and emotional level. The more advanced cognitive functions of grasping and manipulating concepts appears later at 4 or 5 years old.[3] At this age, children are fond of pretending to be different things in the natural world. They can act out being a seedling growing into a tree, a bird flying or a dog barking. This ability makes them compassionate towards living things in the world around them. As they interact with their peers they learn to evaluate the assertions and beliefs of others, whether they are true or imaginative and can do this with their own ideas as well.[4] In this way they come to understand that humans are different from other creatures in the universe—they communicate using language, they can cooperate together to build things and give each other instructions on how to do things or to play a game. As children grow older, working in pairs and small groups they are able to learn to be cognizant of others and respect their thought processes, just as much as they respect their own.[5] Parents can help their children to formulate this intuition in clear language in what is known as the golden rule: *Do unto others as you would have them do unto you*. Through the natural process of the development of the mind and education received from parents and other adults, children come to understand in a natural way that humans are on a higher level of being than other things. It is interesting to note that the book of *Genesis* brings this out very clearly in the early chapters where Adam found himself alone in the Garden of Eden, the perfect natural environment. He knew himself of a higher order than all the creatures God had created because of his spiritual nature. Only when Eve was created did he discover a creature who was his equal and with whom he could share his life.

Children see the world as a huge playground, and as their intelligence begins to mature, they appreciate that for something to happen, there must be something else, either on the inside or the outside that makes it happen. All parents know that there was a stage in the lives of their children when they ask "why" for everything—especially the brighter ones. Just as everything they have comes from their parents, children naturally appreciate that the world around them must come also from a powerful father whom we cannot see. Good parents will orient their children at this stage, providing religious education in keeping with the traditions that they subscribe to. Children will learn about this heritage and naturally tune into the world of the spirit, understanding that there is a spiritual part to their own selves and that this is what is most important.

Thinking about one's own understanding of the world around, it is not difficult to relate to the process described above in general terms. It is common experience to comprehend different levels of being in nature.

1.3 Levels of being in St. Thomas Aquinas

Great thinkers who have built on what John Paul II calls "implicit philosophy", have had a special acuteness to express philosophically that which, in reality, occurs naturally. An important example of this are the levels of being that St. Thomas Aquinas identifies in nature. He saw that as we go from minerals to the spiritual realm there are different levels of being in the things we encounter. We can identify the following hierarchy in being going from lower to higher levels:

Minerals → Plants → Animals → Humans → Purely spiritual beings → Divine being

At each leap to a higher level, the natural things encountered have a greater ability to impact on their surroundings. Aristotle used the term "potency of acting" to refer to the power a thing has to act externally on its surroundings, or internally on its own self, in order to bring about its own perfection.[6] At the level of minerals, things are made up mostly of potential in that they are part of various processes where they are being modified or being changed into something else by their environment. What's more they are hardly ever encountered in their pure form. Their power to act is very small and so their unity is weak. In this state of flux it is difficult for us to know exactly what something is at any given point at this level. The early Greek philosopher Heraclitus famously stated that you never step into the same river twice.

At the level of plants, there are stronger active powers. Plants put down roots and some plants grow into majestic trees that not even a hurricane can uproot. The phenomenon of life appears. Beings encountered here have autonomous activity aimed at their own perfection. The activity of plants unfolds in such a way as to become fully-grown and reproduce. The next level up comes animals. Some species of plants exhibit behaviour that may seem animal-like, but we have botanists to help us determine if they are plants or not in these cases. Animals display a stronger unity in that they move and can acquire information about their environment through their senses of sight, taste, touch, smell, and hearing. They seek out their food or prey and are guided by a well-defined and at times sophisticated instinct in interacting with their environment. Animals exhibit the famous GRIMNER acronym: Growth, Respiration, Instinct, Movement, Nourishment, Excretion and Reproduction.

The next step up comes human beings. Whereas from plant to animal the limit can be blurred, this does not happen in the leap to human beings. Something radically new appears. Humans are capable of abstract thought, language, and free action. The intelligence and will appear along with an awareness of self. These are spiritual powers, as we will discuss more at length further on. Man, at the same time, has a body in many ways like that of the animals. The next step up is to suppose that there are creatures who are purely spiritual. These would be the Angels. Finally, there is another great leap to the one who is the source and origin of all that exists and who sustains them in being. This is God.

We have taken time to go through the exercise above because it is natural for us to see the world in this way with an honest, unprejudiced look. In other words, it is just common sense. The reader is free to have a different perspective but is invited to observe, not himself or herself, but the people around him or her and to see if this is not the natural way their minds perceive reality.

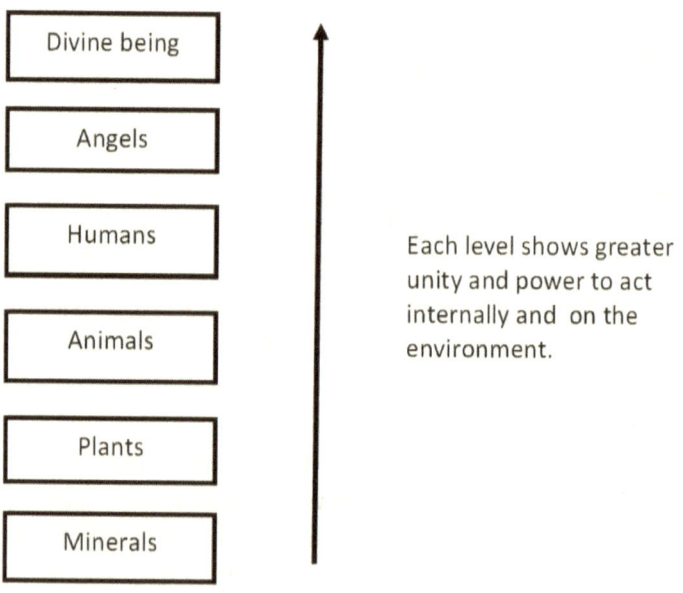

Figure 1.1 Levels of being in nature

1.4 The existence of a spiritual principle in the human person

For the sake of argument, we can present here a few points to illustrate the spiritual dimension of the human person. In the first place, it can be shown that the transmission of meaning in language is impossible without admitting such a dimension. Take, for example, the case of a symbol such as "dog" that is entered into a machine. The machine is asked to say what a dog does. It outputs "barks", "wags its tail", "sleeps", etc. Suppose our machine has a person inside who only understands Chinese. If he follows the computer instructions written in Chinese to answer "what does a dog do?", he will give a correct answer without understanding a single word. In the end he will have regurgitated what was indexed in a table somewhere and that's it. There is no difference even if we make our machine a biochemical one. Changes in the biochemical states of our new machine does not give an understanding of what a dog is, but just a new state that is linked to being presented with the word "dog". Humans, in fact, can pretend to be machines and we immediately know that we have no understanding nor free will but act by following instructions blindly.

There are other realities that we live out every day as well that show man's spiritual side. For example, we hold people responsible for their actions. If my behaviour could be reduced to a physical/chemical process, then I could hardly be held responsible for it. We deal very differently with animals. When a dog bites you, who is responsible? Can you press charges on a dog and demand compensation? You will rather look to see if the owner was neglectful in not having his or her pet restrained. Perhaps it was my fault because I got too close or was teasing the animal.

Another important point is the fact that humans have only been able to thrive when they uphold certain values such as life and family that are regarded as universal, immutable, and obligatory. Historical analysis has shown that when these values are not upheld, civilizations or cultures surely collapse. Such characteristics can only be meaningful if man has a spiritual soul and can thus transcend himself in knowing what is universally good. To know something that has always applied in the past and will always apply in the future is only possible if man has the ability to grasp things that are beyond the here and now and this is precisely what it means to have a spiritual dimension.

Notes

1. St Thomas Aquinas, *Summa Theologiae*, I–II, q. 79 a. 3.
2. R. S. Siegler et al., *How Children Develop*, Fifth edition (New York, NY: Worth Publishers, 2017), 151.
3. Philippe Rochat, "Five Levels of Self-Awareness as They Unfold Early in Life," *Consciousness and Cognition* 12, no. 4 (2003): 727.
4. Rochat, 727.
5. Elizabeth Whitman, "The Impact of Social Play on Young Children," *Integrated Studies* 94 (2018): 11.
6. Aristotle, *The Metaphysics*, trans. Hugh Lawson-Tancred (London: Penguin Classics, 1999), Bekker number 1049b.

2 MAN AS A UNITY OF BODY AND SOUL

Once we have an appreciation that man exhibits spiritual functions, we are in a position to understand how great minds, grounded in implicit philosophy, have articulated this aspect of the human person using precise philosophical terminology. More specifically, we will base our discussion on the writings of Aristotle and St Thomas Aquinas whose works on this topic are timeless points of reference. Just as we can speak about a life principle as a principle of operations in animals that minerals do not have, in man there is a spiritual dynamism that is the principle of the spiritual operations of man. These operations are fundamentally the Intellect and the Will. With these also comes an awareness of self as a Person. The spiritual dynamism in man is not an angelic one, but a human one and it is called the soul. In the second part of the first part of the Summa, St Thomas presents a thorough philosophical study of the human soul and its operations. The intricacies of this study are beyond the scope of this handbook. At this point we can emphasize two points:

1. The human soul has a spiritual nature, transcending time and space with the operations of the intellect and will.
2. Man does not have two souls, a spiritual soul for spiritual operations and an animal soul for his bodily operations. There is one life principle in

man for all his operations, both spiritual and bodily, and this is what we call the human soul. Using terminology from Aristotle: *The body and soul are united in such a way that the soul is per se the form of the body.*

Here it helps to briefly explain the meaning of the term "form" that Aristotle developed. The "form" of a dog for example, is like the mould from which all dogs are made. This may sound silly at first, but Aristotle is not referring to a physical mould but to the type of life principle that underlies the active powers of a dog like barking, tail wagging, seeking food, moving in packs, morphology, etc., that are observable to the senses. Science enables us to detect other active powers on a deeper biological and molecular level that further help us to understand the fundamental dynamisms of this type of life principle, in our case of a dog—not any specific dog but of all dogs, past, present and future. Extending the analogy of the mould, new dogs are formed by uniting the mould or form with a suitable material or matter. The matter takes the form of the mould and is inseparable from it once it dries. Yet we can make a distinction between the matter and the form it has received.

Returning to the definition above, we can say that while we can distinguish clearly between the body and soul, in each individual human being they cannot be separated but are united in a single reality. The rational soul is a single principle of life, and from it the body receives all movement, life, and sensation. A synthesis of this reality is presented in the Catechism of the Catholic Church as follows: "The unity of soul and body is so profound that one has to consider the soul to be the "form" of the body: i.e., it is because of its spiritual soul that the body made of matter becomes a living, human body; spirit and matter, in man, are not two natures united, but rather their union forms a single nature."[1]

2.1 Manifestations and implications of body/soul unity

When we understand the soul as the form of the body, it becomes clear that while the soul cannot be reduced to physical/chemical processes, neither can the body be considered as a mere instrument of the soul. We are not a soul inside a body like a pilot in an aircraft for example. Ordinary experience shows that we deal with our body as part of our very selves. When someone touches your hand, you say they touched me. When someone points at you they are not pointing to your body but to you. As they point, they may call your name saying: "there is so-and-so". Our awareness of self, that self to which our name refers, pertains to the substantial unity and not to the soul alone or the body alone. The case of a pilot and a plane is quite different. Let us assume that we are speaking of commercial aircrafts. When we point to a plane, we can hardly say that we are always pointing to the same pilot. A plane and a pilot do not form a substantial unity as is the case with the body/soul composite of human subjects. Planes can have different pilots and vice versa. This, however, is not possible with bodies and souls.

Going back to St Thomas Aquinas, the body and soul unity is so profound that there is hardly any operation in man where both the spiritual and bodily dimensions are not implicated together. The means by which the intelligence acquires and manipulates concepts for example, is through images that are provided through the external and internal senses of the body. When persons suffer from mental illnesses, the spiritual function is intact but the malfunction of conduits in the brain impedes the correct generation of the images that the intelligence needs. In ordinary experience, when one is tired or sick, it is hard to think straight. Here again, due to fatigue in the brain, the images needed for thought are not effectively produced. Hence the importance of mental health and managing stress for proper reasoning. The Will too must be aligned with the body. By its very nature it seeks what will make the Self happy; but the Self, as noted above, belongs to the substantial unity of body and soul. It follows that the operations of the Will, though spiritual, are related to the body at all times. When the body is tired and worn out, the power of the will to exercise control over the body is diminished. People are more irritable and impatient in those conditions and may yield more easily to saying hurtful things for example, and to intemperance in food and drink. Such behaviour is harmful to self and others.

Confirming the unity of body and soul, medicine is increasingly aware that stress from work, relationships, and guilt, for example, is an important factor in some illnesses.[2]

2.2 The three levels of action of the human person

Up to this point, for the most part, we have been considering the human person in two aspects, body and soul. Given the unity of body and soul, it is not surprising that a great deal of human experience is in part physiological as well as spiritual at the same time. These experiences are called emotions. In the second book of the Rhetoric, Aristotle presented a systematic account of various emotions. He showed how emotions are important for influencing the judgements of others to do what is good and true.[3] His model for analysing the psychological structure of emotions centres around a cognitive element where "there is an unpremeditated evaluation (belief or phantasy) that something positive or negative happens or may happen to the subject or to someone else in a way which concerns the subject".[4] Then there is the affective element where the subject experiences a pleasant or unpleasant feeling about the content of the evaluation.

Aristotle did not develop a systematic taxonomy of emotions. In the rhetoric he analyses emotions such as anger, confidence, friendliness, shame, pity, indignation, and envy. He ended his discourse stating again his purpose: to outline the means by which several emotions may be produced or dissipated for presenting persuasive arguments for right judgement.[5] While emotions are discussed with the practical purpose of persuasion in mind in the *Rhetoric*, he revisits emotions in his discourse on virtue. Virtue is a state of character lying in a middle point between two extremes. He applies this to the emotions as well, so that virtue includes having the right feeling, and this is part of leading a good life.[6]

Aristotle is a milestone for the tripartite understanding of human actions as spiritual, emotional, and physiological. Emotions have been given more or less importance in different philosophical schools following on Aristotle. The Stoics, for example, developed a therapy aimed at *apatheia*, the extirpation of emotions. They considered them to be irrational movements that should have little importance for good citizenship. The stoics divided emotions into four basic types, depending on whether the object was regarded as a present or future good or a present or future evil. For a present good, the emotion is a type of pleasure. For a present evil it is some form of distress. When the good is a future one, the subject feels a type of desire and when the subject is presented with a future evil, he or she feels a form of fear. This fourfold classification of emotions was used well into the middle ages and beyond, although the Stoic understanding of emotions, as such, did not garner followers.[7]

In the thirteenth century, St. Thomas Aquinas synthesized the most important intellectual works up to his time, giving also a new perspective. In moral philosophy he developed the notion of natural law. It is a law that is naturally grasped regarding the fundamental goods of human nature. He brought to the fore a new function of the movements of the appetites called natural inclinations. They are powerful tendencies that lead to the apprehension by the intellect of fundamental goods related to the end of man. The principal inclinations are the inclination to survival, the sexual inclination, and the inclination to know the truth about God and live in society.[8] The angelic doctor did not say that inclinations are emotions. They are present in all aspects of human nature. He clearly states, however, that the inclinations of the concupiscible and irascible parts of human nature, in so far as they are ruled by reason, belong to the natural law.[9] These parts are the origins of emotions. As a result, emotions have an important function of illuminating the natural law and helping an individual to live according to the natural law, when they are properly ordered.

In 1872, Charles Darwin published *The Expression of the Emotions in Man and Animals*. He regarded emotions as mental states that cause stereotypic bodily expressions. This work ushered in a resurgence of interest and research on emotions. There are two main competing perspectives that essentially define the modern psychological approach to emotions. The "appraisal approach" is based on the notion that thinking and mental activities are responsible for emotions. It rests on the assumption that emotions are intentional states. They refer to an object or situation in the world and the meaning ascribed to the event makes an emotion a particular kind of emotion. A different perspective is developed in the "basic emotion" approach. Basic emotion models are based on the notion that responses from the body are what create emotions. Objects and events in the world biologically trigger emotions in an automatic way. Instances of emotions that bear the same name—for example, fear—show the same pattern of behaviour, bodily activation and facial actions so that people around the world can easily and effortlessly recognize the emotion.[10] In humanistic psychology, core emotions have been identified that powerfully influence choice such as the drive to feel safe, the desire for a sense of belonging and the desire for significance.[11]

Emotions will be discussed in detail in chapter 6 of this book. This preliminary discussion is meant to expand on the body/soul unity conception of the human person, introducing the element of emotions. Human action can thus be considered on three levels: the spiritual, the psychological and the biological levels. This is illustrated in the diagram below:

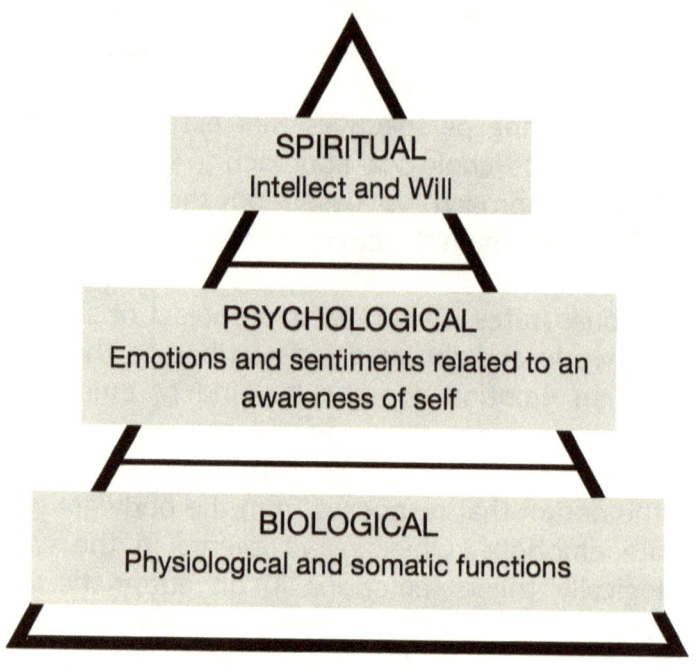

Figure 2.1 Levels of action of the human person.[12]

The activities of the spiritual level are those that we do with our intelligence and will. On this level we reflect, do introspection, relate and connect concepts, and decide to take an action, or not.

The psychological level is an intermediate one that spans the sentiments, the passions, and the emotional states.

On the biological level, actions have a corporal manifestation. Some are involuntary such as reflex actions, the beating of our heart, respiration etc.

The three levels of human action ought to be clearly differentiated. At the same time, it should be affirmed that their proper end is unitary action for the good of the whole person. This process, whereby the different levels interact and are coordinated to produce unitary action for the overall good of the person is the main concern of this book. It is called Integration.

Notes

1. *Catechism of the Catholic Church*, 2nd edition (Washington, D.C.: USCCB, 2019), para. 365.
2. Saundra Montijo, "How Stress Affects You Physically," Psych Central, November 2, 2021, https://psychcentral.com/stress/the-physical-effects-of-long-term-stress.
3. Aristotle, *On Rhetoric: A Theory of Civic Discourse*, trans. George A. Kennedy (New York: Oxford University Press, 1991), bk. II ch. 1.
4. Simo Knuuttila, "Medieval Theories of the Emotions," in *The Stanford Encyclopedia of Philosophy*, ed. Edward N. Zalta (Metaphysics Research Lab, Stanford University, 2018), sec. 1, https://plato.stanford.edu/archives/sum2018/entries/medieval-emotions/.
5. Aristotle, *On Rhetoric*, bk. II chapters 2–11.
6. Aristotle, *The Nicomachean Ethics*, ed. Lesley Brown, trans. David Ross, New edition (Oxford; New York: Oxford University Press, 2009), bk. II ch. 3.

7. Knuuttila, "Medieval Theories of the Emotions," sec. 1.
8. St Thomas Aquinas, *Summa Theologiae*, I–II q. 94.
9. *Ibid.*, I–II q. 94. a. 2. Reply 2.
10. Maria Gendron and Lisa Feldman Barrett, "Reconstructing the Past: A Century of Ideas About Emotion in Psychology," *Emotion Review* 1, no. 4 (2009): 316–20.
11. Saul Mcleod, "Maslow's Hierarchy of Needs," *Simply Psychology* 1 (2007): 1–5.
12. © Alianza Latinoamericana para la Familia (ALAFA) 2021. Reproduced with permission.

3 THE GOAL OF HUMAN LIFE: TRUE HAPPINESS

If someone were to ask you, do you want to be happy? Most surely you would say "yes" without much hesitation. If you were asked "Does everyone want to be happy?" It may not be so easy to answer. To begin with there is so much evil in the world. So many people seem trapped in a logic of addictions, arrogance, violence, revenge, and envy. It's hard to see how any of these things can bring happiness and yet we must affirm that, just like us, everyone wants to be happy. Benedict XVI repeatedly pointed out that our age suffers from a crisis of reason. We no longer accept that we can know the truth but affirm in our arrogance that we are the architects of it. What does this have to do with happiness? This crisis impacts directly on how we interpret the word "happiness". I think that what makes me happy has to do with the lifestyle I choose and am comfortable with. Once I don't impinge on the freedom of others, who are you to tell me that I may not be truly happy?

From the perspective of the anthropology presented here, there is a valid and important subjective dimension to happiness where true happiness is experienced as a personal choice that we are very pleased about. At the same time, we are invited to consider and evaluate the motives and forces behind our choices. Anthropology of integration identifies two scenarios:

In the first, our choices may flow from a built-up store of patterns of behaviour and thought, arising from our experiences and decisions throughout our lives, where all the dimensions of the human person are harmoniously integrated.

In the second, they may flow from a built-up store of patterns of behaviour and thought, arising from our experiences and decisions throughout our lives, where the dimensions of the human person are not harmoniously integrated but oppose and destroy each other.

The internal tearing apart of the human person in the depth of his or her being is a source of unhappiness, even though a subject may choose to ignore it. In this way we can affirm that a person may say they are happy, but with a closer look we can see that they are not. Similarly, a person who I may think is unhappy because they seem externally constrained to me, can actually be much happier than I am. (My perception is tainted from disintegration).

Consider the case of a businessman who travels from time to time to a far away land for work. He is married and has three small children. In this distant country he lives out an affair with another woman who affirms him and makes him feel special, something he feels he is lacking from his wife. This individual is savvy and manages to perfectly cover his tracks. He has a double life and if you ask him, he will say that he is quite happy pulling this off. It may well be that some of his colleagues are doing the same, so he does not see it as abnormal. Would you agree that this person is truly happy? Is there not something wrong with that kind of happiness? The reader is invited to put himself or herself in the shoes of the spouse of this person who is faithful and who has to make innumerable sacrifices every day to care for the children, even more so, when the husband is away with another woman. Is this fair? Is it correct for a man to be unfaithful and for the woman to bear the brunt of carrying the family forward?

Anthropology of Integration recognizes that a businessman in such circumstances may say that he is happy, but this claim has to be tested to see if it flows from a truly human core. In this scenario, the person is divided. He is one way at home and another way abroad. His choices flow from interior disintegration that undermines human dignity and so we can affirm that this is not a truly human happiness.

Another situation that one can consider, is that of a woman who, after several years of marriage, discovers that her husband has a degenerative nerve disease. They have young children, and she is now in a situation where she must care for the children and accompany her spouse through his illness. Managing degenerative nerve diseases is very complicated, both medically and psychologically, not to mention the costs that are involved. A young attractive lady who finds herself in such a situation will have to muster great, if not heroic, interior strength, to keep positive and find meaning in the apparent misfortune. She may come to see it, for, example, as tremendously enriching, because it challenges her to be more humble, to be more understanding to others, and to be a much better person and friend to those close to her. This deepening of interior harmony and strengthening of relationships can be a source of great joy that is not immediately perceptible seeing the external circumstance alone. A superficial person, hearing of the predicament of a woman with young children and a husband with such a complicated ailment, may think that she must be sad. How can she be happy with no time for herself, economic hardship and stress? Yet we find persons in such circumstances who are truly happy. What is more, we admire them and have them as our models for strength and the greatness of the human spirit. The reader can think, at this time, of persons he or she admires. Are they persons who have had an easy life? Or rather, are they not persons who have made great sacrifices for a noble ideal, for love of others and country? Perhaps it is the person who judges that such people have to be sad, is the one whom happiness is eluding without recognizing it.

True happiness hinges on the harmonious integration of all the dimensions of the human person. This perspective connects with the teachings of the ancient philosophers who placed the practice of virtue (*arete*) at the core of happiness (*eudaimonia*).

Speaking of happiness Aristotle used the image of a harp. Happiness consists in the human powers being played in a perfect harmony as a master musician plays a harp or like an orchestra in perfect unison. For Aristotle, this consists in living a virtuous life. For the sake of reference, it is worthwhile to quote here an important passage from Aristotle's Ethics that brings together his thought on happiness:

> We state the function of man to be a certain kind of life, and this to be an activity or actions of the soul implying a rational principle, and the function of a good man to be the good and noble performance of these, and if any action is well performed when it is performed in accordance with the appropriate excellence: If this is the case, human good

turns out to be activity of soul in accordance with virtue, and if there is more than one virtue, in accordance with the best and most complete.[1]

In the *Rhetoric*, he gives a synopsis of what these virtues are, enumerating and describing them briefly:

> The parts or subdivisions of virtue are justice, courage, self-control, magnificence, magnanimity, liberality, gentleness, prudence, and wisdom. Since virtue is defined as an ability for doing good, the greatest virtues are necessarily those most useful to others. For that reason people most honour the just and the courageous; for the latter is useful to others in war, and the former in peace as well. Next is liberality; for the liberal make contributions freely and do not quarrel about money, which others care most about. Justice is a virtue by which all, individually, have what is due to them and as the law requires; and injustice is a vice by which they have what belongs to others and not as the law requires. Courage is a virtue by which people perform fine actions in times of danger and as the law orders and obedient to the law, and cowardice is the opposite. Self-control is the virtue through which people behave as the law orders in regard to the pleasures of the body, and lack of control is the opposite. Liberality is the disposition to do good with money, stinginess is the opposite. Magnanimity is a virtue, productive of great benefits for others, and magnificence is a virtue in expenditures, productive of something great, while little-mindedness

and stinginess are the opposites. Prudence is a virtue of intelligence whereby people are able to plan well for happiness in regard to the good and bad things that have been mentioned earlier.[2]

Aristotle does not give a mathematical formula for judging the "good and noble performance" of actions. The harmony and beauty of it is simply recognized as such by the natural activity of the intellect. He appeals to implicit philosophy, which was discussed earlier. Happiness is caught more than taught in that we know what it means to be happy when we see it lived in the example of others. Ultimately, it is the good man who teaches us what happiness is.

3.1 St Thomas Aquinas

When we turn to St Thomas Aquinas, the discussion on happiness incorporates the Aristotelian perspective outlined above but also goes further. There is a debate, which continues today, of whether it is proper to speak of the philosophy of St Thomas Aquinas since his work is not divided into a philosophical part and then a theological part, but pretends, rather, to be synthesis of reason and faith. This synthesis comes into play in his discussion on happiness. The Angelic Doctor points out that the last end of man cannot consist in the active life as actions are for some other end. The virtuous life can bring a high degree of happiness here below by achieving a harmonious integration of the different dimensions of human life. Underlying the pursuit of virtue, however, there is a natural faith and hope and love that things will work out for us also socially and materially by living in this way. Socrates lived a virtuous life, but he was persecuted and driven to consume a deadly tonic. He refused to retract declaring boldly before a jury of hundreds of Athenians that he must be true to his inner self: "Nothing can harm a good man either in life or after death."[3]

Man is social by his very nature. While the reward for Socrates is in personal growth for doing good, in being treated unfairly, he lacks the recognition and esteem that society owes to him. The reward is in some way incomplete and opens the human spirit to have faith and hope in an all-powerful God who rewards and punishes in the afterlife and satisfies the deepest longing of a noble soul.

As a practical exercise, try to decide what you would do in a situation where you are held captive and presented with two options: kill an innocent person by pressing a button, or do nothing and your captor will press another button that will destroy an entire building killing thousands. If you press the button, the building will not be harmed. Let us suppose that the action of pressing the button directly causes the death of the innocent individual by releasing the axe of a guillotine or triggering a hanging or something like that.

Would you press the button so that your captor would refrain from taking many lives, knowing that you would be deliberately taking the life of an innocent person? Or would you refuse in conscience to take an innocent life, knowing that thousands would die? Whatever the option you may feel inclined to, the reader can certainly respect the decision of a person not to take an innocent life. Consider if such a decision in some way does not rest on faith in a God that will make things work out somehow, most probably in the afterlife.

Building on the wisdom of the Greeks, a central theme of western philosophy is the transcendence of the human person. Values and virtue present themselves as universal, immutable, and obligatory. This means that they transcend the here and now. As an individual becomes aware of this, he or she opens himself or herself to acknowledge, through a natural faith, the existence and of a transcendent cause of one's being, of others and of the world.

St Thomas Aquinas builds on Aristotle but opens up a richer perspective in positioning true happiness in the afterlife, as a reward for virtue. Happiness, however, begins here below in the joyful fruits that a virtuous life brings. In eternal life, the angelic doctor explains, perfect knowledge of the intelligible end, actual attainment of the end, and delight in the presence of the end attained must all coexist in happiness. He describes this state of complete happiness as the contemplation of the Divine Essence in the world to come. The contemplation of the divine essence is not possible for man without the aid of grace. Thus, man's last end is a supernatural one.

3.2 Happiness as harmony

Although Aquinas centres happiness on one thing, namely contemplation in the afterlife, classical philosophers, including Aquinas himself, recognize that many things must come together to attain the best possible happiness here below. From the perspective of anthropology of integration, the concept of *harmony* is a useful one to analyse this reality.[4] The corresponding image is that of an orchestra which has different instruments that play in perfect unison. *Happiness would be the harmonious integration of the different dimensions and aspects of a person in accord with his or her dignity and personal vocation.* Harmony evokes the feeling of a sublime and captivating beauty that is linked to completeness, perfection, full realization and by extension, happiness. The integration of the three levels of action of the human person is important here as well. Integration means that the spiritual, emotional, and biological dimensions of the human person work together to bring about the overall good of the person. This overall good comprises the proper functioning and coordination of the internal faculties, as well as the good that is attained through social relationships and interaction with nature. We can say that harmony is achieved through the integration of the levels. We can identify five aspects of the human person where harmony is a good leading to fulfilment:

1. Interior harmony between body and soul
2. Harmony with others
3. Harmony with creation
4. Harmony with God
5. Existential Harmony

Interior harmony means that the passions habitually follow the dictates of right reason. Essentially the person enjoys interior freedom and lives a virtuous life. The joy that this brings comes to light, for example, in the testimonies of persons who have managed to overcome debilitating addictions. A writer for Sexaholics Anonymous shares: "We discovered that we could stop, that not feeding the hunger didn't kill us, that sex was indeed optional! There was hope for freedom, and we began to feel alive. Encouraged to continue, we turned more and more away from our isolating obsession with sex and self and turned to God and others."[5] There are numerous similar testimonies from alcoholics and drug addicts that are not hard to find on the official websites of recognized support groups. Interior harmony implies self-possession in order to have the capacity to freely commit to a fulfilling life project in relationships with others.

Continuing to the second aspect, harmony with others denotes recognizing the dignity of each and every human being as "another me". This leads to an acknowledgement of the radical equality of all persons and respect for *the golden rule: do unto others as you would have them do unto you.* To live in harmony with others, it is necessary to exercise empathy and to sympathize with others. It entails fostering an attitude of understanding and compassion towards others, desiring their genuine good, in spite of the inconvenience it may cause me. The opposite of this would be indifference, which is an outlook of not caring for the welfare of those near to me and, of course, even less those far away, once I am comfortable and doing what I like. Particularly saddening is the case of profound neglect or abuse of children on the part of their parents or guardians. Children need love and attention from their parents to develop psychologically and emotionally. Neglect has been shown to be a cause of traumatic stress in children that gives rise to personality disorders later on.[6]

In the gospels, Jesus has very harsh words for those who are indifferent to the sufferings and needs of others. In the eschatological parable, those on his left are condemned because they failed to feed the hungry, give drink to the thirsty, welcome the stranger, clothe the naked and to visit the sick and those in prison.[7] They were indifferent to them. It was as though those needy persons may just as well have been dead. Along with empathy and compassion, a condition for finding true happiness in relationships is respect for the freedom of others and their freely chosen life project or vocation. Many other virtues come into play in relationships, but these will be discussed more at length in a later section.

Concerning harmony with creation, we recognize that nature has its own dynamism that we must nurture and respect. At the same time, we have the power to intervene and harness the powers of nature using our minds and hands to create more suitable and sophisticated living spaces for ourselves. When there is overindulgence, this power is abused, natural processes are harmed, and the environment grows ugly and hostile. We know, for example, that plastics take a long time to be broken down by the environment and, as such, are a strain on the ecosystem if not properly disposed of. Yet, when you go to the beach, you often find plastic bottles and wrappers strewn all over, left by people who were not careful to pick up after themselves. This makes you sad because you know that it is damaging to nature as well as being an eyesore for all the people who are getting away to enjoy a nice day at the seaside. Harmony with creation implies finding the proper balance, exercising restraint in consumption, and carefully managing waste so as to ensure a healthy ecosystem.

Regarding God, in the depths of the being of each person, there is a sense that their dignity and worth is a gift from a transcendent, loving, all powerful being. When we act in accordance with our dignity, we honour and please God, and are happy. When we betray our dignity, we dishonour God, feel guilty for taking his gift for granted and recognize that we are deserving of punishment. St Augustine tells in his autobiography, that one of the sins that weighed most heavily on his conscience was the time when he stole peaches from someone's property just for the sake of rebelling against having to follow any rule at all. Our conscience tells us that we should do unto others as we would have them to do unto us. Here, Saint Augustine and his friends went against their consciences. They knew they had all the peaches they could eat at home, but they stole just out of pride, for the twisted pleasure of feeling above good and evil, superior to everyone else, and even above God. That deed left a bitter taste afterwards for St Augustine, which was a constant source of guilt and a feeling of unworthiness before God and others. Only after his conversion and having confessed that sin did he feel restored, liberated, and happy.

Finally, there is existential harmony, which is the integration of our actions into a life project. We are not happy merely drifting from one place to the next doing good things. Man transcends himself and so he seeks meaning and purpose for his entire life. Take, for example, the case of a young man whose wife is expecting very soon and needs him to be around more to help her at home. His mind, however, is focused on getting ahead at work, playing golf to rub shoulders with his bosses and keeping on top of the latest news. He fails to meet his wife's needs and she is overwhelmed and unhappy. Her husband may argue that all that he is doing is good and useful, important for being successful. That may be true, but he has neglected what is most important in his life, caring for his spouse and the child in her womb. Stephen Covey describes such scenarios saying that a person can be very busy climbing the ladder of success, only to realize in the end that it was leaning against the wrong wall.[8] In the case described, the young man failed to see the bigger picture of long-term fulfilment that hinges on caring for family life in small day-to-day things. Existential harmony means having the right priorities and lovingly fulfilling the duties of one's state in life every day, even though other apparently "good" things may have to be set aside.

The importance of meaning and purpose in life was brought home in a very powerful way by Victor Frankl in his research on human behaviour in extreme circumstances, in his case, a concentration camp during the Second World War. Frankl observed that the persons who were able to endure such difficult conditions, were those who were able to find meaning and purpose for struggling every day. In his own case, he did this on three levels. The first or more tangible was that he saw his predicament as an opportunity for his career as a psychologist. The camp could be considered a lab for studying human behaviour and helping others in extreme circumstances. On a more personal level, he imagined his loved ones, also in camps, enduring each day with the hope of being reunited with him. He felt he owed it to them to reciprocate by struggling to survive. Frankl also found meaning in his faith as a Jew in an all-powerful God who rewards those who do good. [9] Speaking about human freedom, Pope John Paul II would often affirm that our freedom reaches its high point in a relationship of total self-giving for love.[10] Happiness is inseparable from a life project that is faithfully followed.

Notes

1. Aristotle, *The Nicomachean Ethics*, Bekker number 1098a.
2. Aristotle, *On Rhetoric*, Bekker number 1366b.
3. Plato, *The Last Days of Socrates*, ed. Harold Tarrant, trans. Hugh Tredennick (London; New York: Penguin Classics, 2003), Bekker number 41d.
4. Germain Grisez, *Christian Moral Principles: Way of the Lord Jesus: 1* (Chicago: Franciscan Press, 1983), 124.
5. "The Problem and the Solution," Sexaholics Anonymous, 2001, https://www.sa.org/solution/.
6. "Complex Trauma," The National Child Traumatic Stress Network (NCTSN), 2023, https://www.nctsn.org/what-is-child-trauma/trauma-types/complex-trauma.
7. Matthew 25:31–46
8. Stephen R. Covey, *The 7 Habits of Highly Effective People* (New York: Simon & Schuster, 1990), 98.
9. Viktor E. Frankl, *Man's Search for Meaning* (Boston: Beacon Press, 2006), 75–85.
10. Karol Wojtyla, *Love and Responsibility*, Revised edition (San Francisco: Ignatius Press, 1993), 135.

4 PERSONAL FULFILMENT THROUGH KNOWLEDGE AND ACTION

4.1 Knowledge and human perfection

Human life is a fact in that we are alive and there are persons around us who are alive. Life is also a task. Living things come into the world with an impulse to struggle and seek out what will enable them to survive, grow to maturity and multiply. To arrive to the fullness of life, creatures that are self-moving must have some form of built in or acquired knowledge of what brings about self-fulfilment. Animals have instincts and built-in ways of learning. Human persons also have instincts and built-in ways of learning but are not as "hard-wired" as other animals. There is a great lack of determination in the emotional and psychological make-up of the human person that is affected by many factors as a subject goes through life. We have "hard-wired" instincts that are similar to those of other creatures, such as the tendencies to self-preservation and to reproduce. In the human person, however, these tendencies are subject to and shaped by higher functions of thinking and free will. The knowledge children are exposed to when they are small and which they choose to pursue as they grow older impacts on the nature and intensity of the challenges they will face in life to grow in virtue. If I grow up with a mother and father faithful to each other, the knowledge of their example will feed my aspirations to have a stable family later in life. If my mother and father are apart and have an antagonistic abusive relationship, this will tend to shape my attitude to marriage later on.

It is well known that Plato gave priority of place to knowledge for the practice of virtue and the attainment of happiness. In the dialogue *Protagoras*, he places Socrates in dialogue with a famed Sophist named Protagoras. Through his protagonist, Plato argues that human virtue hinges on knowing the good and being able to correctly choose the actions that bring about the most good. The argument begins with the premise that everyone wants what he or she believes to be good. From this it follows that when a person does something wrong or bad it cannot be because they want to do it, knowing it is bad. It must be that they want to do it, believing it to be good. What separates the virtuous person from the un-virtuous is not a desire for what is good, but rather the knowledge of what the good really is.[1]

Knowledge certainly influences what a subject does in a given circumstance. Plato seems to place the emphasis on intellectual knowledge. From the perspective of anthropology of integration, there are forms of knowledge or cognition on three levels: the biological level, the emotional level and the spiritual level. A feature of a mature person is the integration of cognition on the three levels, where the biological and emotional levels have been moulded by and are docile to the spiritual or intellectual level. When integration does not take place, a subject is conditioned mainly by the biological and emotional levels. The subject can know and desire what is good on the spiritual level, but if the spirit is "hijacked" and unable to govern, he or she lacks interior freedom.

Carlos Beltramo pioneered a version of this for teaching, in his collaboration with Christine Vollmer in the elaboration of *Alive to the World*, identifying the importance of instructing the three levels in each chapter of their student texts. Each chapter targets the *understanding* of a given objective, or concept, appeals to the *emotions* through the plot of the story, and suggests ways of *doing* which correspond to the harmonious integration of the 3 levels. Beltramo later presented this new pedagogical method as the Pedagogy of the Integration of the Human Person (PIHP) at Navarra University, obtaining with this thesis his Doctorate in Philosophy *Summa Cum Laude*.[2]

The ordinary activity of having a meal can illustrate the importance of intellectual knowledge and how forms of knowledge can be on three levels. A girl, for example, going to a foreign country, is invited to try a popular dish in the home of a friend she made there. She examines the ingredients, asks some questions, and proceeds to try it. On the biological level, as the dish is unfamiliar, she has a certain reservation out of fear that it may be an unpleasant experience. Her hosts are encouraging her, helping themselves to generous servings. On the emotional level, she does not want to disappoint her new and only friend in that country and feels anxious about being rejected in some way if she does not try the dish. On the spiritual level, she weighs the different values at stake such as health, friendship, and the opportunity to learn and acquire culture, in the light of the information available. She judges that it is a good idea to try the dish, and helps herself to a serving, overcoming her fear on the biological level.

The following day, she is very sick and goes to the doctor. The medical practitioner explains that she is having an allergic reaction to something she ate. By process of elimination, it becomes clear that the local dish she had the previous evening was the cause. Unknown to her, it had an ingredient that she was allergic to, which made her feel unwell later on. If she knew at the time that such a substance was in the meal, she would have nicely refused to partake of it, explaining that it adversely affects her. Her hosts, of course, would have understood, and offered her something else.

The above example illustrates how forms of knowledge occur on different levels, producing different reactions. The intensity of the impulses on the biological and emotional levels varies from person to person. By trying to acquire good habits, an individual becomes increasingly adept at having an appropriate response in such situations, in a way that is spontaneous and executed with relative ease and with confidence. A lack of knowledge, however, can still lead to the wrong choice. In the scenario considered, the girl made a bad choice due to lack of knowledge. From a moral perspective, she is not guilty of doing something wrong. Furthermore, this is part of how experience is gained. Mistakes like these are learning experiences that help one to make better decisions in the future.

4.2 Personal growth through action

Linked to knowledge, personal growth and fulfilment is achieved through action. It is crucial to emphasize the importance of every free action for the personal happiness of an individual. At first this may seem an exaggeration. What's the big deal if I don't study today even though I should? It's not a big deal, but at the same time the omission should not be taken lightly due to the special force that free action has for forming habits. Actions we are forced to carry out do not have this power. A father may force his adolescent son, for example, to get up at a certain time each day. The day his son is left to get up on his own, however, it is unlikely that he would stick to the schedule. A young man who, seeing the benefit of getting an early start, asks to be woken up at a certain time, is more likely to find a way to stick to his or her schedule (using an alarm for example) when the help of another is absent. By the simple fact of being freely chosen, I connect it with my own happiness, and it has the power to form a habit in me. Research in psychology and neuroscience has provided interesting insights into how this happens from a scientific perspective. New habits are formed because the behavioural patterns, which humans repeat, become imprinted in neural pathways. When a familiar context appears, the pattern kicks in, putting an individual in a neural state akin to being on auto-pilot. An illustrative example of this is the carrot and M&M study by researcher Wendy Wood. In an interview with Michaela Barnett she explains:

> This was a study that I did with Pei-Ying Lin and John Monterosso. We trained people to choose carrots in a computer game. People played the game when they were hungry and they actually got the carrots. They had to move a joystick in the direction of the carrots when they saw them on the screen, and then they won carrots and got to eat them. All of our participants liked carrots, but they also

liked chocolate. And after we had trained people to choose carrots by moving a joystick toward the carrots whenever they saw them on the screen, we gave them the opportunity to choose M&M's if they wanted to. Now, when the screen was set up in just the same way as it was during training, people continued to choose carrots. Over 60 percent of them chose the carrots. But when the screen changed, and they had to actually move the joystick in a different direction, then they stopped to think. And many more of them chose M&M's.[3]

Interestingly, the study also illustrates how our thinking self can actually undo healthy habits. In the study, beneficial habits were formed, namely choosing a healthy food, carrots. When people thought about it, they disrupted that habit and chose chocolate.

Habitual behaviour often goes unnoticed in persons exhibiting it, because a person does not need to engage in self-analysis when undertaking routine tasks. A large percentage, approximately 50%, of daily behaviours is performed out of habit.[4] Once a habit is formed, it is hard to break, although new habits can be developed that counteract old ones. Some repeated behaviours could become addictions where the subject is uncontrollably drawn to behaviour that is harmful.[5]

4.3 Habits and virtue

The ancient philosophers did not have the scientific information we have now. Nevertheless, they were spot on in underscoring the importance of action for happiness via the formation of good habits. In general, good habits are called virtues. In the context of moral philosophy, this statement needs to be qualified by certain conditions:

> 1. A habit is understood as good because it has the capacity to bring about the overall good of the person and is done with rectitude of intention.
> 2. The actions realized are the fruit of free action.
> 3. Common sense guides the execution of the habit so that it is fitting and appropriate in the given circumstance.

The first point is a clarification that is needed because of the versatility of language, in particular the use of the word "good". In ordinary language we sometimes use the word "good" to refer just to an aspect of something and not the essence of it. The aspect that is in focus is normally clear from the context. For example, I may say that I know several tailors who are very good. Now these tradesmen may all be very bad fathers, but does that make my statement incorrect? Assuming the context of my affirmation is getting an article of clothing made, the word "good" refers to their stitching skills. If the context were that someone was saying that the tailors in a certain town are all scoundrels, then my answer would have an entirely different meaning. It would be referring to their moral uprightness. This may seem trivial, but it is the cause of much confusion in reasoning about good and evil. A person who is very adept at picking the pockets of others can be said to be a very good pickpocket. Here the word "good" is used to describe an activity that is evil. There is an apparent contradiction, but language admits it, which is why it may be regarded as humorous.

Because the word "good" has multiple connotations depending on the context, so too the phrase "good habit" can have a flexible application. I can say that it is a good habit to think before acting. But if the goal is to cover up a crime, then can that be considered something good? The phrase can be properly understood if we assume that the object of the action was morally sound. Similarly, one can affirm that it is a good habit to save money. But if the object is to purchase weapons for an unjust war, then we have an exception.

As language is contextual, it is useful to specify that the good habits that we call virtues are those where the action has the capacity to bring about the overall good of the person and is done with this intention in mind. The virtue of fortitude, for example, does not apply in the case where a person shows resilience in setting up a drug cartel or in establishing a totalitarian regime. One finds, however, that the word "fortitude" is sometimes used in such cases. This is unfortunate, and perhaps it is a degradation of language to use a word that stands for a virtue in such a context.

To equate good habit with virtue, it is also important to establish that the action is freely carried out. An example was given earlier to illustrate how an adolescent boy who is obliged by his father to wake up early every day, does not develop the habit of rising early unless he sees the value of it and appreciates the help of his father. A boy who is constantly badgered by his parents to keep a specific timetable and to carry out certain activities, be they academic, sporting, or religious, will eventually rebel, and none of these supposedly good habits will take root. His parents may have all the good intentions of wanting the best for their son, but sadly they have the wrong strategy. It happens that some adolescents develop an exaggerated feeling of rejection to all that appears to them as restricting their freedom. Life brings many limitations to the exercise of freedom due to the demands of working with others and the constraints on resources that are always present. When a boy does not have a proper and balanced emotional response to constraints, he rejects commitments and suggestions in an unbalanced way, especially if they evoke what he experienced growing up. This can be a source of tension in relationships with people he deals with later in life. If not addressed, this person can find himself increasingly isolated and alone as his peers settle in committed relationships and professional careers.

Beside the fact that good habits simply do not take root without freedom, the very notion of virtue demands freedom. Virtue has as its object the perfection and fulfilment of the human person as a human person. What makes our actions truly human is the fact that they are free. It is contradictory to speak of human fulfilment if freedom is excluded.

Freedom means that an action is carried out with full awareness and full consent. In moral philosophy, full awareness is understood in terms of the moral qualification of the action; in other words, its nature in relation to the affirmation of human dignity and true human perfection. I can be aware that my hand is on someone else's wallet, for example. It may be that I am returning it to the owner who dropped it, or it may be that I am taking money from it that is not mine to take. The simple awareness that my hand is on the wallet is trivial for the understanding of freedom as it relates to virtue. The awareness that I am returning a lost wallet or taking money that is not mine, however, is not. In the first case I am doing an action that affirms my own dignity and that of others. I am living out the golden rule to do unto others as I would have them do unto me. This corresponds to the truth about man and his perfection by being just in his relationships. In the second case, I am stealing, and such an action is evil. It undermines my dignity as a human person as I fail to see the owner of the wallet as "another me" and am unjust towards him. Such actions produce vice and will hinder my progress to true fulfilment.

Together with full awareness, a free action requires full consent. A necessary condition for freedom is the power to act or not to act, to do this or that, and so to perform deliberate actions on one's own responsibility. Some acts that human beings carry out are not free in this sense. Dreaming, for example, takes place with or without the consent of the person who is asleep. The imagination and the memory are engaged unconsciously. I can cheat on an exam in a dream and then even laugh about it with my colleagues when I am awake. The actions done in a dream are neither virtuous nor vices. If I am fully conscious, however, and trade answers with others in an important exam, then I have fully consented to an evil action. I am blameworthy and deserving of punishment.

Even when one is awake, there are things that trigger the imagination and the memory of a person that are outside the dominion of his or her free will. These stimulations can come from the external senses or from interior mechanisms as well, such as those associated with changes in one's affective state. An individual is not responsible for the appearance of these images and memories in his or her mind, even though they may be very strong and may perhaps present a temptation to do evil. Moral philosophy has always upheld that to be tempted is not to sin. In fact, it can be an occasion to solidify virtue, through the deliberate rejection of the temptation by purposefully calling to mind the disorder it entails and the contrary good action that should be pursued. A man may be tempted to say something inappropriate to a woman who visits his office for professional advice. If he resists the temptation by calling to mind the lack of professionalism that such an act entails, and that his purpose is to be a good professional, then he has grown in the virtues of respect and chastity.

Freedom is a condition for virtue, but it also works the other way in that virtue perfects freedom. In the example above, the man who resisted the temptation has affirmed his freedom by choosing to act in a way that is in accord with his role and purpose in life over a disorder that contradicts it. He will find that it will be easier to resist similar temptations in the future and will feel a deep joy for having maintained a high standard of professionalism in the career that he freely chose.

When virtue is lacking, freedom is undermined. Consider the following actions:

- Wasting time,
- Slander,
- Reckless driving,
- Indifference to the needs of others,
- Drug abuse,
- Lust,
- Greed

Now think of a woman in the prime of her life who feels a deep joy about where she is, fruit of many years of dedication to her profession, family, and community. Let's say her field is fundraising and she has a faithful, supportive husband and three children. No one ever forced her to choose her particular career or spouse. She has raised millions for charitable institutions, and she finds that very fulfilling. This young lady can choose to put all this in jeopardy by engaging in the actions listed above. If someone tries to correct her, she could say "don't tell me what to do, I am free!" It is clear, however, that by engaging in those disordered activities, she will no longer be free to have the flourishing career and wholesome family life that she enjoys. Without being judgmental, we can say that she threw away a more fully human and dignified life for something less worthy of her attention. From this perspective, disordered actions are constraining and so freedom is undermined. Sin and vice are a misuse of freedom and can never lead to true happiness.

Full awareness and full consent are conditions for free acts. Because of this culpability and responsibility for an action can be modified by ignorance, inadvertence, duress, fear, habit, inordinate attachments, and other psychological and social factors.

Together with rectitude of purpose and freedom, a good habit that we wish to call a virtue needs to be guided by common sense so that the concrete expressions of the habit in question are fitting and appropriate in the given circumstance. Reading good books, for example, is generally considered a good habit. During vacation it is commendable for a young man to spend a lot of time reading good novels. In the period leading up to exams during the school term, however, this would be a disorder. Charity can be used to further illustrate this condition. It is a good habit certainly. Nevertheless, a charitable action I perform ought to take into account a host of factors about the person to whom I show charity, such as their relationship with me, their social position, physical ability, mood, background etc. Suppose the charitable action is to correct another. It may not be appropriate that I be the person to do it if there is not enough trust and openness between that individual and me. To correct effectively requires choosing the right person, at the right time, and the right place with the right words.

4.4 Classical notions of virtue

The wise men of ancient Greece spoke and wrote a great deal on virtue. For Socrates, Plato, and Aristotle, for example, the practice of virtue was the centrepiece of good living, happiness and civic life. Aristotle wrote the *Nicomachean Ethics* in which he synthesized and developed Greek thought on happiness and the virtues. Later in the Middle Ages, St. Thomas Aquinas wrote a new synthesis from the perspective of harmonizing faith and reason. Here we recap some key ideas that we have inherited from this tradition.

Aristotle defined moral virtue in two ways:

1. As a disposition to behave in the right manner[6]
2. And as a mean between extremes of deficiency and excess, these extremes being vices.[7]

He emphasized that we learn moral virtue primarily through habit and practice rather than through reasoning and explanation.[8]

Before elaborating on the first definition, it helps to clarify what Aristotle is saying when he refers to a mean between extremes. The notion of extremes is not hard to grasp. We all have a sense of when something is too much or going overboard or too little or miserly. For example, someone can sleep too much or can sleep too little. Too much sleep is unnecessary and can make a person lazy. Too little sleep is bad for one's health. The same applies to almost any activity. The mean Aristotle refers to in the second definition above, refers to what is appropriate in each situation. Mean is sometimes confused with a middle ground. It does have this connotation in part, but Aristotle used the term in the sense that it is the response one would expect from a good man in that situation. Depending on the situation the mean is different. Take, for example, the virtue of temperance. On a day of fasting it is appropriate to do without a glass of wine. During a wedding celebration it is fitting to have one. Temperance is lived in both cases though the choice of action is entirely different. The virtue of prudence is needed to discern the mean in a given situation.

Aristotle listed the principal virtues along with their corresponding vices, as represented in the following table.[9] A virtuous person exhibits all of the virtues: they do not properly exist as distinct qualities but rather as different aspects of a virtuous life.

Sphere of action or feeling	Excess (vice)	Mean (virtue)	Deficiency (vice)
Fear and confidence	Rashness	Courage	Cowardice
Pleasure and pain	Licentiousness	Temperance	Insensibility
Getting and spending (minor)	Prodigality	Liberality	Miserliness
Getting and spending (major)	Vulgarity	Magnificence	Pettiness
Honour and dishonour (major)	Vanity	Magnanimity	Pusillanimity
Honour and dishonour (minor)	Ambition	Proper ambition	Complacency
Anger	Irascibility	Patience	Lack of spirit
Self-expression	Boastfulness	Truthfulness	Understatement
Conversation	Buffoonery	Wittiness	Boorishness
Social conduct	Obsequiousness or flattery	Friendliness	Cantankerousness
Shame	Shyness	Modesty	Shamelessness
Indignation	Envy	Righteous indignation	Malicious enjoyment

Figure 4.1 Table showing the principal virtues along with their corresponding vices according to Aristotle.

When we turn to St Thomas Aquinas, the perspective of a mean is affirmed, but he emphasizes, rather, the aspect of disposition of the subject to behave in a right manner. More precisely, virtue concerns the perfection of the active powers or operations in man. We find in the Summa a definition of virtue as *a habit that "disposes an agent to perform its proper operation or movement"*.[10] It is not just that the power is exercised in the right way from time to time. There is a stable disposition towards the proper functioning of the powers to bring about the good of the person. A virtuous subject will seem to naturally act in a way that brings about personal growth and happiness in the various circumstances of life. From this perspective, in accord with Plato, the angelic doctor presents the cardinal virtues as the main habits that regulate the principle drives in man. Plato used an analogy with the human body to illustrate this framework. The lower part of the torso comprising the stomach and groin correspond to appetites for pleasure. The upper part of the torso, which is the chest, corresponds to the drive to struggle and overcome obstacles. Finally, the head represents the powers to know and to love. For each of these powers or drives, we can attach a virtue that denotes its correct operation to bring about the overall good of the human person. These are: Temperance, Fortitude and Prudence (or Wisdom). Justice is the virtue that ensures unity, order, and harmony in the whole body alongside the practice of the other virtues.[11]

Personal fulfilment through knowledge and action

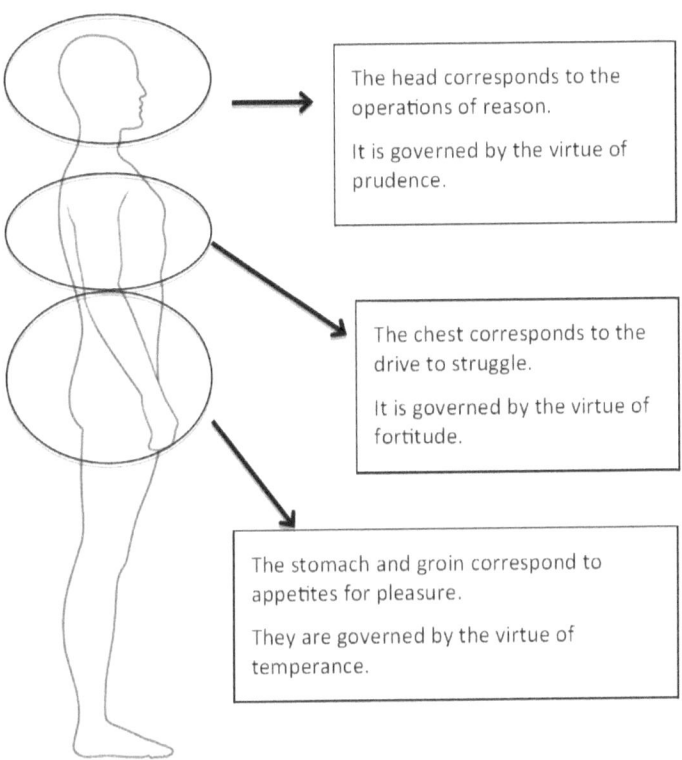

Figure 4.2 Plato's framework for explaining the Cardinal Virtues of Temperance, Fortitude and Prudence. Justice is the state of good health where unity, order and harmony are achieved alongside the practice of the other virtues.

The four Cardinal Virtues can be defined as follows:
Temperance: This is self-control, self-discipline—a rational control over the passions and appetites leading to their proper integration in a personal project of self-giving. Its opposite (also common today) is self-indulgence, a habitual pursuit of pleasure and comfort as ends in themselves.

Fortitude: Fortitude is the moral virtue that ensures firmness in difficulties and constancy in the pursuit of the good. It strengthens the resolve to resist temptations and to overcome obstacles in the moral life. The virtue of fortitude enables one to conquer fear, even fear of death, and to face trials and persecutions.

Prudence/Wisdom: This virtue disposes the reason to discern the true good in every circumstance and to choose the right means of achieving it; "the prudent man looks where he is going." With the help of this virtue, we apply moral principles to particular cases without error and overcome doubts about the good to achieve and the evil to avoid.

The acts of prudence are three:

Deliberation: to take counsel carefully, to ask, to gather information, to seek advice, to study the means that are needed to perform an action in a virtuous way.

Judgment: to sift through the facts and data and come to a conclusion after deliberation.

Command: to apply those counsels and judgments to action, to direct the order issued to the faculties so that the action is performed according to the judgment; this is the chief and most characteristic act of prudence.

Justice: This we would call "sense of responsibility"— giving others what is due to them. It is the sense of duty implicit in recognising others as "another me", and actively seeking their good along with the common good of society as a whole. In one sense, this consciousness of responsibility is the most important mark of moral adulthood—maturity is responsibility.

4.5 A new approach to virtue in anthropology of integration

Aristotle elaborated on a rich list of virtues that can be considered to be elements or features of a portrait of a virtuous man. They are facets of an image of the good man or woman that we should try to emulate. Plato's approach is quite different. He looks not so much at what a good man looks like, but rather how a good man, or any man for that matter is put together. He identifies three principle powers and matches them with corresponding virtues which bring about the proper functioning of those powers for the overall good of the person. In this way he identifies the cardinal virtues. As Plato's model pretends to capture all the powers that have to do with appetite or desire, it follows that all the virtues can be categorized under the cardinal virtues.

While embracing the ideas from Plato and Aristotle on virtue, anthropology of integration looks at human action in a new way. It recognizes that there are three dimensions to the human person, the spiritual, the emotional and the biological dimensions. They are clearly distinct but at the same time should work together to bring about the overall good of the person. The process by which this happens is called integration.

Integration takes place in two directions. There is upward or cognitive integration, whereby the intellect grasps the fundamental goods of human nature, drawing on inclinations or tendencies on the lower levels. These are goods such as life, love and society that the subject is challenged to adhere to as core personal beliefs. They are recognized as constitutive of the dignity of the human person.

There is also downward or formative integration whereby values inform and shape the emotions to give rise to actions that are consistent with the dignity of the human person. As values more deeply inform the actions of a person, habits are developed that make the person more inclined to be aware of and to perceive the fundamental values that are at stake in an action that he or she is about to perform, is doing, or has already completed. Cognitive integration is enhanced.

When there is good will in the subject to adhere to the values that are grasped in upward integration, the enhanced cognitive integration facilitates, in turn, the task of downward or formative integration. The dynamism of integration continues in a cyclic way leading to an overall more integrated way of being. While a subject is still on the journey of life, there is always the prospect of progressing in overall personal integration. One can also regress, unfortunately.

Anthropology of integration provides a new framework, where personal fulfilment and growth is understood in terms of progress in an overall more integrated way of being (see diagram below).

Personal fulfilment through knowledge and action

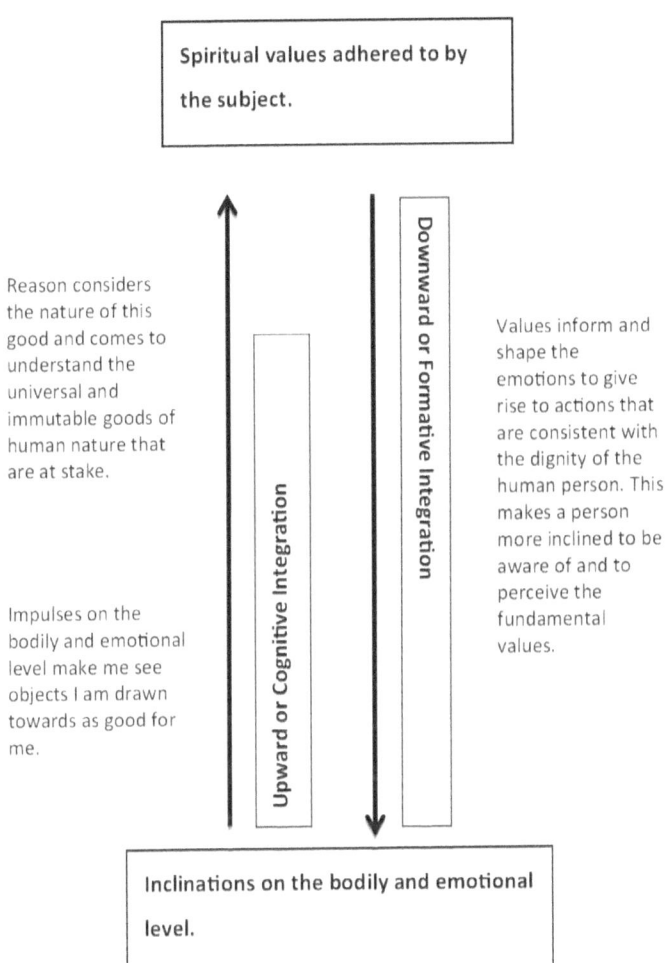

Figure 4.3 Upward and downward integration and how they are related.

From the perspective of integration, a different set of virtues emerge at the centre of unitary action for the human person. These are virtues such as diligence, order, loyalty, charity, and generosity which match the core values for human dignity. The cardinal virtues are also identified as pertaining to human dignity, but alongside other virtues, such as those just mentioned. From the standpoint of this approach, virtue can be defined as:

> habits that integrate the different dimensions of the human person in accord with his or her dignity and vocation. When habits are opposed to proper integration, they become vices.

In the sections that follow, we will articulate in greater detail the different dimensions of the human person and how integration applies. We will also expand on the key virtues that emerge from this framework.

4.6 The role of example and family life

Connecting action to operations as St. Thomas Aquinas does, provides a useful framework for understanding virtue. Out of this perspective, the cardinal virtues emerge as the "hinge" of all the virtues. In other words, all the virtues can be classified under the headings of the cardinal virtues in some way. In practice, however, a theoretical framework is not enough. Persons who are models and examples of virtue are needed to help me to commit to leading a virtuous life. In his writings Aristotle highlighted this reality. He advised to look to the good man to know how to live a virtuous life.

The need for good example can be considered from two points of view. The first is from the perspective of moral conscience. In every individual there is a sort of divine spark that tells us if an action we have done or plan to do is morally good or evil, meritorious or sinful. If my conscience tells me, for example, that I should be fair in grading an exam, then I understand this as an application of an unchanging rule. I should be fair because it is good to be fair and not for any material gain. If material gain were relevant, then I could accept payment to be fair. This is corruption and it is evil. What applies here in the case of being fair, applies to all the virtues as well. In fact, the practice of virtue may often require sacrifice, even to the point of accepting death, as in the archetypal case of Socrates. If even death should be embraced, rather than forsake virtue, then it makes sense to have faith in a reward for virtue in the afterlife, as St. Thomas Aquinas highlights in his study of the topic. The practice of virtue in its pure form needs faith in an all-powerful and benevolent God who rewards virtue and punishes vice in the hereafter. This being the case, the intelligence needs a special aid to adhere to a reality that is beyond the senses, namely the afterlife. This special aid is the example of others like Socrates who adhered heroically to virtue. Their witness is the sensible experience that helps my intelligence and will to grasp and affirm: "I can do it too!"

Revelation in the Judeo-Christian tradition tells us that a special help from God called actual grace is also necessary for an individual to make the leap to having faith in the afterlife. These graces are special lights and strength given by God in the daily life of every person to draw them nearer to Himself through conversion of heart and by opening themselves to a deeper faith.[12] God, however, never fails to grant this grace to those who seek him with an upright heart. Acknowledging the important role of divine assistance, part of the Judeo-Christian tradition is to honour the holy men and women of old such as Eleazar (2 Mac 6:18ss), the seven brothers with their mother (Mac 7:1-14), the three young men (Dan 6:12-28) and also the numerous martyrs and Saints, many of our own times, who lived virtue heroically. This keeps the memory of their lives and deeds alive so that models of heroic virtue are never lacking for the faithful in this tradition.

The good example of others is also critical to the practice of virtue from another perspective, that of the existential dimension of the human person. Man is a being whose life has a trajectory through time. His existence is a journey where he seeks to find meaning and purpose to guide his decisions. This is an important reality for each individual because happiness is contingent on how well one lives out one's life project or vocation. In the journey of life, examples, models and guides are needed to discover one's calling and to progress and mature in it. For example, a person who discerns a calling to marriage will have done so, not just because of a theoretical understanding of marriage, but because there would have been concrete examples and models of married life that he or she would have been exposed to along his or her path. The same applies to someone who is called to the priesthood or apostolic celibacy. These examples and models are what make the choice to seek happiness in marriage or otherwise a real possibility and not a heroic exercise of faith.

4.6.1 The perennial value of the traditional family structure

For persons who grew up in the fifties and sixties in Western Civilization, the traditional intact family was the norm. It was a given that married couples would stay together and be faithful to each other. The reality for many children today is quite different.[13] They may be in a household with a stepfather, or mom's boyfriend, with other children from previous unions of their mother or father or move around between different households depending on the arrangement for custody made by their parents. This is so prevalent today, in fact, that one can be tempted to regard the traditional family as one more among several possibilities, rather than a point of reference or benchmark to which we ought to strive. It can be argued that by favouring the stable natural unit of mother, father, and children, we run the risk of making many children who, through no fault of their own, have not had such an environment, to feel very insecure about themselves and to be stigmatized by others.

The discussion in this section recognizes this challenge. It seeks, however, to present an ethical framework inherited from the Greeks that can help anyone, whether from an intact family or a broken home, to strive for true happiness. In this sense it acknowledges the intrinsic dignity of each person and thereby overcomes the problem of stigmatization and insecurity that can arise when values are not presented in a proper way. It is always important to distinguish between the action a person may perform or a situation that may disadvantage a person from the person himself or herself. Throughout this text we have sought to emphasize the intrinsic dignity of every person, while, at the same time, pointing the way to true happiness that this same dignity demands. The *Alive to the World* programme mentioned earlier does this is a very effective way. Through stories, children who may be disadvantaged in some way, are exposed to a different "normal", which, experienced in stories, they can strive towards in real life. At no point are they made to feel judged or insecure, because they know that they are reading a story with a reasoning and a moral they can all connect with. There are activities and questions related to the story that provide opportunities for feeling rewarded and affirmed. The undeniable strength of this method is that, given the freedom to do so (the privacy of a student reading a book) almost every child will recognise and desire the good options simply described in the story.

In the prologue to his book *Character Building*, David Isaacs presents a very persuasive case for the perennial value of the family.[14] He presents arguments based on the *efficiency* of the family to produce benefits to individuals and to society as a whole, such as providing care for the young and the elderly, personal satisfaction and personal development. Furthermore, statistics show that there is a strong correlation between divorce, poverty, delinquency, and unhappiness.[15]

The arguments presented by Isaacs, together with the hard facts, show that many parents can be in denial about the hurt and pain their children suffer when they divorce. A teacher recently shared with the author the case of a child, who vowed to be faithful to his future wife at a tender age because he did not want his children to go through the pain and agony he felt with the breakup of his parents. Even though this boy grew up in a broken home, the ideal of an intact family was not a source of insecurity, but rather of inspiration for his future life. Many years later he is living out this dream. If a small boy is capable of such a positive response, even though it may have been through his dissatisfaction with his current situation, should we refrain from presenting the beauty of an intact family to children out of fear that they may feel insecure or inadequate? With an appropriate pedagogy, like that of *Alive to the World*, we can help children to feel positive about themselves and what they can achieve, without hiding from them an ideal that they can aspire to in the future. They will understand that by learning to make good decisions now, and learning the skills offered, they can assure a future situation for themselves that may be quite different from what they currently experience, but which they understand as better.

To conclude, a person does well to give attention to individual acts because it is by dint of these that virtue develops or on the contrary, vices become ingrained. Through concrete actions, a person can progress or regress in achieving an integrated life and by extension, the person will progress in true happiness or not.

Notes

1. Plato, *Protagoras*, Revised Edition, Clarendon Plato Series (Oxford, New York: Oxford University Press, 1992), Bekker number 361a - 361b.
2. Carlos Beltramo, "La Pedagogía de La Integración de La Persona Humana" (PhD diss., Pamplona, Universidad de Navarra, 2003).

3. Michaela Barnett, "Good Habits, Bad Habits: A Conversation with Wendy Wood," Behavioral Scientist, October 14, 2019, https://behavioralscientist.org/good-habits-bad-habits-a-conversation-with-wendy-wood/.
4. Wendy Wood, Jeffrey Quinn, and Deborah Kashy, "Habits in Everyday Life," *Journal of Personality and Social Psychology* 83, no. 6 (2002): 1293.
5. Courtney Humphries, "Why We Do What We Do," MIT Technology Review, December 17, 2013, https://www.technologyreview.com/2013/12/17/175086/why-we-do-what-we-do/.
6. Aristotle, *The Nicomachean Ethics*, Bekker number 1106a.
7. Aristotle, Bekker number 1107a.
8. Aristotle, Bekker number 1103b.
9. Aristotle, bk. II ch. 7.
10. St Thomas Aquinas, *Summa Theologiae*, I-II, q. 49 a. 1.
11. Plato, *The Republic*, trans. Desmond Lee, New edition (London: Penguin Classics, 2007), Bekker number 434d–441c.
12. *Catechism of the Catholic Church*, paras. 2000–2001.
13. Patrick Fagan, "Executive Summary: How Broken Families Rob Children of Their Chances for Future Prosperity," The Heritage Foundation, June 11, 1999, https://www.heritage.org/marriage-and-family/report/executive-summary-how-broken-families-rob-children-their-chances-future.
14. David Isaacs, *Character Building*, 23rd ed. (Dublin: Four Courts Press, 2006), 1.
15. Patrick Fagan, "The Impact of Marriage and Divorce on Children," The Heritage Foundation, May 13, 2004, https://www.heritage.org/testimony/the-impact-marriage-and-divorce-children.

Part II
The three dimensions of the human person

In the body/soul unity of the human person we can identify three dimensions: The biological, the emotional or psychological, and the spiritual dimension. The emotional level needs to be distinguished from the purely spiritual and purely biological, because emotions have both biological and spiritual components.

Spiritual Dimension: Operations of the Intelligence and Will.

Emotional/Psychological Dimension: Impulses and sentiments connected to an awareness of self that powerfully influence choice.

Biological Dimension: Morphology, physiological and somatic functions.

Figure 5 The dimensions of the human person.

In this section, the three dimensions are discussed separately. This is done in order to highlight differences that are designed to work together in an integrated way. The differences, in fact, in themselves, hint at this unitary action. This occurs because they function in order to achieve the same end which is the overall good of the human person. The shape and articulation of a wing of a bird, for example, already leads one to think that it is part of something that is meant to fly. A stomach is part of something that is meant to eat and so part of some kind of animal. The end or the whole is implicit in the form and functioning of the part. As we distinguish the three dimensions in this section, this also applies. The overall end of the human person is inherent in the functions performed in each of the dimensions and is the cause for the way it is structured and operates.

The orientation to an end that can be grasped from an objective standpoint also occurs in the interior of living beings. If nature is ordered and beautiful, then it is reasonable to think that creatures inherently carry out patterns of behaviour that bring about their perfection. If creatures were to naturally behave in a manner that harms them and stunts their maturing, then we would have to conclude that nature is disordered, and ugly. Thank God, creatures do in fact spontaneously behave in a way that brings about their well-being and the preservation of their species according to their nature. This is what we call natural inclination. In the words of St. Thomas Aquinas: "All natural things are inclined to what is suitable for them, having within themselves some principle of their inclination in virtue of which that inclination is natural, so that in a way they go themselves and are not merely led to their due ends."[1]

Unlike animals, humans are not led blindly to fulfil their purpose. He or she is free and must engage his or her intellect and free will to orient his or her life to what is truly good for the human person. Within himself, however, the dynamisms in the three dimensions of the human person are oriented in their very nature to full human development. When the dynamism in question has a strong unitary action, it is initially perceived by the intellect and interpreted in regard to a partial good. With further reflection and the use of freedom, a subject is able to relate this partial good to the transcendental goods of man. Consider the example of hunger. It has a strong unitary action. It drives a subject—me for example—to seek out something to eat. The intellect is moved to see food as a good, but initially only in a partial way—it satisfies a need, namely hunger. With further reflection I can come to comprehend that food nourishes the body which in turn sustains life and enables the whole person to pursue full human development.

There are natural inclinations that are implicit in all three dimensions of the human person. On the biological level, inclinations are inherent in the strong physiological impulses that influence behaviour. In the psychological realm, inclinations are implicit in the powerful emotions that influence choice. On the spiritual level there are two basic inclinations which work differently from those on the lower levels. They are linked to the two spiritual faculties. From the intellect, the human person is inclined to the truth, and from the will to what is good.

The heart of Anthropology of Integration is the aim of living in accord with one's dignity as a human being. Achieving this, however, cannot be separated from living in accord with the universal goods of human nature. These goods can be known in different ways. We can be taught them or comprehend them by a special illumination. Anthropology of integration builds on the principle, however, that, constituted as a unity of body and soul, it is only natural that the human person takes his or her cue from the natural inclinations on the biological and emotional level.

Introduction to Anthropology of Integration

Appealing to the insight of levels of being in nature, St. Thomas Aquinas outlined a profound intuition regarding natural inclinations in human beings in his most famous work, the *Summa Theologiæ*.[2] He pointed out that there are inclinations that we share with natural things in general, which is the tendency to preservation in being. Things found in nature will spontaneously resist to different degrees, that which they perceive to threaten their subsistence. In man we can call this the inclination to survival. Then there are the inclinations that are more specific to the animal kingdom. This is the drive to reproduce and care for offspring. Finally, there are inclinations that are more specific to humans. These are the inclinations to know about things and how they work, to communicate with others and to live in society.

In the *Summa*, St. Thomas Aquinas shows how the content of fundamental spiritual goods, which is equivalent to the term *Natural Law* that he uses, flow from the natural inclinations as follows:

> In man there is first of all an inclination to good in accordance with the nature which he has in common with all substances: inasmuch as every substance seeks the preservation of its own being, according to its nature: and by reason of this inclination, whatever is a means of preserving human life, and of warding off its obstacles, belongs to the natural law.
>
> Secondly, there is in man an inclination to things that pertain to him more specially, according to that nature which he has in common with other animals: and in virtue of this inclination, those things are said to belong to the natural law, which nature has taught to

all animals such as sexual intercourse, education of offspring and so forth.

Thirdly, there is in man an inclination to good, according to the nature of his reason, which nature is proper to him: thus man has a natural inclination to know the truth about God, and to live in society: and in this respect, whatever pertains to this inclination belongs to the natural law; for instance, to shun ignorance, to avoid offending those among whom one has to live, and other such things regarding the above inclination.[3]

The text above may be a bit heavy for the reader as it is a long quote from St. Thomas Aquinas. It was important to include it, however, because the perspective developed in this book, goes back, in large part, to the insight of St. Thomas Aquinas that is summarized in this passage. The Natural moral law, which is based on the universal, transcendent goods, follow from the natural inclinations. As the angelic doctor affirms, these inclinations are:

- The inclination to self-preservation
- The inclination to sexual union and care of offspring
- The inclination to truth and knowledge, to live in society and to relationship with God.

In the text quoted above, St Thomas Aquinas identified these as flowing from:

1. things that man has in common with all substances
2. things he has in common with animals and
3. what corresponds to him as a rational being.

The framework that is adopted in anthropology of integration presents these inclinations articulated in three dimensions in each case—the biological, the emotional and the spiritual. The way inclinations work and are articulated together in the three dimensions is discussed in greater detail in the following chapters.

Without going into too much detail, the discussion in this second part of the book will also look at how the different dimensions of the human person have their own dynamism and logic. This is important because the unitary activity on the biological and emotional levels influence thought and decision making. A lack of proper development or defects on these levels helps to explain why persons make bad decisions at times. It can "excuse" them to some extent as they may be coerced inwardly by fears or inhibited to act due to illness. Persons involved in character formation need to take into account physical and emotional health in order to correctly evaluate a person's actions and avoid the pitfall of hasty judgements about a person's character. It is outside the scope of this book to give an in-depth presentation of physical and mental health. Some important aspects will be briefly discussed with a view to highlighting some aspects which are important to have in mind for the task of character formation.

Notes

1. St Thomas Aquinas, *Questiones Disputatae de Veritate*, trans. Robert W. Mulligan, vol. 3 (Henry Regnery Company, 1952), q. 22, a. 1.
2. St Thomas Aquinas, *Summa Theologiae*, I-II, q. 94, a. 2.
3. *Ibid.*, I-II, q. 94, a. 2.

5 THE BIOLOGICAL DIMENSION OF THE HUMAN PERSON

5.1 Human morphology

Biology and medicine have made huge advances in modern times. Interestingly, prestigious institutions place a great emphasis on collaborative work where experts in different fields intervene in the resolution of a medical problem. This is an effective strategy because the human body works as a unity. The parts function together in a coordinated way to give rise to operations that are peculiarly human. In his introductory book on Anthropology, Leonardo Polo takes this a step further to illustrate how certain physiological features of the human being make the body a particularly apt matter or material for being united to a soul.[1]

In the first place, Polo highlights the fact that man is biped as opposed to quadruped like most other animals. This has an extraordinary importance because it frees two extremities from the function of walking. A biped has arms and hands. It can also support a large head for a large brain on a vertebral column. With intelligence, a developed brain and hands become fit for a multiplicity of uses. Aristotle called them the instrument of instruments because, informed by intelligence, they have an infinite number of uses. Hands can produce and develop instruments of production. Man is a technological animal. With his hands he can build an environment to cater for his needs in widely differing conditions.

Added to this, Polo observes that language develops as a parallel to the use of hands as instruments of production and culture. The primary use of language is to pass on know-how and give orders. It is for organization. But to have language, the mouth, lips, and tongue need to be suited to the articulation of varied sounds with relative ease. Fine lips are important for this function and, interestingly enough, as the effort to move them is small, human beings can smile. Polo invites the reader of his book to consider all that a smile brings together—hands, brain, intelligence, language...all the things that makes us peculiarly human. A smile communicates many things without words such as gratitude, friendliness, appreciation, and internal happiness.

5.2 Bodily integrity

Bodily integrity is a notion from moral philosophy designed to safeguard the dignity of the human person when there is a project to restrain, alter or neutralize a bodily function.[2] It establishes that such interventions should be therapeutic when necessary, therapeutic meaning that is has a healing or curative effect. A procedure is unnecessary when no proportionate reason justifies it. Bodily Integrity is often considered in the context of something significant such as kidnapping, torture, amputations, mutilations, forced sterilizations and cruel punishments to enforce laws. A more refined application of the notion is suggested in this section in the light of new perspectives regarding the human body.

Doctors and medical professionals are increasingly aware of the importance of working in a team where different specialities are represented. To perform a heart bypass operation, for example, a surgeon needs to ensure that the patient does not have other medical issues such as kidney failure and lung disease that impact on his or her ability to recover. In the case where the lung function of the patient is compromised, for example, the heart surgeon will need a lung specialist to be involved every step of the way. The mental determination and support that a patient has also impacts on the progress of his or her recovery. What science tells us about the functioning of the human body suggests that the different operations within the human body have been carefully engineered to work together as an integrated whole.

The dynamism of differentiated parts working together in an integrated whole goes much deeper. There are layers of functions going from the molecular to the organs to systems of integration where the systems and processes on the different layers are all connected and work in unison. There are also evolutionary mechanisms at work (or creative if you want) which tune and adapt the various structures and dynamisms at work to enable greater overall autonomy and adaptability in the given external environment.[3] The origin, nature, and functioning of the dynamisms on the different levels and how they interact are far from being fully understood in science today. In 1953 the double helix structure of DNA was discovered, but biology is still very far from understanding how the chromosomes work together for the forming of a new organism from the initial genetic material.

Even though there are gaps in what science has been able to explain about the human body, a new paradigm has taken centre stage in recent times that rejects the outlook prevalent in the past that the human body is a sophisticated machine.[4] In this later framework, as with cars and other machines, parts can be taken out and replaced at will once they meet certain specifications. The new perspective today places integration at the centre. While we can perform organ transplants for example, it is with the clear understanding that an entire self-reorganisation must take place for its proper assimilation. The new organ must be integrated.

In the field of neuroscience, recent research has highlighted integrated action. The activation of neurons in the brain when a subject is aware of and responds freely to a stimulus in the environment does not follow a pattern of a sequential process nor of a set formula that is executed. Large sections of the brain light up on the screens for mapping neuron activation. Different sections of the brain have been associated with specific human activities such as language and emotions. Neuroscience shows that decision making involves input from many different areas. Daniel Siegel, as mentioned previously, has done extensive research to show how this applies in a special way to interpersonal relationships. Unsuspected parts of the brain and of the body are engaged. The integrative activity of the brain is so remarkable that some researchers suggest that there are emergent properties that give rise to some of the intangible aspects of human thought.[5] While this is of course very debatable, the advances in neuroscience point in the direction of complex functions that are brought together by dynamisms that are very sophisticated, involving self-organization and creativity.

The notion of integration in human biology suggests that human intervention to alter or to neutralize a function, whatever it may be, ought to be generally avoided and if necessary, done with the least possible disturbance. In moral philosophy, this is called the principle of bodily integrity. The mechanism at work in the human body are complex and yet finely tuned over millions of years. If you have a highly sophisticated artefact that has been worked on over millions of years, you will be very caring and careful with it. The notion of integrity applied to the human body suggests that it deserves a great deal of reverence and respect. As a community we need to question some practices that are widespread and perhaps entrenched in some places, and even considered as culture. Tattoos and piercings, for example, do permanent damage to a natural organ. It is interesting to note that the medical sciences have discovered long term risks due to allergic reactions and infections that are associated with these practices. Another questionable practice is the use of long-term contraception. These methods alter the functioning of a woman's fertility cycle over an extended period of time. There are also options for permanent sterilization. From the perspective of bodily integrity this practice receives a very negative evaluation. It is not surprising that recent research has shown that the risks of these methods of birth control are considerable in both the short and long term.[6]

5.3 Natural inclinations on the biological level

Saint Thomas Aquinas proposed three fundamental categories of inclinations related to the levels of being. The dynamisms of these inclinations begin on the biological level. Thus, for survival, there is the urge to eat and drink and to seek shelter, for example. For reproduction, there is the sexual urge and for learning and communication, there is the biological drive to curiosity and to manipulate things. These urges compel the subject to seek out and to unite with the object that satisfies the drive. The table below shows the different ontological levels and the corresponding inclinations on the biological level. It is constructed from the bottom up for reasons that will become clearer as we go along.

Natural inclination on the biological level	Survival	Sexual Inclination	Curiosity in order to learn and to communicate
Ontological level	All substances	Animals	Human

Figure 5.1 Table showing the different ontological levels and the corresponding inclinations on the biological level.

It ought to be noted that on the biological level, urges can be experienced at different levels of intensity at different moments depending on varying circumstances. I may be hungry now but in twenty minutes it may have passed, especially if I am engaged in a fun game. The urges can be triggered involuntarily, due to chemical processes in the body and images thrust into the imagination from the external senses and the memory. They are in some way wild, and a person is not considered responsible for the biological urges that he or she experiences but is expected nevertheless to know how to exercise restraint and to manage these urges. Take, for example, the buzz or ring of a cell phone. Curiosity is awakened to know who is calling. Nevertheless, if one is in a meeting or in a conversation with another person, it is not very good manners to put someone you are with on hold to answer a call. Yet how often this happens! Not infrequently one finds people disconnected from others around them because they are on their phones checking messages, websites, and social media. The urge to know and to be connected is very strong, but it ought to be moderated and oriented by the higher powers in man.

5.4 Biological inclinations in action: Sense perception and appetites

Having identified the inclinations on the biological level, it is important to consider how they impact on behaviour.

5.4.1 Sense perception of concrete objects

How is an object perceived as good for a subject? On the biological level, objects are perceived via what is usually termed sense perception. In this section, in order to centre squarely on the biological level, the human person will be considered from the perspective of what he or she has in common with the animal kingdom with regard to perception. If we subtract all that is spiritual from a human person, we are left with something that is more akin to a creature in the animal world. The process of cognition and response in such creatures is also present in the human being. Because of this, the description offered in this section, while applicable to human beings, is essentially a synopsis of perception in animals. As a result, the concepts explained will be mostly illustrated using examples from the animal kingdom.

The process of cognition on the biological level, or, we can say, for animals, begins with the external senses that gather information about the object. There are five external senses: sight, hearing, taste, touch, and smell. This information is then processed by an internal faculty that carries out several functions.

In the first place, the data from the senses need to be coordinated to form an impression of the object as a whole. There is what we can call a coordinating internal sense in the internal faculty that provides an internal projection of the object. Its role is:

> 1. To discriminate between the particular inputs of each external sense
> 2. To unite/combine them into a perceptual whole
> 3. To perceive aspects of the object that simultaneously affect several senses (For example, it both looks and feels smooth)
> 4. To distinguish between input from external senses and from the imagination

Together with the coordinating internal sense, an important function for sense perception is the estimative power. This is the ability to discern whether an object is useful or harmful, based on the information provided by the external senses, their internal projection, the memory, and the imagination. The estimative function connects the current perception of something pleasant, or its imaginary representation, to instinct, which in turn activates desire.[7]

To illustrate sense perception, consider the case of a dog digging in the ground to unearth a frog. The hound smells the frog and may perceive movement below the ground. The coordinating internal sense unites these inputs and relating it to past or future scenarios, the hound may be impelled to draw it out as a possible object of prey. In this case, the internal estimative sense would have connected the current perception and the imaginary representation of the thing in the ground with a "hard wired" notion of something good and desirable for the subject. Not all dogs, however, would actually bite a frog. In fact, frogs are poisonous to dogs. If the hound manages to catch the amphibian, it can then apply its senses more fully to the object in hand. With the new information, the internal estimative sense may judge the trapped animal to be harmful and trigger chemical processes to prevent the dog from biting into the creature and to leave it alone. This reaction may be instinctive or learned.

In the process of sense perception, the memory, and the imagination play an important role. These can be described as follows:

The memory re-presents images or phantasms of previously sensed objects in their absence, within a perceptual experience and a definite temporal context. It identifies past as past.

The Imagination re-presents images or phantasms of previously sensed objects in their absence as possibilities. This is *reproductive imagination,* and it pertains to the biological level. There is also a *creative imagination* that elaborates images or phantasms of things never actually perceived by the senses, drawing on previous sensations. This is more proper to man.

5.4.2 The duality of sensitive reactions—the sense appetites

Classical philosophical psychology deals with the problem of the enumeration and classification of responses to stimuli, establishing two basic categories—the *concupiscible appetite* and *the irascible appetite*. The duality of the appetitive faculties is based on two distinct ways of grasping a good in time. Sense perception of a good in the immediate present is the basis for desire and the enjoyment of possessing that object. On the biological level, this constitutes the concupiscible appetite. The grasping of a good in the context of the past and/or the future according to the manner in which it is perceived by the internal senses, is the basis for *the irascible appetite*. It enables desire to be referred to goods that are beyond the immediate presence of the faculties associated with sensibility.[8] This happens, for example, when a cat has to go out to hunt for its prey or a hound has to seek out its mate. The creature will undoubtedly have to suffer to overcome the obstacles to achieving its goal. The irascible appetite thus corresponds to a spirited core that motivates and stimulates a creature to make the sacrifice needed to overcome the obstacles in the way of its purpose.

It is useful to distinguish two modes of sense appetite because it helps us to understand that a creature's behaviour is not wholly determined by the prospect of immediate pleasure or avoidance of pain. We know from neuroscience that the two dynamisms of immediate satisfaction (concupiscible appetite) and of struggle to obtain a desirable good (irascible appetite), are linked to patterns of interacting neurons in the brain that intervene when a subject is placed in a given environment. As the creature becomes familiar with its environment, it can recognize patterns in its surroundings as well as recall other patterns related to its past interactions with those surroundings. By engaging the imagination, it can also have a future projection of possible scenarios. All this is a dynamic reality where certain courses of actions prevail over others based on competing patterns that are evaluated based on instinct. We can say that there is an underlying pattern that shapes all others, which is the tendency every creature must behave in a way that brings about its own well-being and preservation according to its nature. Every action a bird does must connect with its nature as a bird. Every action of a dog or cat is likewise necessarily related to the specific way of acting that characterizes that species.

5.4.3 The passions

In the Aristotelian model of sense perception and action, after the estimative power has evaluated the desirability of the object perceived, powers are activated to move the subject to possess or move away from the object perceived. Some objects are more difficult to attain and require the overcoming of obstacles. Others are more easily attainable and bring pleasure readily. Traditionally, the powers that are activated to move the subject towards or away from an object are called *passions*. The definition of passion, as gleaned from St. Thomas Aquinas is as follows: *A movement of the sense appetite, which follows the apprehension of the senses, and is accompanied by a bodily transmutation.*[9] Following St. Thomas, there is a classical representation of passions placing them in two categories. The first class of passions are those that correspond to the concupiscible appetite and the second are those that correspond to the irascible appetite.

The notion of *passions* is useful because it helps us to characterize and classify a type of driving force behind concrete action on the biological level. In ordinary language we sometimes use the words "passions" and "emotions" interchangeably. To clearly distinguish the three levels of action in the human person, here we will focus on the passions as they appear in the animal kingdom in general. In this context they will refer to impulses related to a biological sense of self, as opposed to emotions which will be considered as impulses related to a spiritual awareness of self.

Connected to the notion of a biological sense of self, it should be kept in mind that, considered independently, the passions can only present a partial explanation for the behaviour of a subject in a given environment. More importantly is the understanding of its nature. Depending on what a thing is, we derive the first and most fundamental characterization of its behaviour. The passions that are activated when a cat is near water will be entirely different from those of a frog, for example. A cat experiences aversion to a pond, whereas a frog will be attracted to it and most likely will jump in. This happens because they have different natures, different ways of being with regard to fundamental operations such as nourishment, survival, growth, communication and reproduction. They have a

The biological dimension of the human person

different biological sense of self. With this in mind, we continue with the exposition of the passions.

For objects easily attained, the following six passions can be listed in pairs as opposites:

Attraction towards an object (the object is perceived as good or desirable)	Repulsion away from an object (the object is perceived as evil or harmful)
Joy/Gladness (present good)	**Sadness** (present evil)
Desire (imminent good)	**Aversion** (imminent evil)
*__Love__ (good as such)	*__Hatred__ (evil as such)

Figure 5.2 Table showing the passions related to the concupiscible appetite.

For objects difficult to obtain five passions can be listed in pairs as opposites:

A good difficult to obtain	An evil difficult to avoid
Hope (absent but attainable good)	**Despair** (absent, unattainable good)
Courage (a difficult obstacle that can be overcome)	**Fear** (a real or imagined evil that cannot be avoided)
(N/A - a present good difficult to obtain is contradictory)	**Anger** (unavoidable present evil)

Figure 5.3 Table showing the passions related to the irascible appetite.

Love and Hatred were listed with a star because they are passions linked to cognition on a spiritual level, as only on this level can a good or evil be perceived as such. They were included in this list under the biological dimension for the sake of completeness.

All the other passions can be exhibited on the level of creatures with sense organs, that is, animals.

To illustrate the passions, we can consider different scenarios involving the concupiscible appetite and the irascible appetite. The passion of gladness belongs to the concupiscible appetite, and it is felt by a dog, for example, that is given a big bone. A hound will normally take it away and enjoy spending time gnawing at the different parts of it. It may happen that the owner takes it away after a certain amount of time. The dog misses its bone and becomes sad. To prevent this from happening, some dogs bury their bones to hide them.

Continuing with our pet dog, we can point to the passion of desire when the creature sets about to retrieve its hidden bone. The item is not immediately present, but it was hidden in a place where it can be easily recovered. The passion of desire also applies to goods that are not so easy to obtain. An instance of this would be the same animal that must get past a high fence to mate with its friend next door. The mating instinct is very strong in hounds and dogs do extraordinary things to ensure the preservation of their species. In this case, other passions intervene, those related to goods that are difficult to obtain. With hope, the animal will keep trying to get over the fence. If the dog is creating a lot of commotion, the owner may lock it up and the creature will then despair.

Staying with the same creature, a pet dog may experience aversion when he sees its owner coming to tie it. The object is not immediate, but dogs have a way of knowing when they are going to be tied. The animal may try to keep out of the reach of the owner. If it is well trained, it should eventually comply, heeding the pack instinct or out of fear or both.

Turning to the passions of the irascible appetite, these can be illustrated in other ways that a dog behaves. Because of its strong pack instinct, these creatures can show great courage to defend their owners. They are also territorial. As a result, they will also display courage to repel an intruder. In both instances their anger often flares up with loud barking, growling and the tensing of muscles in a posture to attack. When dogs are taken away from their owners and displaced, they become very timid and afraid. The passion of fear is greatly accentuated. Some hounds never adjust well to their new environment and undergo a change of personality.

5.4.4 Conditioning

To the model outlined above, we can add the phenomenon of conditioning which was discovered and developed by the Russian physiologist Ivan Pavlov in the 1890's by observing salivation in dogs. He started from the idea that there are some things that a dog does not need to learn. For example, dogs don't learn to salivate whenever they see food. This 'reflex' is hard-wired into the dog. There are other things like a bell that do not produce this reflex action. Pavlov showed that by ringing a bell, for example, just before food is given to a dog, after a number of repeats of this procedure, the dog will begin to salivate when the bell is rung on its own. This is called conditioning and the response is a conditioned response.

Pavlov's work suggests that animals can be conditioned through repeated experiences they may have had in their history. The internal reaction, and following on that, the external response of an animal to an object in a given situation is determined by how it is "hard-wired" but also by how it has been conditioned.

Added to Pavlov's work, B. F. Skinner developed the theory of *operant conditioning* by conducting various experiments on animals. He used a special box for his work with rats. Rats learned to press a lever to obtain food. His work suggests that changes in behaviour are the result of an individual's response to events or stimuli that occur in the environment.

Bringing together the elements above, what then is the outcome in action before a concrete object? The answer is that it depends on how the object is perceived and its convenience evaluated in the internal senses, and how the appetites are activated in the context of how the animal has been conditioned. Whatever the action may be, in the end, the nature of the subject, manifesting itself through the instincts and tendencies, is the cause that gives unity, consistency and purpose to the behaviour of a particular species of animal.

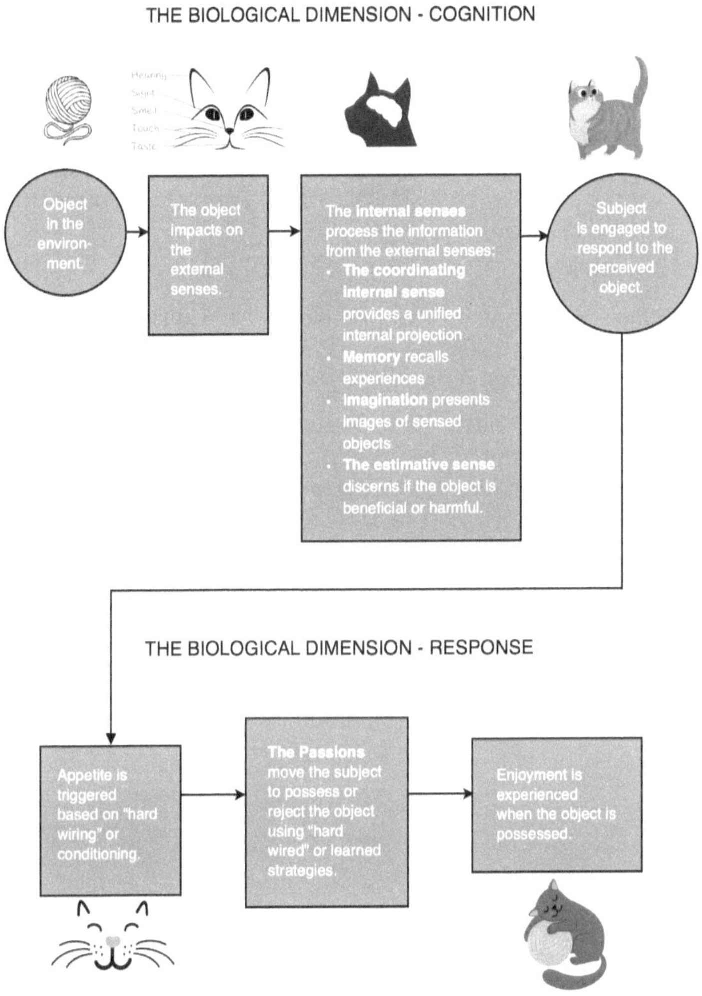

The biological dimension of the human person

THE BIOLOGICAL DIMENSION - COGNITION

- Object in the environment.
- The object impacts on the external senses.
- The internal senses process the information from the external senses:
  - **The coordinating internal sense** provides a unified internal projection
  - **Memory** recalls experiences
  - **Imagination** presents images of sensed objects
  - **The estimative sense** discerns if the object is beneficial or harmful.
- Subject is engaged to respond to the perceived object.

THE BIOLOGICAL DIMENSION - RESPONSE

- Appetite is triggered based on "hard wiring" or conditioning.
- **The Passions** move the subject to possess or reject the object using "hard wired" or learned strategies.
- Enjoyment is experienced when the object is possessed.

Figure 5.4 The cognitive and response sides of concrete action on the biological level.

Notes

1. Leonardo Polo, *Quién es el hombre* (Madrid: Rialp, 2003), chap. 3.
2. *Catechism of the Catholic Church*, para. 2297.
3. Mariano Artigas, *The Mind of the Universe: Understanding Science and Religion* (Philadelphia: Templeton Foundation, 2001), 83–102.
4. Artigas, 83.
5. John R. Searle, "The Problem of Consciousness," in *Consciousness in Philosophy and Cognitive Neuroscience* (New York: Psychology Press, 1994), 105–16.
6. Louise Kirk, "A Bitter Pill to Swallow: Sex Education Must Face the Facts about Contraception," Adamah Media, April 20, 2022, https://adamah.media/a-bitter-pill-to-swallow-sex-education-must-face-the-facts-about-contraception/.
7. Robert Edward Brennan OP, *Thomistic Psychology: A Philosophic Analysis of the Nature of Man*, ed. Cajetan Cuddy OP (Tacoma: Cluny Media, LLC, 2016), sec. IV–XI.
8. St Thomas Aquinas, *Summa Theologiae*, I, q. 82, a. 2.
9. *Ibid.*, I–II, q. 22.

6 THE EMOTIONAL-PSYCHOLOGICAL DIMENSION OF THE HUMAN PERSON

Spiritual Dimension: Operations of the Intelligence and Will.

Emotional/Psychological Dimension: Impulses and sentiments connected to an awareness of self that powerfully influence choice.

Biological Dimension: Morphology, physiological and somatic functions.

Figure 6.1 The three dimensions of the human person

In the drawing above showing the three dimensions of the human person, the emotional/psychological dimension was identified as partly spiritual and partly biological. It is partly spiritual because the more important drives at this level are set in motion and sustained by rational judgement linked to the awareness of self. They are partly biological because they are felt as powerful spontaneous physiological impulses. Modern Psychology has identified three fundamental needs at the emotional level. These are:

1. Feeling safe
2. A sense of belonging
3. A sense of significance

These distinctions are clearly set out, for example, in the well-known Maslow hierarchy of needs that appear in many texts on motivation.[1] In this text they are not considered as a hierarchy, but side by side as three vital categories of emotions. Furthermore, while these longings can be regarded and needs, perhaps more importantly, they are also inclinations which, when properly integrated, help the individual person to achieve authentic human fulfilment. The discussion in this chapter looks at emotions from this perspective in the first place.

Emotions are being considered in this book to differentiate a clear dimension of the human person, which has its own structure and dynamism. At the same time, it is with the view of showing how these realities are oriented towards integrated action for the overall good of the human person. To this end, it helps to bring to the fore two aspects of emotions. Firstly, as previously mentioned, the core emotions are also natural inclinations or tendencies. Secondly, they are drives that are related to a judgement linked to an awareness of self. In an important work, Antonio Malo lists the core emotions from this perspective. The three fundamental tendencies on the emotional level can be formulated as:

1. Personal survival (Independent "I")
2. Personal relationship ("I" valued by another for who I am)
3. Personal recognition ("I" valued for my role in a community or in society)[2]

Taking a close look at these tendencies, one can observe immediately that there is a correlation between them and the inclinations on the biological level. In

The emotional-psychological dimension of the human person

other words, we can now add another row to the table that was done earlier, to give the following scheme (to be looked at from the ground level going up):

Tendency or inclination on the emotional/ psychological level	Feeling safe (Independent "I")	Sense of Belonging ("I" valued by another for who I am)	Sense of Significance ("I" valued for my role in a community)
Natural Inclination on the biological level	Survival	Sexual Inclination	Curiosity to learn and to communicate

Figure 6.2 The corresponding inclinations on the biological and emotional levels

6.1 Feeling safe or independent "I"

It is not hard to appreciate that feeling safe is a core emotional tendency. We need to feel free from harm in the present and also have a minimum of guarantee for our future well-being. Consider, for example, how much money we spend on securing our homes and possessions, even though there might not be an immediate threat. As crime heightens in a city, people make great sacrifices to build bigger walls, limit their movements, hire guards and so forth. For the sake of feeling safe, you have the impression that some houses are like prisons, except that, rather than keeping people in, they are meant to keep people out. So, we choose to live in prisons, something that you would never imagine doing if the offer were made to you. Feeling safe drives us to behave in this way. On a more spectacular scale, it is shocking to observe the situation of refugees all over the world. To escape their countries, they take huge risks with all their savings and possessions and with their very lives as well, on a chance that they may find a more secure living in a foreign land. These telling examples reveal how powerful this emotion is. It orients our actions, more than just to a single object to be obtained as on the biological level, but to patterns of behaviour over a sustained period of time.

6.2 A sense of belonging or "I" valued by another

Consider what life would be like without someone who values and loves you just for who you are—a gift. You may see yourself as useful to someone because of what you can do, but you know that when you are no longer useful you will be basically worthless. It is easy to see how someone can easily fall into anti-social behaviour if he or she has no love to live up to; a love that says: "you are not worthless and never will be"; "I am always here for you and count on you to be there for me". Without love, suicide becomes attractive as that way you solve the agony of not belonging.

Another way to see the importance of a sense of belonging is to consider the many situations of dependency that one finds in relationships and gangs. It is mind-boggling to observe how frequently women, for example, remain in abusive relationships just to feel appreciated and loved by someone. We see this too, in gangs where young boys and girls join gangs to have a sense of belonging. Unscrupulous men and gang leaders know how to prey on this powerful emotion to manipulate others. These are things that are plain to see by everyone. In addition, there are many psychological studies that place healthy relationships at the centre of a happy life. Brené Brown, for example, highlights this point in her popular Ted Talk on vulnerability.[3] She describes her extensive research on the importance of human connection for happiness, showing the importance of belonging and love, and the role of vulnerability for developing this aspect of life.

There is also the well-known Harvard study on longevity and happiness that identified healthy relationships as the most important factor for living longer and being happier.[4]

6.3 Sense of significance or the "I" valued for a role in a community

It is very embarrassing when you can't give straight and simple answers to questions about your studies, work, profession, and career. Think how hard it is to tell someone that you failed an exam or lost your job. There may be good reasons, but one fears that the esteem of others will be lost. Ordinary experience tells us that this is a very deep and powerful emotion. To be recognized by others, some people will go to the extent of lying about their achievements and cheating to look good. Seeking recognition, others may have an exaggerated dedication to work or some other task, losing the balance with other important things such as health, family and faith.

When an individual is mature and settled in a life project, sense of significance is mostly tied to living for something that is bigger than oneself. At times the word "vocation" is used to express this reality. Vocation comes from the Latin root "vocare", which means "to call". Thus one is dedicated to a task that one has been called to perform. Vocation is felt as responding to a divine initiative that explains the very purpose for one's existence. An example of a vocation is to be a good husband and father or a good wife and mother. It is a task that embraces one's entire life and gives it a particular shape. The impact of having a happy marriage and a good family transcends the lives of the parents and reaches generations into the future. When a person has a vocational sense to life, he or she does not need the affirmation or esteem of others to persevere. It certainly helps, but the very nature of vocation means that one trusts that the "Caller" will make things work out if one does one's part. Sense of vocation makes a person capable of enduring great hardships and persevering to overcome obstacles for the sake of love and fidelity.

The deeply spiritual character of the sense of vocation does not take away from the fact that the desire to be recognized for a role is a strong emotion. The way a rocket works may be a helpful analogy. When a rocket takes off, it has a propulsion module attached that enables it to climb and reach a certain speed. At a certain height and velocity, the module is dropped, and the rocket must continue its trajectory on its own without the aid of propulsion. Similarly, a young man entering the professional world, for example, is attuned to positive feedback and recognition as he matures and develops his talents. He will need to be helped to discover a vocational sense to his life so that his desire to be valued by others for his abilities does not become disordered, leading him to an excessive dedication to work. If the individual responds to this help and has faith, then as he matures, the drive for significance will be channelled more internally than externally. It will be fulfilled in knowing that he is faithful to a life project and is trying to do his best. External recognition still has a role, but it will be of less importance. The individual continues his trajectory without this propulsion module.

The desire for significance has an important role of helping a person to be objective about their contribution. A woman who is a teacher, for example, may not be seeking recognition per se for educating students, but being valued by others for her work is a sign that she is doing a good job. This positive feedback will motivate her to continue coming out each day to fulfil her duties to the best of her abilities.

Society is made up of many interacting systems where each individual has a part to play. The larger part of the day of most citizens in a nation is spent carrying out the demands of the role they have in these systems. In the first place there is work, both in and outside of the household, and then there are obligations that arise from the various institutions and communities in which one is involved. These include, for example, school, sports clubs, religious groups, the neighbourhood community, political activities etc. Being held in high regard and admired is an affirmation that one is fulfilling one's function adequately, just as the opposite is an indication that one needs to improve, perhaps acquiring new skills. As a mechanism for gauging one's performance, the recognition of others that we are powerfully attuned to, has an important role.

6.4 Educating emotions

In the introduction to this handbook, the analogy of a boat was used to illustrate that emotions need to be managed and directed. The emotions are the motor and then there must be a braking and navigating system in place. Otherwise, the vessel will surely end up lost or shipwrecked. This does not undermine in any way the importance of the engine. Assuming there are no sails, without it, the vessel does not get anywhere. Persons who work with power boats understand that an engine is a complex system with different parts that need to work together in unison. Similarly, it is important for persons who work in character development to understand that there are a number of factors that influence how the emotions are engaged and expressed by different individuals in similar circumstances. These affect the ability of a child, for example, to connect with, assimilate and move towards concrete goals in the practice of good habits. It is useful to expound a bit on some of these dynamics. The following points will be considered:

- Genetic bias or temperament
- Emotional affirmation and regulation during childhood
- Family life, good example, and guidance
- Traumatic experiences in childhood and later years as well
- Psychological conditions

6.4.1 Genetic bias or temperament

Temperament includes behavioral traits that remain fairly consistent, particularly throughout adulthood.

For the sake of simplicity, we will adopt the following definition:

Temperament is a stable pattern of behaviour and reactions that proceed from the physiological constitution of an individual.[5] It is something unique in each person and there is no such a thing as a good or bad temperament per se. People of different temperaments tend to respond to identical stimuli in very different ways, and this way of responding tends to be consistent throughout the person's life. For each type of temperament there are advantages for practicing certain virtues as well as disadvantages for living others. It helps to be aware of one's temperament to better understand why one tends to react a certain way in similar situations. By educating one's emotions and cultivating virtue, this tendency can be managed to harness the positive aspects and to correct the disadvantages that it may carry.[6]

A common classification divides temperament into four categories: choleric, melancholic, sanguine, and phlegmatic.[7] This division does not mean, however, that a person can be classified, strictly speaking, as belonging to only one of these. A person may have some characteristics from each of them, but usually one is more predominant. Some of the salient features of these temperaments are as follows:

> *Cholerics* react quickly and intensely. They are decisive, extroverted and action-oriented. A choleric is challenged by humility.
> *Melancholics* tend to value the ideal—whether it be truth, beauty, justice, or unity. They are deep and idea-oriented, given to solitude and reflection. Persons with this

temperament are compassionate and devout. A melancholic is challenged by daring.

The *sanguine person* is creative, fun-loving, and high-spirited with a natural tendency to look at the bright side of things. They are spontaneous and people-oriented. A sanguine is challenged by endurance.

Phlegmatics are reserved and mindful in their behaviour. They are loyal and committed, tolerant and supportive and are not easily insulted or provoked to anger. Persons of this temperament are restrained and peace-oriented. A phlegmatic is challenged by magnanimity.

Our temperament is quite stable and does not change much throughout our lives. As much as one may try to hide it, it shows itself in underlying patterns in our behaviour that others pick up on eventually. There are simple psychological tools to discern a person's temperament. Some persons are trained to perceive these stable patterns in handwriting or in certain drawings that a subject can be asked to do.

A danger surrounding temperament is that it can lead to stereotyping others to the extent that one can make rash judgements about a person's ability to handle a given situation based on their temperament. Genes are of great importance when assessing a person's athletic ability for example. In the realm of emotional maturity, however, its influence may not be significant if the individual in question has cultivated the virtues needed to properly manage his or her temperamental reactions. It is important for parents and educators to keep in mind that they ought to have

The emotional-psychological dimension of the human person

the same high expectations for everyone, regardless of their temperaments. It would be sad if a teacher, for example, denies a little girl an opportunity to show courage just because she has a timid disposition. In fact, just the opposite is needed. The child needs to be put in situations requiring courage in order to overcome her fearfulness. She may not react well, but this should be overlooked as far as possible, encouraging the girl to keep trying to handle those situations better.

An example of a fear that may come with a nervous temperament is the case of a young man who is terrified to speak in pubic. To make things worse, he may even stutter. There are very inspiring stories, such as that portrayed in the movie *The King's Speech*, of persons who have overcome this disability through tenacity and of course, the support of others. Children can be cruel, making fun of the apparent shortcomings of others. Parents and teachers need to correct this when it arises, explaining that we need to help each other and that by ridiculing someone, we show ourselves to be silly. We will most likely be embarrassed later on when we will need that person's help. Imagine that the colleagues of St Thomas Aquinas in university called him the dumb ox! He was a bit chubby and taciturn. Their teacher, St Albert the Great, corrected them saying that one day the bray of this ox would encircle the whole world. His words were prophetic because this Saint is one of the greatest theologians of all times.

In forming the character of young people, it helps to explain the notion of temperament and to help young people to identify some of the temperamental traits that they possess. At the same time, it is important to transmit this information in the context that one can lean on the strengths that these traits bring and, at the same time, develop habits to counteract the weaknesses. The *Alive to the World* programme, for example, devotes a large part of Book 5 to helping the student to recognise and improve the strengths as well as the weaknesses that come from their temperament and to enhance their own particular talents.

6.4.2 Emotional affirmation and regulation in early childhood

Research in Neuroscience enables us to affirm that emotional development begins as far back as the womb of the Mother! Investigators have been able to identify the part of the cerebral cortex that governs our sense of self, emotions, self-control, and many other elements that make for a happy and balanced person. It is called the limbic system. Alongside this discovery, studies show that the cerebral cortex does not grow automatically but develops according to the stimulation it receives in the period of greatest growth, that is, during the first years, beginning in the womb.

The psychiatrist Daniel Siegel states: "The most common everyday experiences also shape the brain structure. Brain development is an 'experience-dependent' process, in which experience activates certain brain pathways, strengthening existing connections and creating new ones".[8] The goal is to achieve *integration*, which he defines from a neurological/psychological perspective. On his webpage he asserts: "Defined as the linkage of differentiated components of a system, integration is viewed as the core mechanism in the cultivation of well-being. In an individual's mind, integration involves the linkage of separate aspects of mental processes to each other, such as thought with feeling and bodily sensation with logic. In a relationship, integration entails each person being respected for his or her autonomy and differentiated self, while at the same time being linked to others in empathic communication."[9]

The lack of experiences can lead to cell death in a process called 'pruning'. Sometimes this is called the principle of 'use or lose' brain development.[10] Applied to emotional development, proper stimulation in the early years is crucial for emotional health. It starts with the love and caresses that the mother and father give their child from the first moments after birth. A remarkable scenario researched by Alan Shore and others is the mutual gaze of the baby and Mother. An energy emanates from the mother's brain, is transmitted through her eyes, stimulating the limbic lobes of her baby. This stimulation causes the secretion of elements similar to endorphins which cause the limbic lobes of the baby to develop as well as giving both mother and baby feelings of great joy.[11] The entire future emotional welfare of the baby is based in this exchange.

Together with stimulation, parents also play the role of emotional regulators, helping their child to develop the capacity to control his or her emotions. Mothers usually know perfectly well how much stimulation to give and when to calm her child. In a nutshell, science tells us that it is undeniable that mothers, in their constant contact with their children, are really forming the child's brain! When a mother is emotionally mature this is passed on to the child. Unfortunately, the reverse can happen as well. Emotional upheavals or immaturity on the part of the mother have negative effects on the child's emotional "wiring".

6.4.3 Family life, good example, and guidance

(i) Family life and education in virtue

Given the significant role of attention in early childhood, it is not hard to appreciate, on a broader level, the importance of family life. In the family a child is continually affirmed as a gift and blessing, worthy of love and affection. This forms his or her identity as worthy of such love and called to show it as well. During childhood another important way that affections are formed is through the acquisition of virtue.

The first steps in virtue are taken in the family. It is here they take root and the foundations for emotional maturity are laid. C. S. Lewis highlights this dynamic in this way: "St. Augustine defines virtue as *ordo amoris*, the ordinate condition of the affections in which every object is accorded that kind and degree of love which is appropriate to it. Aristotle says that the aim of education is to make the pupil like and dislike what he ought. The little human animal will not, at first, have the right responses. It must be trained to feel pleasure, liking, disgust, and hatred at those things which really are pleasant, likable, disgusting, and hateful."[12]

The importance of educating the emotions in childhood is clearly not new. Modern research has provided new insights to support this time-tested practice. Between the ages of 5 and 12 the minds of children are particularly tuned to grasping high ideals and to value the practice of virtue. In fact, it is regarded as a "window of opportunity" for schooling children in proper behaviour. This means that during this stage of life, there is a chance to lay foundations for reasoning and living according to the virtues that one may not have later on. This happens because a child's brain has a great deal of "plasticity" in this period, and they do not have preconceived ideas that they stubbornly hold on to. He or she is able to learn new concepts very quickly and to relate them to each other.[13] Together with this, children see their parents like "Gods", so they do not question the ideals and virtues they transmit to them through their example, stories, explanations and what they tell them they should and should not do. Part of what makes the 5-12 stage suitable for education in values, is that fact that the sexual drive is asleep. The minds of little boys and girls are free to wonder at the marvel of creation and to think of the power of its maker. Their imagination takes them on wonderful adventures of saving the world, destroying evil and exercising superpowers to ensure that good triumphs. An atmosphere of trust is the key element for effectively transmitting values and virtues during this stage and the family is precisely the environment where this loving confidence is assured.

(ii) The important role of good example

In the process of educating emotions, the importance of good example cannot be understated. The child's mind is in a stage of extraordinary growth and grasps patterns in his or her environment with great agility. One never ceases to marvel, for example, at how naturally and quickly children learn to understand and use the language that is spoken in their environment. This happens with proper conduct as well. Children pick up and imitate naturally the patterns of behaviour of their parents and other trusted persons in their environment. It is thus very important that they give a good example.

The presence of role models has another important function, which is that of reinforcing desired conduct that is communicated in language. There is a popular saying: "seeing is believing" and also "action speaks louder than words". A young person, for example, may be able to articulate many reasons for not using foul language with their peers. Faced with a concrete situation, however, they may give in to peer pressure. Deep down they do not believe that it is realistic not to use bad language at all in the given circumstances of their life. The moment one member in the group has the courage to act differently, others will begin to believe that it is not unrealistic and take the leap to live by a higher standard.

(iii) Guidance from trusted adults

In the education of the emotions, the guidance of trusted adults has an indispensable role. It is worthwhile to consider the contribution of the Russian Psychologist Lev Vygotsky. He perceived that an element missing in the entire Piaget system was the role that the social environment and the intervention of adults play in the development of the child. Vygotsky saw that in order to learn concepts, they must be internalized. The surrounding environment and the help of adults play an important role in this second phase.[14]

To explain his research, Vygotsky developed the concept of "zone of subsequent development". It refers to functions in the process of development that are not yet fully developed. In practice, this "area" represents the gap between what the child can do for himself or herself and what they can do with some help. So, when a balance between adult guidance and confidence in what the children can do by themselves is attained, the child conquers the next zone and is growing in abilities. Parents and educators are challenged to find that delicate balance where they communicate clear demands and expectations and at the same time allow the child to be as independent as possible and the protagonist of his or her own learning. Some parents spoil their children, doing everything for them. They may have good intentions, but in fact they are undermining the proper development of their children. Their offspring will fail to internalize the concepts and behaviours that the parents wished to pass on and will continue to be dependent on their parents into their adult life.

6.4.4 Impact of traumatic experiences on emotional development

When children experience abuse at a tender age, be it physical or sexual, from someone they trusted wholeheartedly to provide care, love and security, their emotional health is severely and at times irreparably damaged. Extreme neglect also has this effect and is another form of abuse. With exposure to such stress at a young age, children may feel that they are not worthy of love or affection and see the world as a hostile place. Later in life they will have difficulties in romantic relationships, in friendships, and with authority figures, such as teachers and police officers. They may find it difficult to think clearly and calmly, which is necessary for learning and planning for the future. Extreme stress in infancy impacts deeply, affecting the body's stress response systems, giving rise to reactions that are out of proportion when faced with a threat. The behaviour of abused children can be unpredictable, volatile, and extreme, where they do not calm down easily and fail to exercise self-control.

The reactions of a child who has experienced traumatic stress may also be the other extreme of being unresponsive and detached. Being numb to external demands is a way to protect oneself from further trauma.

A source of traumatic stress that should not be overlooked is that of neglect. To make ends meet, parents may find themselves often away from their children, and when at home, lacking the energy to properly engage them. Traumatic stress can build up bit by bit in children under these circumstances. Research shows that in neglectful environments, an absence of mental stimulation hinders brain development, which gives rise to difficulties in identifying, expressing, and managing emotions later on.

Returning to trauma in general, professionals use the term *Complex trauma* to refer to exposure to varied and multiple traumatic events, often of an invasive, interpersonal nature. Dissociation is often seen in traumatized infants where they disconnect from reality or past experiences. The National Child Traumatic Stress Networks affirms that "Complexly traumatized children are more likely to engage in high-risk behaviours, such as self-harm, unsafe sexual practices, and excessive risk-taking such as operating a vehicle at high speeds. They may also engage in illegal activities, such as alcohol and substance use, assaulting others, stealing, running away, and/or prostitution, thereby making it more likely that they will enter the juvenile justice system."[15]

Persons who have suffered traumatic stress often need professional help to come to terms with their situation and to make headway in reversing the psychological damage done. The usual self-help strategies aimed at forming new habits are ineffective as the person is not in a normal situation emotionally. They may need to be medicated and closely supervised in specialized institutions. Of course, it must be recognized that the behaviour of children exposed to complex trauma is not their own fault. Much of the responsibility lies with the adults who have perpetrated the abuse and neglect.

In leading children to emotional maturity, it is important to take into consideration that traumatic experiences in early childhood can lead to emotional disorders. At times it will be necessary to seek professional help to deal with these issues. A very accessible and well put-together resource for information and assistance on this topic is the National Child Traumatic Stress Network (NCTSN). Their mission is to raise the standard of care and improve access to services for traumatized children, their families, and communities throughout the United States.[16]

6.4.5 Psychological conditions

Science and medicine have identified conditions on the emotional or psychological level that follow certain patterns, and which may require specialized treatment. Symptoms of these syndromes could be learning difficulties, the violation of cultural standards of behavior, the exhibition of behavior harmful to self or others or the experience of distress from chronic and painful anxiety.

The frequency of these illnesses is high. Globally, for example, more than 264 million people of all ages suffer from depression.[17]

It is beyond the scope of this book to discuss special conditions related to the psychological sphere. Nevertheless, persons who work in the formation of children and young people should try to become familiar with some of the symptoms of these syndromes. In this way they could help the persons in their care to consider specialized help when there are signs that they may need such assistance. When conditions are picked up early they can be more effectively addressed.

6.5 Emotional and psychological inclinations in action: Cognition and response

How do tendencies on the emotional level govern human behaviour? For the biological level, we were able to describe how concrete action takes place with examples from the behaviour of irrational creatures. When we go up to the emotional/psychological dimension, there is a different dynamic in play for several reasons:

> 1. The object is now perceived rationally. It is considered under the aspects that affect the subject's emotions. (How does it make me feel?)
> 2. It is evaluated as convenient or not in terms of deep emotions connected to the sense of self.
> 3. On the biological level, the subject seeks to enjoy a concrete object. At this level it is more a state of contentment or happiness that is affirmed or enhanced.
> 4. Any emotion, regardless of the time frame in which its object is placed, is experienced in the present.

Concerning the first point, whereas on the biological level the objects are mostly concrete, on the emotional level the object can be any reality that can affect a subject's personal feelings. We are not referring to raw feelings that are the mere satisfaction of biological urges, but deeper needs linked to the awareness of self. Something concrete like food, for example, when possessed gives me a sensation of satisfaction. This same object can have a different impact on the emotional level if I consider it from the perspective of making me fat and unattractive (something I try to avoid). On the biological level food is normally desired to placate hunger, but on the emotional level, the same food can provoke a powerful rejection when associated with feeling unattractive. The object of emotions can be complex objects in the present such as playing with a child, or a future situation such as taking an examination.

An object affects a person emotionally because it is considered by the intellect under the aspects that affect the subject in this way. This perception is rational because it is connected to self-awareness, which is a capacity that pertains to the spiritual nature of man. The object is perceived in terms of its actual or possible impact on feelings or the emotional state of the subject. Take, for example, the case of two children who are quarrelling and teasing each other in class. The teacher asks them to stop and five minutes later they are at it again. The first time, the instructor would most likely have remained calm, trusting that the pupils would obey and that he would be able to get on with the lesson. He sees that there is no reason to get upset because what is happening is normal among kids, and the interruption is a small hiccup that should disappear after his intervention.

The third time the teacher has to correct the students, he may find it difficult to maintain the same serenity. He will begin to see the situation as losing control of the class and being an incompetent teacher. This thought process may be very subtle and hidden. It relates the situation to one of the fundamental tendencies on the emotional level, which is the "I" valued by others for my role. When deep longings related to the sense of self such as this are threatened, strong impulses of fight and flight are awakened. When the teacher has to speak a third time, he will experience strong feelings of frustration and anger towards these children. Evil thoughts may pass through his mind such as screaming at them or punishing them very harshly. Depending on how one has learned to be aware of and manage one's emotions in a situation like this, especially the deeper ones, the outcome could be disastrous. The teacher could end up "losing control", shouting at the children in front of the class and saying hurtful things.

Researchers in neuroscience have identified a part of the brain that triggers reactions of fight, flight, or faint. It is located in a complex, seemingly disordered mass of brain cells called the Amygdala. Daniel Siegel puts it in an interesting way. Imagine the brain as a closed fist with the thumb tucked in. The amygdala would be the centre of our palm, which is covered over by our fingers. In our brain, this covering corresponds to other centres of regulation and control that buffer the eruptions in the amygdala, integrating them into the whole cerebral system. We can compare them to a lid that contains the explosions inside. If we lift the lid, then the eruptive core dominates, and our reactions will be unbalanced and easily destructive. We metaphorically "blow our top".[18] By educating the emotions, strategies can be learned to better manage situations like the case mentioned. It is hoped that, in their training, teachers would have been prepared for circumstances such as these so that they would not be caught off guard. They may feel frustrated, but then be capable of distancing themselves from the reality, seeing it as a textbook case of class management to be studied and discussed later with other teachers. So rather than seeing the misbehaviour of the children as threatening their prestige, they understand it as an opportunity to improve.

6.5.1 Emotional regulation

Emotions are good and necessary, but they need to be regulated by the intelligence in order to correspond to what is reasonable. In the regulation of emotions, there are various functions of reason that intervene. Antonio Malo suggests three principal categories: interpretation, valuation, and rectification.[19]

Interpretation

Interpretation is the function of discerning the meaning of affective experiences. In the first instance it allows one to be aware of one's emotions without confusing them with others. The fear that one has from strange noises on a camping trip, for example, can correctly be interpreted to be jumpiness from being in an unfamiliar setting, rather than a real threat to one's safety. The help of others is crucial in forming how we interpret emotions. Using the example of the camping trip, the camp leaders who have experience can explain what the strange sounds are and make light of them by showing amusement at the reactions of the first timers. Little by little, comforted by the leaders, the newcomers themselves will make light of the strange noises and even see the humour in their initial reactions.

The interpretation of affections can be complex in emotions such as envy and revenge, and even more in dispositional moods such as rage and dejection. Persons often need advice and support to adequately interpret these sentiments. A point of reference is the three core personal longings that powerfully influence and orient the entire emotional systems of human beings. In the terminology of Antonio Malo, they are: the "independent I", the "I valued by another" and the "I valued for my role". By considering how the envy, rage, or dejection that a subject feels may be linked to these core tendencies, one can discover important clues for understanding and interpreting them.

Valuation

In interpretation, reason is applied to answer: "What is making me feel this way?" Valuation concerns the impact of an experience on the kind of person I am. It asks the question: "Am I happy with having this experience?" Or "Do I want to feel this way?" Humanity is broken, so we all have experience of feeling disordered desires that we wish would disappear. A woman may feel jealous of a colleague who is getting married to a fine young man while she herself is still single with no prospects on the horizon. When she stops to reflect on this emotion, she may not be happy with it at all. She understands that jealousy can lead her to be unfair to that person, speaking badly about her behind her back for instance. She may even feel a certain twisted pleasure in seeing her colleague experience setbacks in her work, health or finances. Meditating more deeply, she may conclude that she does not want to be that kind of person and take steps to overcome those feelings. It may happen in a similar circumstance that a woman with these negative feelings may allow herself to be carried along by them. Perhaps she is proud and does not want to face up to a disorder within herself. Sometimes people fail to recognize these destructive feelings because they do not take the time to reflect on their behaviour and to examine the motivations of their actions to see if they are wholesome and honest.

Another scenario would be that of a married man who is tempted to have an affair with a colleague. He feels a strong desire to be intimate with that other person. Upon reflection it is clear that the emotion he feels is driving him to actions that can hurt his wife and destroy his family life.

Emotions are not always disordered of course. A girl may feel a wholesome affection towards a good friend and show it in tangible ways. She feels calm and relaxed with that person and can share openly about things dear to her. At some point she may wonder if her affection for this person is too great. Upon examining her motives and perhaps after consulting with others, she can feel assured that she has nothing to worry about. This is a positive evaluation of an emotion.

A negative assessment can also apply to a lack of emotion. A mother may be cold and distant to one of her children, for instance, if she feels that her child is on the side of her estranged husband. A professional doctor can be clinical to the extreme of lacking empathy with the suffering of his patients and their families.

Value judgements are not always straightforward. They are made in the light of knowledge of self, one's place and one's purpose in life. It takes into account future goals, commitments acquired, responsibilities assumed and, in general, life in all its personal aspects.

Evaluating emotions rationally is very important as it allows for their proper integration into the unity of the human person. Emotions can be very intense and can completely invade the consciousness of a person, driving the subject to act in a determined way. For example, a man who feels offended feels impelled to respond by saying embarrassing and hurtful things to stop the offender from further humiliating him or to defend himself. It is often recommended that one should take deep breaths, exit the situation, and let some time pass before responding in circumstances like these. In that way, one can then approach the difficulty more objectively and rationally. Some emotions drive our behaviour in very powerful ways, such as the need to feel safe, to belong, and to be valued for a role, as explained earlier. The intervention of reason is crucial to objectify feelings that may be confusing, to understand their origin and meaning and to allow for their education.

To ensure proper valuation, young persons should be encouraged to have clear demanding goals, a personal mission and to examine the motives of their actions. It is also indispensable to practise the virtues. The word itself implies that the emotions are properly educated. Furthermore, a person who strives to live the virtues has clear points of reference for evaluating his or her feelings and behaviour. These criteria are the principles and good habits that they would have cultivated over time. As humility is the cornerstone of all the virtues, it will not be hard to recognize disorders when they arise and to implement the necessary strategies to remedy them.

Rectification

Sometimes, even when there is a proper interpretation and valuation of emotional impulses, a person may be unable to control his or her behaviour. A boy, for example, may have little motivation to study. With the guidance of trusted adults in school, he can interpret his lack of enthusiasm to be, in part, a reaction to an exaggerated impression of the work that he needs to do. He can also be helped by a mentor to work out a plan for his studies and to set short and long term academic goals. Having worked all this out, the young man feels good about himself. He has rejected his negative attitude to study and is happy about his goals. He is even clear that they are not inspired by selfish motives but a desire to contribute. With all this in place, this student may still find himself unable to settle down to study. The pull of the distractions at home to play games, wander around and do nothing overpowers him all the time. It may be that this individual is addicted to games and too accustomed to having things easy. This can happen when parents neglect their children over long periods of time and give in to their whims and fancies to avoid conflict or to "buy" their affection. The result is that even though the student may see clearly what to do, he can't because of ingrained bad habits.

Rectification means changing one's behaviour based on interpretation and valuation. Virtue is needed to bring about this change. This is why parents ought to be diligent to cultivate good customs in their children from a tender age. While needing a certain prerequisite of virtue, rectification also implies the cultivation and acquisition of new virtues. The virtues of integration that are outlined in a later section are particularly recommended for a happy life.

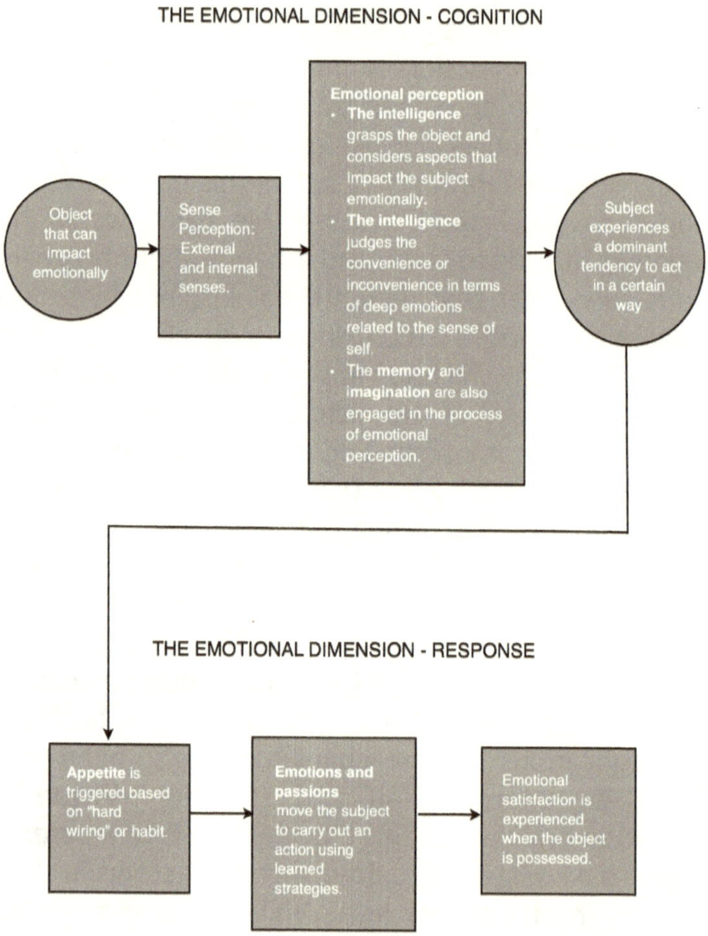

THE EMOTIONAL DIMENSION - COGNITION

- Object that can impact emotionally
- Sense Perception: External and internal senses.
- **Emotional perception**
  - **The intelligence** grasps the object and considers aspects that impact the subject emotionally.
  - **The intelligence** judges the convenience or inconvenience in terms of deep emotions related to the sense of self.
  - The **memory** and **imagination** are also engaged in the process of emotional perception.
- Subject experiences a dominant tendency to act in a certain way

THE EMOTIONAL DIMENSION - RESPONSE

- **Appetite** is triggered based on "hard wiring" or habit.
- **Emotions and passions** move the subject to carry out an action using learned strategies.
- Emotional satisfaction is experienced when the object is possessed.

Figure 6.3 The cognitive and response sides of concrete actions on the emotional level

Programmes for character building should engage students in the process of interpretation, evaluation and rectification outlined above. The Alive to the World series, for example, does this in an effective way by narrating episodes in the lives of two characters, Alice and Charles, as they grow from infancy to adulthood. Every story is structured around the successful integration of the three levels of action of the human person—the spiritual, the emotional and the physiological. This involves the proper interpretation, evaluation, and rectification of emotions. Being a continual story, it has the important feature of showing how proper actions and attitudes are assimilated over time, taking advantage of windows of opportunity in the developmental stages of growth. Helped by adults, the characters mature as they grow because of the decisions they make and attitudes they learn.

Notes

1. Mcleod, "Maslow's Hierarchy of Needs," 1.
2. Antonio Malo, *Essere Persona: Un'antropologia Dell'identità* (Roma: Armando editore, 2013), 175.
3. Brené Brown, "The Power of Vulnerability," TED Talks, June 2020, https://www.ted.com/talks/brene_brown_the_power_of_vulnerability.
4. Liz Mineo, "80 Year Harvard Study on Happiness," *Harvard Gazette*, April 11, 2017.
5. Art Bennett and Laraine Bennett, *The Temperament God Gave You*, 4th edition (Manchester, NH: Sophia Institute Press, 2005), 6.
6. Alexandre Havard, *From Temperament to Character* (New York: Scepter Publishers, 2021), chap. 1.

7. Bennett and Bennett, *The Temperament God Gave You*, 15.
8. Daniel J. Siegel, *The Developing Mind*, Second edition (New York; London: The Guilford Press, 2015), 22.
9. Daniel Siegel, "Interpersonal Neurobiology," Dr. Dan Siegel, March 8, 2023, https://drdansiegel.com/interpersonal-neurobiology/.
10. Siegel, *The Developing Mind, Second Edition*, 22.
11. Allan N. Schore, *Affect Regulation and the Origin of the Self: The Neurobiology of Emotional Development* (Hillsdale, NJ: Lawrence Erlbaum Associates, 1994), 72.
12. Clive S. Lewis, *The Abolition of Man* (San Francisco: HarperOne, 2015), 16.
13. Gail Gross, "Your Baby's Brain, Part 3: Windows of Opportunity," Huffington Post, November 12, 2014, https://www.huffpost.com/entry/your-babys-brain-part-3-windows-of-opportunity_b_5806108.
14. Lev Vygotsky, *Mind in Society*, 2nd ed. (Cambridge, Massachusetts: Harvard University Press, 1978), 86.
15. "Complex Child Trauma - Effects," The National Child Traumatic Stress Network (NCTSN), June 11, 2018, https://www.nctsn.org/what-is-child-trauma/trauma-types/complex-trauma/effects.
16. "The National Child Traumatic Stress Network," The National Child Traumatic Stress Network (NCTSN), 2023, https://www.nctsn.org/.
17. "Depressive Disorder," World Health Organization, March 31, 2023, https://www.who.int/news-room/fact-sheets/detail/depression.
18. Siegel, *Mindsight*, 98.
19. Antonio Malo, *Essere persona. Un'antropologia dell'identità* (Roma: Armando Editore, 2013), 189.

7 THE SPIRITUAL DIMENSION OF THE HUMAN PERSON

Spiritual Dimension: Operations of the Intelligence and Will.

Emotional/Psychological Dimension: Impulses and sentiments connected to an awareness of self that powerfully influence choice.

Biological Dimension: Morphology, physiological and somatic functions.

Figure 7.1 The three dimensions of the human person

The premise of this book is that man is a unity of body and soul. The soul is spiritual in nature and is the form or life principle of the body. With a spiritual nature there emerges the faculties of intelligence and will, together with an awareness of self. With these powers, a subject has the capacity to transcend itself, to know and choose what is objectively true and good. The opposite can also happen. A person can choose to turn in on himself or herself, settling for what is false and evil. We are free and responsible for our actions. In this section, we wish to elaborate on these realities in the context of an anthropology of integration.

7.1 Human intelligence

Intelligence is such an amazing power that many people refuse to trust it. Contemporary culture holds that knowledge is relative and that it is impossible to be objective. This relativism that reigns in the world today is rooted in the mistrust of the intellect that goes back to the radical doubt of Descartes on which modern philosophy is built. He sought a new foundation for philosophy and felt that he had to doubt all the impressions that he was aware of, both in his senses and intellect, in order to reach a new foundation for philosophy. Ultimately this led to a theory of knowledge where what we know are our clear and distinct thoughts and not reality itself. Certainty replaced truth.

Anthropology of integration rests on what we may call "popular common sense", where a natural trust is exercised in the powers given to us to know the world around us as it really is. I have no good reason to doubt that when I see a cat for example, and call it a "cat", pointing to it, that in reality a cat is there. When I grasp the nature of a thing such as a cat or dog, which has evident unitary behaviour, the notion possessed by my intellect conforms to the nature of that thing in reality, in this case a cat or a dog. Some things do not display a clear unitary behaviour, or at least one that is accessible to the human senses. For example: rivers, clouds, rocks, and inanimate things in general. Their behaviour seems to be determined more by the environment than their own operations. Machines and artefacts do not have unitary behaviour like natural living things, because they exist as tools or objects that humans use to shape their environment.

The spiritual dimension of the human person

Philosophy helps us to understand how our concepts relate to reality, but it would be terribly misguided to dispense with common sense and deny what is most proper to the intellect, that is, the simple apprehension of the nature or essence of created things, in particular, living beings. To sum up we can say that the intelligence is a power of the soul by which we are able to possess notions of things that conform to their nature in reality, and make assertions about them. Everyone has the power to grasp objects that have an evident unity and activity. We do not have to wait on experts to tell us whether we are deceiving ourselves or not. From the fact of being human, we have the power of simple apprehension. Once the activity of a thing is sufficiently strong and unitary, we are able to grasp its nature.

Aristotle synthesized an important insight regarding simple apprehension in a key statement in Book III of De Anima: "The soul is, in a way, all existing things."[1] He presents the activity of knowing as a power that transcends the individual. This means that through it, a soul comes out of itself and, in a way, becomes the reality known. As an analogy, if you were to grasp a Ping-Pong ball in your hand, your hand would take the shape of the ball. Suppose the air is somehow sucked out of the ball and it collapses. Your hand could have the same shape, but without holding a full-blown Ping-Pong ball. Yet you can still imagine that you are holding a Ping-Pong ball. You are not aware of anything round in your hand, but you are aware of the shape that your hand took when you held it. Something similar happens in knowledge. An object is at first in our senses as the ball in our hand. But then when it is removed, we still have it because of our awareness of how our mind was modified by it.

The capacity of the intelligence to have the shape or form of something, even though it is removed, is called intentional possession. Using the analogy of grasping and removing the ball from our hand, possession is intentional when the spherical object is taken away because what you know from the shape of your hand points or tends to the reality that was once there, even though now it is no longer actually held. Continuing with the example of the ball in our hand, the shape our hand takes is no longer of a specific ball, but the shape of any Ping-Pong ball in general. Similarly, our experience of different kinds of things in nature, such as cows or horses, leaves us, not with the shape of a specific cow or horse, but with the fundamental characteristics that define them. In other words, we grasp the essence or nature of cows and horses. Thus, when we grasp the essence or nature of something like an ant or a bird, it is because we know our own selves, having possessed (grasped) the essence of that thing intentionally. With our imagination and memory, we can recreate past experiences or new instances of the cow, horse, bird or whatever it is whose nature we possess.

The notion of intentional possession developed by Aristotle ties in with what we see in children as their intelligence develops. They enjoy pretending to be different animals and getting others to play along. They can pretend to be a dog, or cat, or cow, without it being a specific dog, cat, or cow that they would have seen in the past. This is because their intelligence has grasped the nature of these animals, and then by engaging their memory and imagination, the children come up with different ways that these animals can behave. This power is proper to human beings. We never see an animal pretending to be another. They can only be themselves because they lack intelligence. Man transcends himself and has a spiritual soul that is in some way all things as Aristotle affirmed.

When an object is grasped by the intelligence, its essence can be manipulated by the mind in ways that are not possible in reality. The analogy of the Ping-Pong ball is again useful here. When the ball is removed, my hand still has the shape of it. But now I can close in my hand a little and imagine that I have a small Ping-Pong ball. I can close in my hand even more and imagine that I have a tiny Ping-Pong ball. In reality no such Ping-Pong ball may exist. Similarly, when the intelligence grasps the essence or nature of a cat, it can now come up with the idea of a tiny cat or a cat with huge ears or paws, even though such a cat does not exist in reality. Engaging the imagination, I can form an image of what such a creature would look like.

In our minds we can shrink, enlarge, pull apart and put together things in a way that is not possible in reality. This is because we have left the real object behind and are now working with just the "shape of our own soul", in a manner of speaking. By manipulating things in my mind in this way, I can create a fantasy world and write fantasy novels that others can relate to because they have souls as well. In this imaginary world I can even attach to the behaviour of a creature whose form I possess, powers that it does not have in reality such as speech and emotions. Children love doing this and also to watch and read fantasy stories. They are naturally exercising their intelligence as it develops, to make it strong, just as they love to run when their legs begin to develop, to make them more robust.

The ability to unite and separate aspects of things in our minds also has an application in science and technology. As we grow and learn more about the world around us, we are able to formulate hypotheses and models that can help us to understand better and to manipulate our surroundings. This activity can have a more sophisticated and structured practice, giving rise to professional scientific research and technological innovation.

In the *Summa*, St Thomas Aquinas explains that there is an order in things that are grasped by the intelligence. In the first place, a thing must *be* before it can *be something*. So, the notion of "being" is included in all things whatsoever a person apprehends. From this follows the first indemonstrable principle that *the same thing cannot be affirmed and denied at the same time*. This is *the principle of non-contradiction*, and it is at the basis of correct reasoning.[2] We just affirmed above that man can be intentionally all things. We can pretend to be different living things in the created universe such as plants and animals. We cannot however actually become one of these things without ceasing to be human. This is an example of how the principle of non-contradiction applies. We can imagine a human being that turns into a frog but, in reality, this is impossible. You can't be a human person and a frog at the same time.

7.1.1 The practical reason and the principle of synderesis

The function of the intelligence to grasp and reason about the nature of things is referred to as its speculative power. It is the application of reason to the question: What is this? As one's understanding of the world around grows, there arises perhaps a more important question: What should I do? Our deliberation regarding our choice of actions is a function of our intelligence termed the practical intellect. There is just one intelligence, so at times this distinction can lead to confusion. Speculative and practical refer to two functions of the same intellect. The distinction is used because it follows the custom of the classical tradition inherited from Aristotle and St Thomas Aquinas. One of the reasons that it is useful, is because it builds on the metaphysical principle that *action follows being*. When we understand what a thing is, then we understand why it behaves in a certain way. If someone were to point towards an animal in the air and ask you: why is that creature flying back and forth, getting twigs, and arranging them together in a kind of bed? You would probably answer that it is a bird, and it is building its nest? Small branches and leaves are useful for this project. If we stop here, we have understood why those inputs are useful. There is a further question that could be asked, which is: and why is it building a nest? One then explains that a nest is a secure place where the bird can lay its eggs and care for its offspring when they hatch. If the person continues asking questions, it could become annoying and the answer in the end would be: because it is a bird and all that we have said just describes what birds do. This is what we mean when we say action follows being.

There is a deeper aspect to this principle that is even more important for the discussion in this section. Action flows from being but it also flows back to it. In other words, a creature acts to bring about its own perfection. Going back to the example of a bird, it acts in order to become a full-grown mature bird and to perpetuate its species. This is the end or purpose of its actions. When one is able to articulate the end or purpose that a being seeks, one can then judge whether something in the environment of that creature will have a positive or negative impact on it. Continuing with the example we are using, a predator for a bird such as a cat, will have a negative impact on its existence. Someone who insists on knocking down the nest of a bird because it creates an unsightly addition to their veranda has a negative impact on the bird and its offspring. The judgement of something being good or bad for the bird is only possible when we understand its nature in a full way that includes its purpose and end.

Taking this discussion a step further, in whatsoever a man apprehends, such as a bird or a tree, included in that notion is the idea of something that is, or "being". Just as "being" is included in the concepts of all that a person apprehends simply, so to the notion of "good" is the first thing that falls under the apprehension of the practical intellect. "Being" and "good" go together, because a thing that "is", necessarily is "something". In philosophical terms, this is called the formal cause of a thing. Inseparable from the formal cause is the final cause or the meaning and purpose for something to exist. As the intellect grasps that a thing "is," and that it is "something", it also grasps that it has an end. In terms of how a subject should relate to a thing in creation, the intelligence sees that it is good for a thing to achieve its end, and evil for it not to do so. This understanding of what is good guides the answer to the question: what should I do? The notion of "good" captured in relation to a thing's natural end therefore guides the practical intellect. St Thomas Aquinas sums this up saying: "Now as 'being' is the first thing that falls under the apprehension simply, so 'good' is the first thing that falls under the apprehension of the practical reason, which is directed to action: since every agent acts for an end under the aspect of good."[3]

Following on what has been affirmed above, we can assert that the first principle of the practical reason is one founded on the notion of good. In other words, "good is that which all things seek after."[4] From this derives the first natural precept or law that governs human actions: "good is to be done and pursued, and evil is to be avoided." It is called *synderesis*.

The rule of *synderesis* is a core metaphysical principle that is inscribed in the nature of every human being. Understood as we have formulated it, however, it refers to what is good in an abstract way. Each individual is now engaged to seek out the content of that good. What are the core or fundamental goods that we should seek as human beings? The human person is free, and so he or she can choose to move towards the good or away from it. Every individual thus faces two important tasks in life. The first is to discover and understand the core elements of what is good in terms of the nature that we have in common. In classical terminology, this is called the Natural Law. The second is to adhere freely to these points of reference and, in this context, seek out one's personal path, purpose and calling in life.

Regarding the first task, building on the classical perspective that we have outlined up to now, the angelic doctor points us toward the natural inclinations as the point of departure for knowing the core elements of the good of human nature. In the same question and article that we have had in focus throughout this section, he affirms:

> Since, however, good has the nature of an end, and evil, the nature of a contrary, hence it is that all those things to which man has a natural inclination, are naturally apprehended by reason as being good, and consequently as objects of pursuit, and their contraries as evil, and objects of avoidance. Wherefore according to the order of natural inclinations, is the order of the precepts of the natural law.[5]

Following on this intuition, anthropology of integration proposes that the way to discover the fundamental elements of what is good is by following the cues that are inscribed in our nature. These cues are the natural inclinations. This book suggests a framework for understanding how this is articulated.

7.2 From inclinations to fundamental values through cognitive integration

Going back to the biological level, the natural inclinations are revealed in drives such as hunger and sexual desire that seek to be satisfied. When these desires are aroused, an object that appeases these cravings will appear as good to my intelligence from the point of view of being satisfying. Upward or cognitive integration takes place in an incomplete way.

It is upward because bodily impulses influence the spiritual intellect. It is incomplete because the intelligence has only perceived a good that is satisfying and not one that is related to the overall good of the human person.

On the emotional level, the inclinations are revealed in more powerful ways. They are linked to deeper more lasting tendencies related to the sense of self. There is a parallel between the inclinations on the biological level and those on the emotional level. On the emotional level, we can match the survival instinct with a drive to feel safe. The bodily instinct for survival is related to impulses such as hunger, thirst, and reflex avoidance of harm, which seek immediate satisfaction. On the level of feelings, the subject is drawn towards a more stable provision of comfort in general, now and in the future. Objects and situations that bring this security are perceived as desirable in a more important way than on the biological level. Students, for example, will forsake eating and sleeping when they have exams. This is because they have in mind their security in the future, which is conditioned on having qualifications.

On the emotional level, the parallel to the physiological sexual urge is the sense of belonging. Here too, objects such as the affirmation, company and warmth of friends and family are perceived as more important than the immediate satisfaction of sexual desire, or of any other impulse on the purely bodily level for that matter. A young man and a young woman in a relationship will be careful to avoid doing and saying things that may hurt or disappoint each other. They will feel a deep aversion to such things due to the powerful drive on the emotional level to be valued by the other. On the positive side they will make great sacrifices to please each other. A young man, for example, will endure the tiredness of a long drive to be with his fiancée who lives far away, if only just for a short time. As on the biological level, perception plays an important role in sentiments. To practice chastity, for instance, it helps to have a keen awareness that a child may be conceived from sexual intercourse and the implications which that can have for the couple's life and that of the child. A young lady who is emotionally sound will feel a strong rejection to having a child outside of marriage. She will know from her nurturing instinct that her son or daughter may suffer a great deal from not belonging to a nuclear family if the relationship does not work out. Furthermore, having a baby will throw off her professional plans and put great financial strain on her and the father of the child.

The third inclination identified on the biological level was curiosity. On the level of emotions, its parallel is the sense of significance. This is a strong emotional drive that compels a subject to seek out and embrace his or her place in the world and in God's eternal designs. As with the other parallels, the objects that satisfy this need are perceived as goods that are much more important than those on the biological level.

Like those on the biological level, the drives on the emotional level influence the intelligence to perceive certain objects as good. The influence on the intelligence is more intense and powerful in the case of the emotions we have highlighted that are related to the sense of self. The objects that are desired can be more sophisticated and complex such as being perceived as beautiful. Upward or cognitive integration takes place, but again, only in an incomplete way. It is incomplete because the intelligence perceives a good from the point of view of meeting a subjective longing and not with the features of an objective good that is intrinsic to the dignity of every human being.

As we go up to a purely spiritual level, applying *synderesis*, we seek a good that is absolute, unchanging and immutable, which are the features of spiritual goods. On the biological level we observed that the goods a subject seeks are those that satisfy physiological urges such as thirst. On the emotional level, a subject seeks goods that meet needs such as being valued by others which are longings related to an awareness of self. On the spiritual level, a subject seeks goods such as human life, family life and justice, which transcend the individual person. They are not goods that merely satisfy carnal urges nor are they just goods that meet emotional needs. They are notions of things that are good in themselves. They are perfections that apply to human nature as such, and not just to John, Frank or Jane who share in human nature. As they regard the essence of what it means to be human, these goods establish a basis for the radical equality among all human beings. We are equally endowed with human life, equally entitled to family life, and equally owed justice.

Stepping back a bit, if I apply the process of simple apprehension to human creatures, when I go through the process of "grasping" the nature of another human being, something happens that is very different from when I "grasp" the nature of other creatures on the planet. While I can take the shape of or pretend to be the things that are not human, when it comes to another person, this becomes impossible. I cannot pretend to be a human being because I simply am one in everything I do, even pretending. Other human beings are perceived differently from other creatures. When I capture the essence of what it means to be human, I understand that it belongs to the nature of a human being to be a unity of body and soul. Other persons have the same nature as I do. They are "another me." Flowing out of this exercise, the golden rule emerges as an important principle of moral life: "Do unto others as you would have them do unto you". The other is "another me", which means that the evil I do not wish on myself, I should not wish on others and the human perfection I wish for myself, I should wish for others. This rule, called the golden rule, helps to understand why some goods are perceived as universal. These are goods such as life and friendship that I understand through the golden rule as good for everyone.

The activity of the intellect that seeks and grasps universal goods that are constitutive of human dignity completes the upward aspect of integration. The influences of bodily desires and emotions on the intellect are not suppressed but rather processed in the context of the spiritual nature of the human soul. The intellect, once is not inhibited to do so by the will, embraces the incomplete goods that it is drawn to consider from the lower levels, and tries to discover their purpose or end as phenomena that are part of universal human experience. Conscious of the radical equality between human beings and the golden rule, the end or purpose is grasped by the practical intellect as a series of universal goods, that are intrinsic to human dignity. Cognitive integration is complete.

Incorporating the subjective dimension, we can also regard the goods of human nature that are perceived on the spiritual level, as fundamental values that are known and adhered to as conditions for a radical sense of personal dignity and identity. Some authors prefer not to use the term "value" because it is often used in common language to denote freely chosen criteria for decision making that can vary from person to person, depending on their personal experiences, context, and convictions. One person may value cleanliness, for example, in a way that another person may regard as stifling and exaggerated. The term is also often used in economic affairs linked to the price of commodities and subjective utility. We say "getting value for your money", but the "value" is dependent on the subject's purchasing power, needs and knowledge with respect to the commodity in question. In this text, we are using the term in its philosophical sense. Authors Lombo and Russo defend this position in their book on Anthropology. Its core element is the objective human good that is at stake.[6] At the same time, the good is considered from a subjective perspective, which is the condition that it establishes for a sense of dignity and identity when perceived.

The subjective dimension that the term "fundamental values" incorporates on the spiritual level is useful for the goal of integration that anthropology of integration seeks. It's not enough to say that something is a good of human nature. A subject must adhere to it personally as a foundation of his or her human dignity and purpose in life. The self is free. It can internalize and adhere to a good of human nature, making it a part of his or her core belief system, or choose not to adhere to this good, ultimately undermining his or her own dignity.

The core belief system of an individual ought to be built on fundamental values. This core forms the kind of person that one becomes and by extension, the way one sees and values one's own self. In this sense we understand *values as universal goods of human nature, naturally known by the intellect, which, when perceived, are simultaneously internalized as constitutive of one's dignity and identity as a human being.*

As the object of values coincides with fundamental spiritual goods, they are *benchmarks for right and wrong*. Personally internalized, they have the following features:

- *Immutable* (They cannot change over time. They are the same yesterday, today and tomorrow)
- *Universal* (Are the same for every human being past, present, and future)
- *Obligatory* (They are grasped as precepts that we are obliged to uphold)
- *Vocational* (They give dignity, meaning and purpose to one's existence)

Thus, the inclination to self-preservation that St Thomas identified is considered on three levels. On the biological level it is the survival instinct. On the emotional level it corresponds to feeling safe or the independent "I", and on the spiritual level, through cognitive integration, it is present as the universal good that is life itself. The inclination to sexual union and care of offspring is also articulated on three levels. On the biological level it is the sexual and reproductive instinct, on the emotional level it is the sense of belonging, and on the spiritual level, through cognitive integration, it is present as the universal goods of friendship and family. Finally, with regard to the inclination to truth and knowledge, to relate to God and to live in society, on the biological level we can identify the drive to be curious. On the emotional level, there is the sense of significance or being valued for a role in a community. On the spiritual level, through cognitive integration, it is present as the universal good of society. The following sections take up this discussion in greater detail.

7.2.1 Self-preservation and the value of life

From the natural inclination to self-preservation, the intellect can come to understand that human life itself is a fundamental good of human nature. There are two dynamics at work. Firstly, the natural inclination makes me see as good what corresponds to it as an object: I am hungry or thirsty so this food or drink that attracts me must be a good for me in some way. Through experience, I know that there are times when it would be harmful for me to eat and drink. Overeating, for example, can cause indigestion and drinking too much alcohol adversely affects one's ability to perceive and respond to situations in reality. Nevertheless, the inclination or drive is always there, though at times dormant. I can apply my intelligence more deliberately to grasp the nature of the good that I am inclined to, and to consider why it is truly good for me. In the case of food, it is not difficult to comprehend that a meal provides nourishment that enables me to be healthy and to grow. Another example is that of a home. Persons who are starting a family feel powerfully driven to acquire their own home. The intelligence can perceive that a home is a stable environment where one can secure the commodities one needs and create an environment that is beneficial for having a family.

In the reasoning process described above, the intelligence advanced from seeing an object as satisfying to seeing it as useful. In the case of food, it is initially seen as placating an urge. When I grasp that it is nourishment to keep me healthy and make me grow, I understand it as useful for this end. The other scenario was acquiring a home. I may initially see this as meeting a need to feel safe. When I grasp that the objective is to have a space I can count on to have a family, I comprehend that a home is useful for this end. Having made the step from a satisfying good to a useful good, my reason can deliberate further. In the example we have been using, health and growth was the end for having a meal. It is a superior good to the mere satisfaction of eating. Going a step further, my reason can discover that when health and growth are lacking, a subject is at risk of death. This good, therefore, is ordained to a higher good, which is life. From the initial carnal inclinations, the reason comes to grasp something that is good in itself for the subject, which is human life.

A second dynamic at work is the golden rule. It arises when a person recognizes another person as "another me". A basic good that I desire for myself, I should also desire for others. This naturally also applies to realities such as life that are goods in themselves. The notion of a good-in-itself such as life, that I come to possess, I understand as a good that applies to others as well. It is a good of human nature and therefore has the characteristics of being universal and immutable. Applying *synderesis*, it is also perceived as obligatory.

In the process described above, in order to reach the notion of a universal good, the intelligence moved from a partial good suggested by the inclinations to a universal good. This is upward or cognitive integration. Just as the intellect can proceed from the partial to the universal, it can also descend from the universal to the partial. This is downward or formative integration. Once the will adheres to the good of life as a value, it will then seek to safeguard life, not just for his or her own self, but for all, in partial and practical ways. In the first place, a subject will need to cultivate a series of virtues that are related to safeguarding life. These are virtues such as diligence, industriousness, temperance, and order which are discussed in greater detail in a later chapter. As we move from the universal to the partial, the virtue of prudence intervenes to establish criteria and norms regarding the best way to safeguard life and to be secure in a given circumstance.

There are more things that could be added to this list of course. How these goods are provided for and distributed depends on the economic resources available, the systems of organization in place, the priorities of the different communities in a society and many more factors. Whatever the state of affairs in a given moment might be, the guiding principle is the value of life and the accompanying desire to seek the wellbeing and a better standard of living for all.

7.2.2 The sexual inclination and the value of the family

The sexual inclination in the human person shows itself in different ways. A woman, for example, may feel spontaneously elated in a chance encounter with a man. The sexual inclination is at work, but there is a strong element of perception that brings on the physiological reaction of feeling elated, and even mild loss of consciousness if the feeling overwhelms her. This reaction is triggered by seeing something touching or courageous, or something like that in the other. A tension is felt to have this person as a lifetime partner in a way that includes sexual intimacy. There are powerful evolutionary mechanisms of selection at work, which, like all feelings, need to be understood and guided by reason.

Another way that the sexual inclination spontaneously appears is in the feeling of being aroused. If a man, for example, allows his eyes to wander around the physique of a woman, it is not unusual that he would experience a bodily reaction that tends towards sexual gratification on the purely biological level. The individual feels an increasing sense of sexual tension. This motivates a drive to relieve this tension by engaging in sexual intimacy and ultimately intercourse. These feelings have their purpose, but they need to be understood and guided by reason to give way to integrated action.

From the natural inclination to a relationship or acts that are characterized by sexual union, the intellect can come to understand that spousal love and the family is a fundamental value. The transition from sexual inclination to a value takes place because the intellect reasons that the good is not just in the personal satisfaction of a feeling, or the relief of a tension, but in the perfection of spousal love in which a man and a woman establish between themselves an intimate partnership for their whole lives, ordered to the well-being of the spouses and the procreation and upbringing of children. The first dynamism at play is the inclination that makes me see that a relationship with the opposite sex that includes sexual intimacy, must be good for me in some way. The intellect considers this good further to see what may be the nature of this good. The inner logic of the sexual act reveals that an essential feature of its nature is to unite the male and female sexual gametes, which can then fuse to form a new human being that develops in the womb of the mother. Science has helped us to understand the complexity and yet powerful unity in this process, beginning with the mechanisms of fertility in the male and female body, to the birth of a new child.[7] Put succinctly, the sexual act is oriented to procreation.

a. The complementarity of the sexes

There is a deeper good in the nature of the sexual act that is not grasped as easily as the procreative element. A more in-depth process of reasoning is required, where the heritage of culture and wisdom play an important role. The sexual inclination brings to the fore the *complementarity between men and women* that is manifested in the various ways that men and women can work together and live together for a common purpose.

The affirmation that men and women are complementary in no way pretends to fit human behaviour into rigid categories. Here we are seeking to understand the nature of this complementarity, and not how a concrete person may feel towards someone of the opposite sex in a given circumstance. For the purpose of this book, complementarity can be looked at from the perspective of three fundamental features: radical equality, natural differences, and harmonic collaboration with a unitary purpose to reach further than the possibilities of the individuals alone.

Radical equality means that men and women are equally human beings, with the same origin, nature, and destiny. Every human being is "another me", and this applies to men and women alike. Someone with the attitude that men are superior to women in some way, and so more deserving of certain opportunities and rights in society, is dishonest and self-seeking. Men and women have the same fundamental dignity and deserve the same protection and guarantees for basic goods under the law.

As we affirm equality, we can also affirm differences between the sexes. The genetic basis for sex-based differences lies in the fact that females have two X chromosomes but no Y chromosome, whereas males have a Y chromosome but only one X chromosome. The chromosomal differences between men and women set in motion a sophisticated system of production and reception of sex steroid hormones during the entire life of an individual that gives rise to important differences in men and women. The most obvious feature that distinguishes the sexes is the reproductive apparatus. Women are equipped with the biological apparatus for childbearing and child rearing in the early stages when the baby is particularly dependant on the mother. Men are equipped with an apparatus to impregnate a woman in sexual union. On the psychological and spiritual level, this union is understood as mutual belonging and a sign and expression of spousal love.

The differences between the sexes goes much further than differentiated but complementary reproductive functions. The sex steroid hormones include androgens, oestrogens, and progestins. Receptors for the sex steroid hormones are present in numerous non-reproductive tissues, including the heart, bone, skeletal muscle, vasculature, liver, immune system, and brain.[8] In all these tissues there are features that are characteristically male and others female.

Enlivened by a single unitary principle that is the soul, it stands to reason that the differences on the physiological levels are manifested on the psychological and spiritual levels as well, giving rise to important differences. In her book *The Female Brain*, neuropsychiatrist Dr. Louann Brizendine writes:

> It's not as if we all start out with the same brain structure. They are different by nature. Think about this. What if the communication centre is bigger in one brain than the other? What if the emotional memory centre is bigger in one brain than the other? What if one brain develops a greater ability to read cues in people than another? In this case, you would have a person whose reality dictated that communication, connection, emotional sensitivity, and responsiveness were the primary values. This person would prize these qualities above all others and be baffled by another person with a brain that didn't grasp the importance of these qualities. In essence, you would have someone with a female brain.[9]

In her other book, *The Male Brain*, she highlights other characteristics:

- Faced with a personal problem, a man will use his analytical brain structures, and less so his emotional ones, to find a solution.
- A male thrives under competition, instinctively plays rough and is attuned to rank and hierarchy.

- A man has an area for sexual pursuit that is 2.5 times larger than the female brain, causing him to think and fantasize about sex more often.
- A boy experiences such a massive increase in testosterone at puberty that he perceives others' faces to be more aggressive.[10]

The differences highlighted here are general patterns but are not absolute. The way hormones are produced and received vary in different stages of life. Furthermore, through free choice, a man or a woman can cultivate patterns of behaviour that may be very different to those specified above for his or her sex. Thus, a man can come to exhibit the qualities listed under the female sex and vice versa.

Though the differences highlighted above do not apply in every case, they are not arbitrary. They allow men and women to work together in a way that unlocks new potentials that are foreseen in nature. A perhaps silly example to illustrate complementarity is to imagine two persons picking avocados from a tree. One is tall with strong broad shoulders and the other shorter, weaker, more narrowly built, but with nimble fingers and good balance. Working separately, each can pick the avocados within their reach. Let us suppose that neither can climb the tree and that there is no pole or stick for reaching the higher fruit. Now if the shorter one were to stand on the shoulders of the taller stronger person, then they would be able to reach avocados higher up as well. Working together in this way, we can say that their differences were complementary with regard to getting more produce.

In the case of men and women, there is a similar dynamic. Each on his or her own is not able to reproduce and adequately care for offspring. A man must unite with a woman in the sexual act for a child to be conceived. As spiritual beings, human procreation is more than a biological process. A child is a son or daughter and, with the parents they form a family. When two persons freely enter into a stable union to form a family, their union is called marriage. It is a bond that is established between the two in virtue of their radical equality as spiritual beings and, at the same time, the complementary differences that work together to form and build up a community of life and love. If equality were lacking, then consent would not be needed, as one party would be in a condition of dependency with respect to the other. And if complementarity were lacking, then there would be no reason for uniting. Each would have all they needed on their own to form a community of life and love.

Going back to the example of picking avocados. With one person standing on the shoulders of the other, there is an apparent loss of freedom. Neither is now able to freely run around, trying to pick the fruit that they can reach. They are now attached to each other, and they now need to come to a consensus as to how they will gather the produce on the tree. The loss of freedom is only apparent because now they have new possibilities open to them that enrich their lives. They can gather more produce and so there is more to go around for themselves and for others. In addition, they develop important skills and habits for communicating, teamwork, and self-control that bolster human dignity. Similarly, when two persons marry, they mutually belong to each other and so there is an apparent loss of freedom. This loss is superficial because they now have the incredible new potential of having children and forming a family. Such creative power ennobles their lives, and the couple is challenged to acquire new skills for communication and raising children, and to grow in all the important virtues for family life such as charity, loyalty, and self-control.

The way in which the differences between men and women are complementary become clearer in the context of marriage. It is important for the spouses to recognize these differences and use their knowledge of them to understand how they could better communicate, and to work out their roles and responsibilities in family life. Take, for example, male aggression. This is often regarded in a negative way as a feeling that leads to unfairly harming another person. In marriage, male aggression can be understood as a complementary gift that ought to be channelled into protecting and providing for one's family. Another example is the drive for emotional connection in women in general. This could become exaggerated and disordered if what is sought is only a good feeling. In marriage, emotional connection can be understood as a complementary gift that ought to be channelled into building a sense of belonging and self-confidence in others so as to bring out the best in them.

Wise men and women throughout the ages have handed down to us very rich teachings about marriage and the family. The dignity and importance of this institution is not immediately evident and, in fact, in some places it is sadly devalued. One hears of children being "married" off to ensure their social status and material wellbeing for example. There is the so-called "marriage of convenience" where two people marry because of the legal benefits that accrue to them. Some marry for sexual pleasure and material gain. Many marriages today end in divorce, which points to the need of returning to the wisdom of the ages regarding this most noble, dignifying, humanizing and holy institution. During his pontificate, Saint John Paul II worked very hard to harness this wisdom, bringing it up to date with the times. His writings on marriage and the family are a sure point of reference on this topic. Two important documents, for example, are the post-synodal apostolic exhortation *Familiaris consortio* promulgated on 22 November 1981 and the *Letter to Families* that was made public on 2 February 1994.

b. The integrity of the sexual act

The objective of the brief discussion above was to elaborate briefly on the context in which the nature of the sexual inclination must be understood. In the light of the complementarity of the sexes, sexual union has meaning when a man and a woman are united in marriage. It is in view of marriage that we can articulate the complete nature of sexual intercourse and how it can be a good for the human person.

An analogy that could be helpful is the difference between the functioning of an eye and seeing. The eye is a very complex system of nerves, sensory cells, muscles, and lens tissue designed to capture and process light so that the brain is able to form an image of an external object. How an eye works is different from seeing in a fully human way. The eye has done its work when it transmits neurological information to the brain. Seeing, however is something active. A young man with his new car in front of him, for example, does not see just light reflecting off the car. He sees his new car. Emotions related to ownership are engaged, making the individual see something that he must care for. He will be aware of the sacrifice made to purchase the car and so his eyes are very tuned to details that may reveal defects. His memory and imagination will be engaged to a high degree. This is a special moment and he would already be imagining taking out loved ones and friends. Someone passing by who is not very interested in cars, may have a look at the vehicle and see just another new car. A few minutes later, he or she may not even remember the model or the colour. It is always a person who sees and the experience of seeing is different for each person, even though the way his or her eyes function is the same.

Applied to the sexual act, there is a function which is the inner logic of the procreative act. The function is meaningful as an avenue for a couple to live out a happy marriage. A girl in an intoxicated state has eyes but does not see in a fully human way. She may drive recklessly even though her eyes are working. Similarly, a couple may engage in sexual activity. If they are not married, it is analogous to the intoxicated girl. The function is not integrated, and they fail to use the act in a fully human way.

Properly understood, the sexual act has two aspects that cannot be separated. There is the inner procreative logic that defines its function, and married love which integrates the function into a truly human act. In classical terminology, the two aspects are needed for the integrity of the sexual act. As an analogy, one can consider these two elements as two sides of a single coin. If one side of a coin is erased, that token does not have value as currency. Similarly, if one of these elements is lacking, the act does not have value as a truly human action.

There is a different analogy involving the eye that can also be useful. In his book, *Theology and Sanity*, Frank Sheed, uses the example of an eye in the face of a human being and one on a dish: "Take the human eye as a convenient example", he writes. "The human eye is very beautiful, as all lovers have seen. But the most ardent lover might find it hard to recapture his emotion if the lady, taking his praise of her eye too literally, decided to present it to him on a plate. The eye needs to be seen in the face; its beauty, its meaning, its usefulness all come from its position in the face; and one who had seen eyes only on plates would never really have known them at all, however minutely he might have examined the eye thus unhappily removed from its living context."[11]

Similarly, the sexual act needs to be seen in the context of marriage. Its beauty, its meaning and its usefulness all come from married love. One who considers sexual activity outside of marriage may have an advanced scientific knowledge about its inner functioning. That person, however, would never really know the exalted value and richness of the marital act.

The move from the sexual inclination to marriage may seem quite intricate, but it is in many ways intuitive when one considers the consequences of premarital sex. When persons are sexually active before marriage, if they are healthy, it is not surprising if a child is conceived from those relations. As they are not married, there is no guarantee that the male party will remain committed. A tremendous burden is placed on the mother to bear a child and care for it when it is born. If she does not have a solid network of support, she may see having an abortion as a way to escape the looming horror she imagines her life would become. The highly rated movie *Unplanned* shows in a dramatic way how women who are in such a predicament can easily end up doing what they never imagined they would do, which is seeking to abort their child. Later the horror is worse when they have to struggle with the guilt and shame of what they have done. Alternately she may choose to have her child and struggle the best that she can as a single mother. A woman can find meaning in this task, but it is a huge setback that can lead to depression from feeling inadequate and from struggles with unresolved guilt and shame. Is it worth the risk? Can premarital sex be a good choice for a truly happy life?

There is an additional danger that should not be underestimated, which is linked to the overriding good feeling that sexual intimacy brings. We say overriding, because this good feeling can lead couples to "drift" into marriage, when they neither understand nor are prepared for such a commitment. In an unmarried couple, the pleasure of sex can easily become addictive, introducing a destructive seed of carnal self-seeking in the relationship. This undermines proper communication as sexual indulgence becomes more dominant as the reason for being together. The couple may 'liken' their relationship to marriage because of the intimacy they share and then actually get married to give it legitimacy and to "piggyback" off the dignity of the institution. When the constraints of having a family become more apparent, things can easily break down and the couple drift apart, often ending in divorce. Sometimes these divorces can be bitter and crippling, wreaking havoc in the lives of the couple and also on those around them, especially on the children if there have been offspring. Premarital sex may bring a good feeling, but that cannot be trusted. Feelings should not be suppressed, but they can be relied on only when properly integrated into values. Again, outside of marriage, is sexual intimacy worth the risk? Is this choosing happiness? There are hosts of other factors that could be presented to show the negative consequences of premarital sex. The reader is left with the choice to further research and deliberate on this matter as she or he may determine. A recommended resource is Jason and Crystalina Evert's Chastity Project.[12]

It has already been discussed that an important dynamic on the spiritual level is the recognition of and adherence to the golden rule. We can apply it here as well. Once the will adheres to the good of marriage and family as a value, it will then seek to foster family life, not just for his or her own self, but for all, in concrete and practical ways. This is the application of integration. In the first place, a subject will need to cultivate a series of virtues that are related to family life. These are virtues such as loyalty, chastity, and charity, which are discussed in greater detail in a later chapter. As we move from the universal to the particular, the virtue of prudence intervenes to establish criteria and norms regarding the best way to safeguard family life in a given circumstance.

7.2.3 The inclination to truth and society

The framework adopted in this document seeks to link inclinations on the bodily and emotional dimension with spiritual goods that can be adhered to as values. When St Thomas Aquinas outlined the three principal inclinations, he pointed immediately to the spiritual goods of truth and society as the aim of one of the inclinations. This was the inclination, he said, that arises from our condition as spiritual beings. When the Angelic doctor leaps directly to spiritual good as the object of an inclination, he presupposes powerful drives and tendencies on the bodily and emotion level that are related to these spiritual goods. On the bodily level there is the drive of curiosity. From a very tender age, small children are curious about the world around them. Typically, a pram will have a baby mobile attached, and the baby will enjoy interacting with it to see what happens when he or she plays with it. As children get older, curiosity is heightened as they discover their own bodies and the world around them. The natural outlet for this is play. Curiosity often has a negative connotation, but here it is a healthy curiosity and children even need to break things to develop their brains and bodily coordination.

On the emotional level, curiosity has a parallel with a desire to be valued for a role in a community. At first glance the two may appear unrelated. The connection becomes clearer when we consider that the purpose of the healthy curiosity in the child was to develop his or her ability to manipulate his or her environment. The drive is thus oriented toward being comfortable in one's surroundings. As one matures, one comes to realize that one's environment is most importantly the systems of human interactions that one is part of. There are systems, for example, for organizing economic activity, education, politics and much more. The large part of the day of an ordinary citizen consists in the execution of a role in the various systems that are in play in a society. Taking this into account, we can comprehend that feeling well regarded or valued for the part one has to play in society is a powerful emotional need. When a person habitually falls short or fails in the fulfilment of his or her role or roles, that person feels embarrassed and insecure and wants to hide from the world. He or she may seek to impress by doing extraordinary things such as partaking in high-risk sports or by showing off with expensive wear and merchandise. Such behaviour can become self-destructive, which points to the important place of this emotional inclination to a sense of significance.

An example related to professional prestige can help to understand the dynamics of this inclination. A young lady who has recently qualified as a doctor is normally driven to know more about her profession. Her curiosity will be spiked whenever she hears about cases related to her field. As she studies, she will feel the satisfaction of knowing a lot about the workings of the human body, and this is a source of motivation. More importantly, this young lady is aware of her role in society, and desires to be valued and recognized in the career she has chosen. The prospect to advance in rank and prestige would encourage her to work hard and work well. Up to this point we have not moved beyond drives on the biological and emotional level. For this woman to give a truly human value to her work, it is necessary for her to reason further and to consider in what way that recognition and rank is good for her. She can come to understand that the good is not merely in the pleasant feeling of being well regarded or admired, but rather in the effective execution of a role she plays in a system of human interaction. It is the good of society that is at stake, which is a good in itself. If she adheres to this good as a value, she will understand that it is her dignity as a human being that is at stake in doing her part or failing to do so. Her true human fulfilment is in knowing that she has been faithful in living this important value at the heart of human dignity. The young lady may rise to be recognized as an outstanding medical practitioner, but she should be happy, not just because she is esteemed, but because the prestige and rewards she obtains tells her that she is fulfilling her function well before God and men.

When I come to appreciate that society is a good in itself, I perceive that it is a good for everyone. It is a good of human nature and therefore has the characteristics of being universal and immutable. Applying *synderesis*, doing my duties well in society are also perceived as obligatory. This completes upward or cognitive integration.

As with the other inclinations, just as the intellect can proceed from the partial to the universal, it can also descend from the universal to the partial. Once my will adheres to the good of society as a value, I will then seek to lovingly fulfil my social obligations and to participate in the betterment of society. I will seek to do this, not just for my own self, but for all, in concrete and practical ways. Here we are on the downward side of integration. In the first place, I will need to cultivate a series of virtues that are related to society. These are virtues such as justice, generosity and social love which are discussed in greater detail in a later chapter. As we move from the universal to the concrete, the virtue of prudence intervenes to establish criteria and norms regarding the best ways that I could contribute to improving society in a given circumstance.

7.2.4 Conclusion

Given that the fundamental values match the inclinations, they can be incorporated into the table drawn earlier as follows:

Spiritual level: Knowledge of fundamental goods and adherence to fundamental values	Life is a fundamental good worthy of adherence. "I" value Life	Family and friendship are fundamental goods worthy of adherence. "I" value Family/Friendship	Society is a fundamental good worthy of adherence. "I" value Society
Natural Inclination on the emotional/ psychological level	Feeing safe (Independent "I")	Sense of belonging ("I" valued by another)	Sense of significance ("I" valued for my role)
Natural Inclination on the biological level	Survival	Sexual Inclination	Curiosity to Learn and to communicate

Figure 7.2 The matching inclinations on the biological and emotional levels, and the related fundamental goods on the spiritual level.

It should be borne in mind that the table is read from the bottom up. The goal of grasping and personally adhering to the fundamental values related to the dignity of the human person takes place through the integration of the lower levels into the spiritual level.

7.3 The will

In the discussion on the biological and emotional dimensions of the human person, we distinguished between a cognitive side and a response side of concrete actions. On the response side the appetites were revealed in the passions and the emotional impulses. When we move to the spiritual level, which ought to dominate over the other levels, the chief appetite is the Will. *The will is the appetitive power of reason.*[13] He explains the will by relating it to the intelligence. It is the appetite that is responsive to the intellect's estimations of what is good or choice worthy. By its very nature the will tends to the good of the human person.[14] In matters of free choice, this good is first captured by the intellect.[15].

Understood in this way, all acts of the will are dependent on antecedent acts of intellect; the intellect must point the will towards the object to which the latter inclines. That object moves the will as a final cause "because the good understood is the object of the will and moves it as an end."[16] Understood in this way, it appears that the will is subordinate to the intelligence as it necessarily tends to the good presented to it. Surprisingly, it actually works the other way as well. The intelligence is subordinate to the will in that the will can direct the intelligence to consider objects from different perspectives just like a light can illuminate a statue from different angles. The proper function of the intelligence regarding moral action is to grasp the main characteristics of an object under the aspect of good, evaluating its convenience in the light of fundamental values. The will, however, can direct the intelligence to lose sight of the values at stake and to focus on the pleasure or emotional satisfaction that it affords. In this way the will is self-directing and human persons are free.

To illustrate this action, consider the scenario of buying goods in a supermarket. Perhaps you come across a costly treat that you don't really need, that will bring you beyond your budget and perhaps is neither in accord with your recommended diet. But you justify it saying: "I deserve a treat today for working hard".

Objectively, there is a lack of temperance here because there is no special circumstance to justify the treat. Wanting to indulge oneself, the will "hijacks" the impassioned proper functioning of the intelligence, directing it to consider the purchase of the delight as an immediate reward for work done, leaving behind considerations of temperance. In this way, the disordered desire is brought to fruition in the purchase and consumption of the treat.

7.3.1 True and apparent goods

It is useful here to distinguish between what can be called an apparent good and a true good. In the example above, the genuine good is in the exercise of restraint and making purchases that correspond to real needs that are within one's means. A treat is justified when there is a special circumstance. When the intelligence is allowed to and helped to carry out its proper function, the intelligence will show the will that it is good and reasonable to exercise temperance. The practice of this virtue is a true good that is genuinely capable of bringing about human fulfilment. When the intelligence fails to carry out its proper function for different reasons, the good that is presented to the will does not correspond to what is truly fitting or appropriate in the situation and context in which the individual acts. In the case at hand, it was the excuse that I need to be rewarded for working hard today. This good is an apparent good. It is not capable of bringing about authentic human progress and fulfilment.

We have considered how the action of the will can distort the proper operation of the intellect. Given this reality, it is wise to examine the motives of one's actions from time to time and seek to rectify if they are found to be disordered.

7.4 The spiritual dimension in action: cognition and response

Having briefly outlined the powers of the intelligence and will, we can consider more closely how these spiritual faculties are engaged in the two aspects of concrete action, namely cognition and the response.

7.5 The moral conscience

The cognitive process involves the apprehension of the moral object by the intellect and its evaluation of convenience or inconvenience in the given context according to the true good of the human person that is expressed in spiritual values. This evaluation or judgment based on spiritual values is called the moral conscience in ethics. *Conscience is a judgment of reason whereby the human person recognizes the moral quality of a concrete act that he is going to perform, is in the process of performing, or has already completed.*[17].

In any given situation, there are often several possibilities of acting and means that can be employed, including the choice of simply not acting at all. Because of this, apprehension and judgement is an iterative process that involves deliberation over several possibilities. While it pertains to the intellect to judge, the will is present in this process, directing the intelligence to focus on this option or other and as to whether more data or counsel ought to be sought. There may be disorder in the will and so it is imperative that the will allow a self-examination by the intelligence from time to time so ensure that its directives are not guided by selfish motives but rather by a genuine disposition of humility, love and service. Eventually the intelligence and will settle on a determined course of action. The will is then the spiritual appetite that commands over the other powers to possess and enjoy the good in question.

To illustrate the dynamism at work in cognition and response, we can revisit the scenario of the lady in the supermarket who deliberates over treating herself on an ordinary day after work. Physiologically she is drawn to purchase the item by the pleasure it can give. Feelings are also engaged. Her emotions can tell her that it is a reward for work well done or that it is needed to cope with the stress of life. There can be negative sentiments as well. Seeing the high calorie content of the snack, she may connect eating it with becoming unattractive from putting on weight. Perhaps she is sensitive to how she looks and so this thought makes her feel aversion to the treat. Reason is present weighing the options and the consequences from different points of view: cost, calories, motive, and so forth. The reader will most likely agree that if good sense prevails, our subject will see the purchase as superfluous, and by practicing temperance, reject the temptation.

In this example, the clear and certain judgement that the purchase would be superfluous is the judgement of conscience. There are four aspects to it:

> 1. Prior to the judgement, the intellect deliberates so that the subject may know the good involved according to the truth of human dignity and one's duties and purpose in life.
> 2. Prior to judgement, the intellect examines the motives of one's action to see if they are upright.

3. Prior to judgement, the intellect deliberates about the various circumstances to see how they affect the moral goodness of the action (supposing it is good).
4. The judgement is taken when there is a clear and certain evaluation of the object as good (and so should be done) or evil (should be avoided).

A conscience is called true or false according to whether it is in conformity with the true good of the person or not.

It may happen, that the lady in question could have been confused and thought that day to be a special occasion such as the anniversary of her engagement or a day of a special celebration in her family or religious community. Based on that she may have purchased a small treat. In this case she would have still spent money unnecessarily, but she would not be guilty of a sin as it was due to a misunderstanding. Weighing the options, her conscience would have told her that the purchase was something good. This would be a false conscience.

When a conscience is false, it means that there is an error in a judgement for some reason. As another example, consider the case of someone who mistakes one medicine for another. One hears of cases, for example, where persons have mistakenly used glue as eye drops. In this case the person is not guilty of an offence. They certainly have done harm to themselves or to others, but it was a mistake. This ignorance is called invincible ignorance because there was no way of knowing.

There are cases where a person cannot be completely exonerated from guilt because of ignorance. Take for example the case of someone who has neglected to be properly informed about the time of an examination and ends up missing it. One can say that he or she confused the time, but this ignorance could have been easily overcome if the person were more responsible to properly inform himself or herself of the time and place of the exam. This kind of ignorance is difficult to justify.

An important principle regarding the moral conscience is that it is never upright to follow a doubtful judgement of conscience. We can go back to the scenario of mistaking one medicine for another. If one suspects that the drug may be mistaken, then the judgement of conscience would be doubtful. It is then necessary to try to be more informed before proceeding. When one is clear that one has the correct drug and has confirmed the dose, then the judgement will be true and certain.

There are cases such as stopping for gas when you are running late to the airport, for example, when a decision has to be made without having time. Stopping could mean missing the plane and not stopping could cause the vehicle to shut down on the way. It is difficult to know for sure what is the best thing to do. There is a risk either way, and the certainty one can have is that of taking what seems to be the least risky option. This is not the same as following a doubtful conscience. The expression is used for cases where one can refuse to act until more information is obtained. When it is expedient to act immediately, a person has to make a decision based on the information available at the time.

In the end, one should seek clarity and truthfulness in judgement. A dictate of conscience that is certain and true can be trusted to lead one along the path of happiness. It is important to note that while certainty and truth would normally accompany each other in a wise person, the two things do not necessarily go together. We saw how this occurs in the case of mistaken medicine. There is a more subtle way that this can happen as well. If a person's conscience is not well formed due to deficiencies in their formation or negligence in seeking the truth, then he or she may feel certain about a decision that is actually disordered. A case of this would be a person who chooses to spend many hours playing video games or wandering around social media on vacation. The subject in question may feel sure that such behaviour is acceptable because he or she is on vacation. The truth of the matter is that it is a lack of temperance, or, to put it bluntly, a waste of precious time. That time could have been used to do other things that are not schoolwork, but which are more beneficial to family and social life, and which can help to be better prepared for the future. In such a case, we say that the conscience is lax because it is more attuned to feelings of comfort and pleasure than the true good of the person. The intelligence is barred from carrying out its proper function by a disordered attachment to comfort and entertainment, and perhaps the fear of making an effort to do something difficult but more worthwhile. In the light of this, one can appreciate that certainty does not guarantee freedom from error. It refers to the psychological conviction with which one holds a view. It is worth emphasizing, however, that certainty normally accompanies truth when the subject has a proper functioning conscience.

As can be seen, there are different scenarios that govern the way that certainty, truth, and guilt are articulated. The following table summarizes these possibilities.

Moral nature of the object in terms of its capacity to bring about the true good of the human person	Judgement of Conscience	Relation of Conscience to the moral nature of the object (True or False)	Type of defect
Good	Good	True	
Good	Bad	False	Scrupulous Conscience
Bad	Good	False	Lax Conscience
Bad	Bad	True	

Figure 7.3 The relation of conscience to the moral nature of the object.

As can be observed, the lax conscience judges something not to be a sin in instances where a properly formed conscience would determine that it is. This occurs, for example, when an individual judges as acceptable things such as wasting time, taking advantage of others and watching immoral content in shows.

The scrupulous conscience fears a disordered action, yet in certain instances has no grounds for this fear. A person may become over-anxious, for example, about having a bad thought, feeling convinced that it was a sin when at best it was a temptation. Individuals who suffer from scrupulosity are normally advised to ignore these fears and to trust that they are still in good standing with God, even though they feel strongly that the reality is otherwise. This is good advice because, as we have affirmed previously, the essence of conscience is not a feeling, nor an intuition, but an act of judgement based on reason, which applies the true good of the human person to a concrete situation. As a person learns to recognize instances of scrupulosity, he or she will also be more at peace in putting aside the fear of having committed a sin, when, in fact, it was not.

Following the judgement of conscience, an individual can choose to act in accord with what conscience dictates, or to act against it. When one acts in accord with one's conscience, then that action is meritorious. If the conscience is neither lax nor scrupulous with regard to the action in consideration, then that action will bolster the human dignity of that person. This happens because he or she would have done something to bring about his or her authentic good. A deep feeling of peace, self-esteem, and satisfaction of being in harmony with the divine plan will accompany the action. To illustrate this dynamic, we can revisit the case of the lady in the supermarket who is tempted to treat herself unnecessarily. If she manages to reason clearly, her conscience will tell her that it would be a lack of temperance to indulge herself. If this is in fact the case, and she acts in accord with this judgement, refusing to treat herself, then this is a meritorious act. To do this, she would have had to control her urges for that compensation, and this would have required some effort and suffering. Nevertheless, having conformed to the dictate of a clear conscience, she would also feel, on a deeper level, the satisfaction of having lived and strengthened an important virtue. This improves her character, makes her feel more in harmony with the divine plan, and boosts her sense of self-worth. Actions such as these bring authentic happiness. Other examples would be choosing to make good use of time, being punctual, truthful, fair, and so on. The reader is invited here to come up with his or her own examples from ordinary life, and to consider how the dynamic discussed here applies. There are numerous possible scenarios, corresponding to the many different virtues that perfect the human person.

When one acts against the dictate of a clear conscience, then that action is disordered or sinful. If the conscience is neither lax nor scrupulous with regard to the action in consideration, then that action will undermine the human dignity of that person. This happens because he or she would have done something destructive and harmful, opposed to his or her authentic good. There may a feeling of satisfaction on the level of pleasure or the good feeling that is sought by one or more of the emotional drives. On a deeper level, however, such a choice will be accompanied by a feeling of uneasiness, loss, shame, and unworthiness for having turned away from the divine plan.

To illustrate this dynamic, consider the case of a fellow who is tempted to spread a rumour that is damaging to the reputation of another which he does not know to be true. He may have heard that the person being spoken of is doing poorly at work, cheats on his wife, only cares about money, is racist, a fake or something of the sort. His conscience tells him he should hold his tongue, as spreading such rumours can do great harm to the reputation of the person in question. He knows for certain that he would not like someone to do such a thing to him. The judgement of conscience is a clear condemnation of the act. In spite of all this clarity, the fellow can still choose to pass on the defamatory gossip. Envy, pride, and the pleasure of getting the attention of others can prevail over good sense. In a quiet moment, the protagonist of this deed would see clearly that he had done something wrong. He failed to show charity and loyalty in an important way. Guilt sets in and he feels uneasy and unworthy to stand and be respected before God and men for having betrayed his own dignity that he received from God, and which he also shares with his fellow men.

The feeling of guilt can be likened to the feeling of pain in the body. Pain is an indication that something is wrong, and it is important to feel pain so that one may have a signal that something is awry and some indication of what and where the problem might be. In the case of guilt, one may feel tormented by it, but its purpose is to signal that there is something broken in us spiritually and our conscience tells us where the problem is. In the example of spreading gossip, reason tells us that we have unjustly defamed another person. As with pain, once the ailment is detected then the remedy is applied. With that the discomfort should disappear. Often we take painkillers for the pain when it has done its job of signalling and pointing to an illness. With guilt, when we have come to terms with the wrong we have done, the remedy needs to be sought. The cure is to seek reconciliation with the creator by asking for pardon in prayer, and the help not to sin again. In addition to this, the harm done to the person maligned needs to be repaired.

To the extent possible, someone who has spread gossip should tell the persons he or she spoke to that the information given was just hearsay and apologize for transmitting unfounded and false information. At times it is not possible to fulfil the latter for various reasons. Perhaps the truth would have already come to light, or the persons spoken to cannot be contacted. In such cases, the subject can choose an alternate course of action to make up, such as speaking well of the individual offended when the opportunity arises and showing compassion and understanding to those who may have offended him in the same way.

The moral conscience not only judges an action to be disordered or not, but also evaluates the degree of good or evil. With regard to evil actions, such deeds directly contradict the essence of fundamental values. They are deeds such as taking the life of another or causing him or her grievous bodily injury. Actions such as adultery, robbery, destroying the property of others, drunkenness, rape, and pornography are gravely evil. Neglect can also be a grave evil if it concerns important responsibilities such as caring for one's children or parents or fulfilling one's duties at work. Over time the accumulated effect of this neglect causes grave harm. When a disorder is a small matter, as in the case of a lady who treats herself unnecessarily with a snack, the conscience judges it to be of minor importance. The corresponding feeling of guilt, shame and unworthiness would also most likely be slight. It is more like being defeated in a skirmish knowing that another opportunity is around the corner to make up.

When the conscience is lax or scrupulous, there is an added element that needs to be taken into consideration. A lax conscience is one that judges a disordered action as permissible. A father, for example, may think that he is entitled to be waited on by his family members on arriving home from work. Yes, that person may have had a long day, but so too, the other members of the family. The case of a lax conscience requires special attention because an individual may have developed that lax way of judging by deliberately neglecting or refusing to look at things from a different angle. His wife and children may have frequently complained about the father's attitude, only to find that he always has excuses and justifications for his conduct. In this case, even though the individual is following a clear judgement of conscience, he or she is guilty for the harm that is done by his behaviour.

At times a person may judge a disorder as good as a result of deep-rooted stereotypes or prejudices cultivated in childhood that the individual is not aware of. An example of this that one finds in many places is the propensity to function in cliques. This is not necessarily bad, but it goes awry when persons in a clique favour each other unfairly in the allocation of benefits and opportunities. When this is widespread, politics also becomes skewed, where the winning party uses its power to favour a certain group, class, or tribe in a disordered way. A young girl who has grown up in such a system may regard this as acceptable. She may have never been challenged about her way of thinking. In fact, her peers in her social group most likely think the same way. Such a status quo, however, is disordered because politicians are charged with the common good, which means seeking the good of all. Without any qualms of conscience, this lady may consent to benefits being unjustly distributed, especially when she is being favoured.

There are cases no doubt, where such a woman would have made this bad judgement out of genuine ignorance. In such instances, she cannot be held guilty for having a lax conscience. The woman in question has not sinned when she acts in accord with this conviction. In fact, it is just the opposite, she would have acted meritoriously. Her will would have acted in accordance with the judgement of a clear conscience that was erroneous out of genuine ignorance. This being the case, it remains true that her actions would have caused harm and have been destructive. It may happen that in a given instance this woman would have chosen to go against the judgement of her lax conscience. She may have conceded an important benefit to someone of the rival party for personal gain for example. In her ignorance, her conscience would judge this as a betrayal. In this case she would have sinned and would be guilty of offending God. It is unfortunate, because the sin would be for having done something that was in accord with justice and so objectively beneficial to society.

These two scenarios may seem confusing to the reader as it appears to condone stereotypes and prejudice. It does not do so at all. It is all too clear how these can undermine social harmony and cause strife. They are meant to illustrate the moral principle that merit and sin are linked to obedience or disobedience to the judgement of conscience. This applies whether the judgment is true or erroneous out of genuine ignorance.

Something similar happens in the case of a scrupulous conscience. A young doctor, for example, may feel obliged to overwork himself to follow up on his patients. He may be over scrupulous, following up on cases unnecessarily. An occasion may arise where he feels obliged to follow up on one such case but refuses to do so in order to get a break. In this instance he commits a sin, even though the patient did not need such close attention. It may happen that he chose to follow the judgement of his conscience and extended himself unnecessarily to attend to that patient. This would be a meritorious action, even though his need for rest in that moment was probably more important.

The various scenarios of how conscience, choice and merit/sin are articulated can be summarized as follows:

Objective moral nature	Judgement of Conscience	Choice of the Will	Guilt value
Good	Good	Commit	Merit
Good	Good	Omit	Sin
Good	Bad	Commit	Sin
Good	Bad	Omit	Merit
Bad	Good	Commit	Merit
Bad	Good	Omit	Sin
Bad	Bad	Commit	Sin
Bad	Bad	Omit	Merit

Figure 7.4 The different scenarios for the judgement of conscience, choice of the will and guilt value for objectively good and evil actions.

The reader is invited to look closely at the guilt value for the corresponding good and evil actions that are judged erroneously by the conscience in the highlighted rows. Can you give examples of such scenarios?

7.5.1 Using and improving conscience

Socrates was sentenced to death for standing up to the sophists of his day who prided themselves on twisting the truth for political gain and influence. In the trial he gave a defence of his actions that is convincing and inspiring. During this speech he famously said: "a life without examination is not worth living."[18]

If we fail to use our conscience we are like a vessel with a powerful engine, but no system for guidance. Our life will lack order, harmony and meaning. Perhaps this is what Socrates would call a life not worth living. When we fail to consider our actions in the light of the true good of the human being and our personal calling or mission in life, then our actions can easily be determined by the force of physical impulses and emotions. This is very unfortunate because our urges and feelings are sometimes disordered. The dignity of the human person lies in freedom. But true freedom lies in the power of the intelligence and the will to know and choose that which would bring about the authentic happiness of an individual. It is not that the temporal goods that satisfy the bodily appetites are bad. Rather it is the numbing of the intellect to consider what the true good may be that leaves the person under the dominion of physical and emotional satisfaction. St Thomas Aquinas wrote: "When our mind is intent on temporal goods to rest in them, it remains at their level. But when it seeks them with a view to eternal happiness, it is not lowered by them, but rather raises them up."[19]

There is a well-known adage that says: "use it or lose it." As long as we are human, we have the capacity to reason and evaluate our actions according to universal moral principles. If an individual habitually fails to do so, just giving in to feelings, then the practice of judging according to values becomes unfamiliar and the conscience is weakened. On the other hand, using one's conscience will strengthen it, especially as one will also feel compelled to study and understand how morality works more in depth. A highly recommended custom is the daily examination of conscience. It consists of putting aside a couple of minutes each day to allow the intellect to examine one's actions, thoughts, and motives in the context of one's dignity as a human being and the duties and commitments that one has freely accepted. At the end of this exercise, a soul can give thanks to God for the good deeds done, ask pardon for sins and shortcomings and resolve to do better the following day.

In the discussion so far, several obstacles for the proper action of the conscience have been identified. There may be ignorance of the proper criteria that needs to be applied, lack of proper knowledge of the nature of the action being evaluated, and the emotions may dominate, inhibiting the proper functioning of the intellect. By defending against and counteracting these obstacles, one can improve the functioning of conscience.

Ignorance of criteria can be addressed through study and by seeking the advice of wise persons in one's family, social and religious communities. It is important to seek advice before reading books that deal with questions of ethics and faith. Instead of acquiring greater clarity on moral issues, one can end up becoming more confused.

With regard to knowledge of the nature of the action, it helps to ponder the situation at hand carefully before judging. At first glance it may appear that a person is trespassing, for example, when it turns out that they have permission to enter. A closer look would have revealed that the individual had the keys and was entering normally. Jumping to conclusions without understanding what was taking place is a rash judgement. It may be necessary to ask question about the facts and inquire about motives in order to grasp the nature of the moral act in question.

The third obstacle concerned the impact of drives and feelings. To counteract this important obstacle, a subject needs to cultivate the habits of self-control, good discipline and the various virtues that make it easier to perform different species of good acts. The importance of self-examination has already been highlighted. For this the virtues of humility and sincerity are particularly necessary.

As an exercise, let us consider the case of a subject who is up late at night preparing for an important exam the following day. She is very tired and has been doing late nights for several days. While she is deliberating about whether to go to bed or to study a little more, she sees on her phone a friend calling who she knows is distraught because of a bad breakup she is going through. What would you do in her situation?

Following the diagram below, the subject is faced with competing objects of choice, which she must consider one by one. She is tired, so her body is pushing for going to bed, presenting that option to the intelligence via the emotions and imagination. The intellect knows that rest is good, and the conscience can concur appealing to the value of safeguarding life.

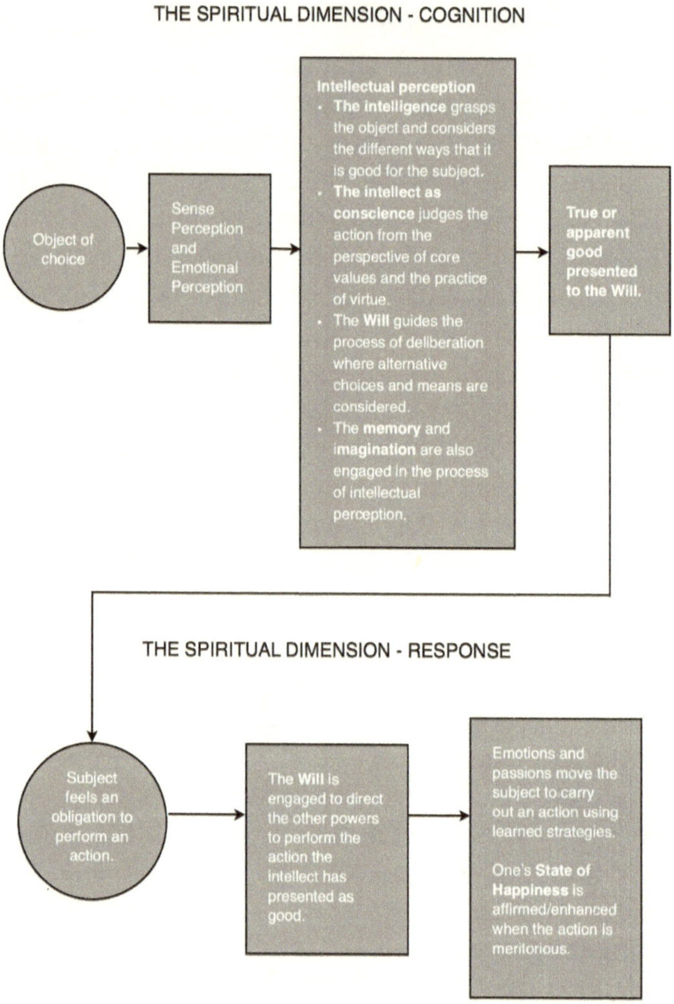

Introduction to Anthropology of Integration

THE SPIRITUAL DIMENSION - COGNITION

- **Object of choice** → **Sense Perception and Emotional Perception** →

Intellectual perception
- **The intelligence** grasps the object and considers the different ways that it is good for the subject.
- **The intellect as conscience** judges the action from the perspective of core values and the practice of virtue.
- The **Will** guides the process of deliberation where alternative choices and means are considered.
- The **memory** and **imagination** are also engaged in the process of intellectual perception.

→ **True or apparent good presented to the Will.**

THE SPIRITUAL DIMENSION - RESPONSE

- **Subject feels an obligation to perform an action.** → **The Will is engaged to direct the other powers to perform the action the intellect has presented as good.** → **Emotions and passions move the subject to carry out an action using learned strategies.**

One's **State of Happiness** is affirmed/enhanced when the action is meritorious.

Figure 7.5 The cognitive and response sides of concrete actions on the spiritual level.

The will is present as the master and does not allow the subject—let's call her Anna—to go to bed but directs the intelligence to look at the pros and cons of her action more thoroughly. Going to sleep means interrupting what she is doing, which is her study. While working more does not bring immediate gratification, there is the satisfaction of being better prepared for her exam and feeling more secure about her future. Furthermore, study is a duty and responsibility for her. The intellect suggests various benefits to this course of action, and her conscience can approve this way of acting by appealing to the values of being productive and practising justice.

There is a third option that also needs to be considered, which is attending to her friend who is calling. Here our protagonist should consider the friendship at stake in giving support to her friend who needs her at that moment.

After weighing the options, Anna will consent to what the intellect presents as the best choice—This is what you should do!

An outcome to a circumstance like this is that Anna may say to herself: "I don't care, let the chips fall where they may, I am going to bed right now." Is she following a true good or an apparent good? The reader may say: well, that may be the best thing to do, who knows? Most probably, however, it may be a rash decision where the will has "hijacked" the intelligence, directing it to focus on the gratification of sleep, ignoring other considerations. Anna may be going after an apparent good as well if she indulges in an unnecessarily long conversation with her friend because she is emotionally attached to that person who gives her a greal deal of attention.

The best choice in this case is most likely to be a combination of two or all of the options in a balanced way.

It is interesting to note that the best choice is not exactly the same for any given person in such a circumstance. It is sufficient that the will does not manhandle and twist the intelligence into settling on an apparent good that aims to please selfish desires and pursuits. It is important to cultivate the cardinal virtues to ensure that this does not happen. These habits facilitate the proper functioning of the operations involved in the genesis of choice and of all action in general. The cardinal virtues are Temperance, Fortitude, Prudence, and Justice.

Another reason that the best choice can vary from person to person is that there are never two identical circumstances. Each individual is a person with his or her unique characteristics, history and calling. This is why we must respect the choices of others if we know that they are upright and seek to form their consciences in accord with the dignity of the human person.

Given uprightness, a person may judge in hindsight that they could have made an even better choice. Their conscience, however, will not judge them as having done something bad, but rather of weighing the options inadequately. In other words, they made a mistake. The subject can learn from this mistake to make better choices in the future when faced with similar situations.

Notes

1. Aristotle, *De Anima*, trans. Hugh Lawson-Tancred (London: Penguin Classics, 1987), Bekker number 431b.
2. St Thomas Aquinas, *Summa Theologiae*, I–II, q. 94, a. 2.
3. *Ibid.*, I–II, q. 94, a. 2.
4. *Ibid.*, I–II, q. 94, a. 2.
5. *Ibid.*, I–II, q. 94, a. 2.
6. José Angel Lombo and Francesco Russo, *Philosophical Anthropology. An Introduction*, ed. Jeffrey Cole (Woodridge, Ill: Midwest Theological Forum, 2014), chap. 17.
7. Alexander Tsiaras, "Conception to Birth—Visualized," TED Talks, December 2010, https://www.ted.com/talks/alexander_tsiaras_conception_to_birth_visualized?language=en.
8. Martha L. Blair, "Sex-Based Differences in Physiology," *Advances in Physiology Education* 31, no. 1 (2007): 23–25.
9. Louann Brizendine, *The Female Brain*, Reprint edition (New York: Harmony, 2007), 13.
10. Louann Brizendine, *The Male Brain: A Breakthrough Understanding of How Men and Boys Think* (New York: Harmony, 2011), 1–9.
11. Frank Sheed, *Theology and Sanity* (San Francisco: Ignatius Press, 1993), 26.
12. Jason Evert and Crystalina Evert, "Chastity Project," Chastity, August 18, 2023, https://chastity.com/.
13. St Thomas Aquinas, *Summa Theologiae*, I, q. 83, a. 3.
14. *Ibid.*, I, q. 82, a. 2.
15. St Thomas Aquinas, *Questiones Disputatae de Veritate*, q. 22, a. 12.
16. St Thomas Aquinas, *Summa Theologiae*, I, q. 82, a. 4.
17. *Catechism of the Catholic Church*, para. 1778.
18. Plato, *The Last Days of Socrates*, Bekker number 38a.
19. St Thomas Aquinas, *Summa Theologiae*, II–II, q. 83, a. 6, ad 3.

Part III
Formative integration

It was explained earlier that a source of disintegration of the human person is the "hijacking" of the intellect by the will. This can happen imperceptibly when a person is not able to exercise proper dominion over his or her emotions. A boy playing video games excessively may have the sensation of acting in a self-fulfilling and self-realizing way, when, in truth, he may be driven by an addiction that he is not aware of. Attachments such as these undermine interior freedom as the person is forced interiorly to make a choice that is not in accord with their best interest and dignity as a human being.

An important aim of anthropology of integration is to propose a framework where decisions and actions are working together harmoniously. The intelligence and the emotions are in accord, and the will dictates the actions accordingly. This is formative integration. It is the integration of the three levels of the human being, unique and unlike any other creature. The hallmark of the dignity of the human person is the submission of the impulses and emotions to the intelligence and the will, resulting in actions which are harmonious with the overall good of the human person.

Building on what has been discussed so far, we can point to four key elements:

> 1. Rectitude in the will where it is guided by the "golden rule" as opposed to selfish pursuits and desires.
> 2. Knowledge of the fundamental values and the ability to think logically, evaluating options based on values.

3. Good health and the proper conditioning of the biological impulses so that they are aligned to the development of good habits.

4. Proper education of the emotions, so that, harnessing their energy, they are engaged, controlled, and directed according to patterns that affirm the dignity of the human subject, and bring about true happiness.

To the extent that these elements inform the choices and actions of a subject, a more integrated way of being is achieved. Human dignity is enhanced, and with this, authentic personal fulfilment and joy is attained. In the previous chapters, we centred on the knowledge of fundamental goods from the natural inclinations, and the adherence to these goods as values. This was upward or cognitive integration. In this section, we will focus the discussion on the descending side where these elements inform concrete action. This we have termed downward or formative integration.

Cognitive integration terminated in knowledge of the fundamental goods of human nature that are constitutive of human dignity. As we enter the downward side of integration, priority of place ought to be given to the cultivation of those virtues that are more directly related to these goods. As discussed, previously, virtues are stable dispositions to do good. There are different ways of classifying and ranking virtues. The most widely used is that which Western civilization has inherited from Plato and St Thomas Aquinas. This classification is based on the idea of achieving the right operation of the appetites. For the proper functioning of the concupiscible appetite, there is the need for temperance. For the irascible appetite, fortitude is required. The appetite of the will requires prudence to discern the most appropriate course of action to safeguard and bolster true happiness in a given situation, and to command that they be employed. Justice is the state of harmony or order that is achieved in the body/soul unity that defines the human person. These four virtues are called Cardinal Virtues, which come from the Latin root *cardo*, which means hinge. It is implied that all the other virtues hang on these as a door hangs on a hinge. In other words, they can all be classified, in one way or another, under the cardinal virtues, depending on the appetite that is in question. Chastity, for example is under temperance. Industriousness would fall under fortitude and so on.

The perspective adopted in this text recognizes the value of grouping all the virtues under the cardinal virtues. Added to this, a new model is proposed where the virtues highlighted are those directly related to the goal of human life which can be understood in terms of the dignity of the human person expressed in the fundamental goods of human nature. When we consider these fundamental goods, a series of virtues emerge as the most important or key virtues from the perspective of anthropology of integration. Another row could be added to the table we have used to illustrate cognitive integration with a proposed series of related virtues. The following scheme is suggested:

Virtues for downward or anthropological integration:	Diligence, Industriousness, Order, Fortitude, Temperance	Chastity, Loyalty, Charity	Justice, Generosity, Prudence
Spiritual level. Knowledge of and adherence to Fundamental Values:	Life is a fundamental good. "I value Life"	Family and friendship are fundamental goods. "I value Family/ Friendship"	Society is a fundamental good. "I value Society"
Natural Inclination on the emotional/ psychological level:	Feeling safe (Independent "I")	Sense of belonging ("I" valued by another)	Sense of significance ("I" valued for my role)
Natural Inclination on the biological level:	Survival	Sexual Inclination	Curiosity to Learn and communicate

Figure 8 Virtues related to the fundamental values.

The table shown is read from the base up. If we start with the inclination to survival on the bodily level, we can identify a matching tendency on the emotional level, which is the longing to feel secure. Reason can discover that these urges and tendencies point to a universal, unchanging good of human nature, which is life itself. An individual who adheres to the principle that life is a fundamental good, must now live in accord with this ideal. This demands the exercise of the virtues related to the value of life. A similar dynamic occurs when we centre on the sexual inclination. The matching tendency on the emotional level is the desire for belonging. Reason can discover that the immutable good at stake is that of the family and friendship. A

Formative integration

person who uses this principle to guide their actions will need to practise the virtues related to the value of family and friendship. In the third column, we begin with the inclination to curiosity. The matching yearning on the emotional level is the desire to be valued for a role. Reason discovers that these tendencies point to society as a fundamental good. The corresponding virtues ought to be practised to guide one's life according to this ideal.

8 THE VIRTUES FOR INTEGRATION RELATED TO LIFE

As we recognize that life is a fundamental value, it is important to acknowledge that life is a struggle. This is true of all life. The creatures we find in the forest have to struggle to survive, grow to maturity and reproduce. A bird, for example, has to work very hard to build its nest to lay its eggs. After all this effort, snakes and other predators go through great pains to get at their eggs to eat them. Birds can have a hard time defending their nests and their young. Adult birds themselves are prey to cats, foxes, racoons, and other animals. At times these feathered animals will find it hard to find food and be adversely affected by the weather. A bird may succumb to all these trials and lose its life. Yet having to struggle is the way that it develops its capacity to survive and overcome obstacles.

We should not be surprised that what applies to the entire animal kingdom, is also true for the human race—life is a struggle. There are always difficulties that must be overcome to have meals every day, a shelter to live in and the means to grow and mature physiologically, psychologically, and spiritually. As with the animal kingdom, an individual may not survive the threats to his or her life. Nevertheless, having to fight to overcome difficulties is the way that a person acquires the capacity to prevail over the obstacles that life brings.

Humans and animals coincide in having to struggle and develop through struggle. As rational creatures, however, we are completely different because we come together to organize the means of production so that everyone can have what they need. A monkey is quite comfortable helping itself to the watermelons I may have planted even though it is not welcome on my premises. If an individual does this, that would be stealing. Humans can't just grab what they need from anywhere to satisfy their hunger. We see in others "another me" and so I know that we must work together to find ways to secure the necessities of all. It is incumbent on every individual to be productive and to contribute. As St. Paul affirmed writing to the Thessalonians: "If someone is unwilling to work, neither should he eat".[1]

In general, we can say that fortitude is needed to overcome the obstacles that threaten life. Temperance is also needed for the rational use of material things and pleasures that regard sustaining and nurturing life. For the human person, security is achieved primarily through work. By contributing to the means of production and culture, persons are able to provide for themselves and their loved ones, and, at the same time, help to secure a higher standard of living for all. Here, fortitude emerges as a needed virtue in general, but more specifically, the virtues associated with work stand out, and concretely, we can identify the virtues of diligence, industriousness, and order.

It is interesting to note that diligence comes from the Latin *diligere*, which means "to love" or "to take delight in". Applied to work, it means having a positive attitude to work, seeing it as a way of serving others and building up society, while ensuring an income for oneself and one's family. Out of this positive outlook, the diligent person shows care, persistent effort, and conscientiousness in the fulfilment of his or her duties. To quote the founder of an institution whose aim is to help people to seek God in work: "We don't persevere in work because we feel like it, but because it must be done; and then we do it willingly and cheerfully. Above all, we have to continue our professional task even when our initial enthusiasm fades away. Usually, people celebrate the laying of the first stone of a building; I like to celebrate placing the last one." [2]

Linked to diligence is the virtue of industriousness. The two words are practically synonyms. Industriousness, however, emphasizes the aspect of being hard-working.

The third virtue listed was order. This is the habit of being neat, methodical, and organized. It is necessary for being effective and efficient in work, and also for having a balanced lifestyle where a reasonable amount of time is given to rest, family life, health and social life. There are different methods that are recommended for being organized and effective. A simple one is having a schedule, for example, and a things-to-do list. There are very good tools and methods available for getting organized and being effective. In the end, it is up to each person to find and use the ones that work best for him or her.

If you consider the virtues related to life discussed so far, you may discover that they can be tied back to the four cardinal virtues in some way. It is nevertheless important to separate and highlight them because they are related to the natural inclination to security in a direct way, and as such, have a more powerful and natural appeal. It is easier and more intuitive to relate to diligence and order than to fortitude and temperance.

This happens because these virtues connect to powerful emotions driving us to be independent and to secure a better standard of living for all. To illustrate this, consider the scenario when diligence and order is lacking. If you are an employer, think of an employee that is lazy, late with everything, never punctual and unreliable. The thought of that employee most likely gets you frustrated. We all have the experience of someone coming to do some sort of repair and doing a poor job, dragging it on and wanting the same pay or more. Terribly frustrating! On the other hand, when you find a handyman, for instance, who is diligent, you are very happy and feel affection to that person. You are happy to pay him a little extra, give him more work and recommend him to your friends.

It is very interesting to listen to the interviews of persons who have won open scholarships based on the CAPE exam in Trinidad and Tobago. With this scholarship, the government of Trinidad and Tobago will cover all expenses for university studies at any institution anywhere in the world. Winners are often showcased in the newspapers, as it is a prestigious award. The common denominator of all winners is very simple—study very hard and study smart. These individuals testify that they had very little free time and studied over 20 hours a week, setting higher and higher goals for themselves. There are many persons who perhaps have the ability to be scholarship winners, but don't make the grade due to lack of effort and that is very sad. Because work is a reality that fills most of the hours of our days, and is the setting in which we have the opportunity to practise and grow in all the virtues, it makes sense that the virtues directly relating to work be highlighted and emphasized. These virtues have a special humanizing value because, nudged by the inclinations to security, we come to know that man was created to work. An important part of his intrinsic dignity is his sharing in the creative power of the divine being through work. The virtues of work affirm and bolster human dignity and when lacking, just the opposite happens. Human dignity is undermined and degraded.

Once we accept the emphasis that is due to the virtues of diligence, industriousness, and order, then it is important that parents and teachers give high priority to teaching and inculcating these virtues. Leaders and educators on all levels, in fact, should consider how they are contributing to creating a culture of work in their surroundings, their communities and in society as a whole. Where there is a culture of hard work and order, countries tend to prosper and show resilience in the face of difficulties.

Notes

1. 2 Thessalonians 3:10 (New American Bible Revised Edition)
2. Saint Josemaría Escrivá, letter dated 15 Oct 1948.

9 THE VIRTUES FOR INTEGRATION RELATED TO RELATIONSHIPS

Along the vertical axis linking the biological sexual inclination, the emotion of belonging, and the value of family and friendship, the virtues that emerge for formative integration are those that foster family life and noble friendships. Three important virtues can be identified: Chastity, Loyalty, and Charity. Given that the family is in crisis in many places in the world today, character building programmes ought to place special emphasis on the cultivation of these virtues. Alive to the World is one such programme. It makes comprehensible and palpable how to integrate the virtues related to family and relationships.

9.1 Chastity

Chastity is a virtue that moderates and governs the emotions related to the sexual drive according to right reason. There is a powerful energy in the human person related to the sexual drive, and so, returning to the analogy of a boat, it is important to have a well-functioning braking and navigation system. If this is lacking, the drives and emotions that are related to human sexuality can greatly distort a person's personality, rendering them, effectively, slaves to their passions and emotions. A young man who habitually gives in to lustful acts such as pornography, masturbation and premarital sex will inevitably have a skewed vision of women, seeing them as objects of sexual pleasure. These disordered acts give rise to addictions that absorb large amounts of time, lead to risky behaviour, and can plunge persons into depression and anxiety from the fear of being found out and the low self-esteem of not being able to change.[1] There are many stories of seemingly happily married men who end up ostracized from their wives and children as a result of sexual escapades with outside parties. There are cases where, when confronted about their infidelities, these persons react angrily and even violently, as though their lives were being threatened. This is completely irrational behaviour.

A challenge faced by society regarding chastity, is the heritage of the sexual revolution. This movement, which began in the sixties, encouraged women and men to be sexually liberated. Governments and institutions around the world mobilized to make contraception and abortion easily available to girls so that they could enjoy romance involving sex without the fear of getting pregnant, and should they conceive, have the "remedy".[2] The current culture pressures a young girl to have a boyfriend and to start having sex in their teenage years. There is a double attraction here for girls. Women are attracted to men who can provide stability, among other reasons because they need a lot of help during pregnancy and when their children are small. The figure of a "boyfriend" has an air of stability and can come across as immediately desirable. At the same time, a girl can find gratification in the romance in the relationship that includes sex. The reader is invited to consider if this is not a classic case of an apparent good. Through cognitive integration, the desire for stability and romantic intimacy accords with human dignity in the context of marriage and the family.

The stability a "boyfriend" pretends to provide is fake as it lacks the consent to marriage. The intimacy is disordered and reckless as the persons are not spouses. It follows that girls should resist the pressure to have "boyfriends" and seek rather to do what is prudent to have good marriages in the future.

Is a sixteen-year-old ready for marriage? In Western society this is very rare. A person needs a certain independence to be ready for marriage. A couple journeying towards marriage ought to have a clear plan for how they will provide for their family. Most sixteen-year-olds are nowhere near having the independence for settling down. If we follow this reasoning, then a "boyfriend" for a sixteen-year-old would most times be an apparent good. She would rarely be in the condition at that age to have a serious relationship. When we look closely at the widespread practice of a sixteen-year-old seeking a "boyfriend", we must wonder whether it is not often an excuse, in the end, to feel good having attention and gifts and to enjoy romantic moments that may involve sexual intimacy. Furthermore, she escapes the stigma of being "loose". Ordinarily, the true good for a girl at this stage is to prepare for having a serious relationship later in life by working at being independent and mature.

The discussion above applies to men as well. A boy at sixteen or seventeen feels drawn to have a "girlfriend" and engage in sexual activity. There is a difference however. In some sectors, a young man can boast about having sex with different women. In fact, it is often the case that a boy will be ridiculed by his friends if he had the opportunity to sleep with a pretty girl and chose not to. At the same time, he needs to avoid the reputation of being a womanizer, as girls will then avoid him. With girls the dynamic is different. The evolutionary force at work in women to perpetuate the species makes them powerfully drawn to stability. Females tend to form strong emotional bonds with the men they become intimate with and feel very jealous if their "boyfriend" shows an interest in another woman.

In an earlier section, it was explained that sexual intimacy ought to be understood in the context of the complementarity of the sexes. It has meaning as an affirmation of a marriage commitment where there is openness to life. A boy of sixteen or seventeen is far from being ready for such a commitment. Yet the term "girlfriend" has the air of being faithful and supportive to a person of the opposite sex, admirably meeting her needs. A closer look leads to question whether having a "girlfriend" in the end, is not just an excuse for sexual indulgence without the stigma of being a womanizer. If this is the case, then it is an apparent good. Ordinarily, the true good for a boy at this stage is to prepare for having a serious relationship later in life by working at being independent and mature. It is unfortunate that many adolescent boys and girls neglect this serious duty by investing an inordinate amount of emotional energy and time in meeting each other's emotional needs.

The pressure that our present culture puts on adolescent girls and boys to have "boyfriends" and "girlfriends", and under this guise to start being sexually intimate, suggests that there is a gap in the socialization of young people that needs to be addressed. Perhaps there is some wisdom from older generations that was lost in the sexual revolution, that needs to be recovered. Persons who reached adolescence prior to or sheltered from this cultural shift acted according to an unwritten "social script" in social dealings that helped to keep them safe and chaste. Interactions between persons of the opposite sex began through interactions between families who moved in similar social circles. Parents were interested in having their children interact with children of the families they were connected with in some way, whom they held in high esteem. This provided a sort of selection for socialization as parental approval was important for choosing one's friends. There was also a well-developed script for dating. A "date" meant setting a date for a school dance, outing or movie. There was no connotation of intimacy or commitment which the term has today. A young man was expected to be a gentleman and to treat his date like a lady. This meant many things. For example, the male party would be expected to come into the house and interact with the parents of his date before taking her out. He would guard his speech and gestures in order to be very correct, staying far from anything that might be disrespectful. Boys and girls interacted around events and institutions. There were dances, outings, parish activities, school events, family celebrations and so forth, which provided the context for persons of the opposite sex to mingle. At a dance, a girl would dance with several boys and vice versa and these events ended at a decent hour. Parents and other adults were usually around to keep an eye on things and the mothers looked for young men to match-make with their daughters and for girls with their sons.

The context for socialization has changed, and the presence of an unwritten script has largely been lost. Professor Kerry Cronin at Boston University has been studying this phenomenon for many years. Her research showed that half of America is single and yet people desire meaningful committed relationships. A "hook-up" culture dominates—especially on campuses—where young people meet at parties at which temperance and decency are meant to be left at the door. The atmosphere lends itself to boys and girls becoming wild with alcohol, sensual music and erotic dancing and then ending up in bed with someone they hardly know. She observes that texting and social media culture have profoundly altered the dating landscape. Many boys and girls do not know how to connect face-to-face in a well-mannered, engaging and meaningful way with someone of the opposite sex with no intention of being sexually intimate or having a serious relationship. Based on her experience, the movie *The Dating Project* was produced in 2017 which provides a useful tool for discussing these issues with young people. Her goal is to encourage young people to have scripts for meaningful and chaste relationships in the context of a globalized, digital, sensual world.

The peer pressure that girls and boys experience in adolescence has been further complicated by the widespread influence of the gay movement. Feminism in the 80's and 90's was heavily swayed by Judith Butler who, in 1988, rolled out the theory that what we perceive to be gender is actually an unconscious, socially compelled performance that creates the illusion of an essence. Reality, gender, sex—everything, even truth—is socially constructed. It is up to each individual to discover within himself or herself, if he or she identifies as a boy or a girl or non-binary, irrespective of biological sex, and society ought to respect this choice.[3] This way of thinking has become mainstream in academia in western civilization. Many institutions have gender policies to ensure that choice of sexual identity is respected. Thirty-four countries now allow for same sex marriage, and the gay lifestyle is increasingly portrayed as normal in the media and entertainment and taught to be so in sex-education programmes sanctioned by the European Union and the

United Nations. Some places allow for gender transitioning which is very harmful to an individual.

A concern among parents, educators and medical professionals is the recent upsurge in adolescent girls claiming gender dysphoria. Formerly known as "gender identity disorder", gender dysphoria is a psychological condition characterized by an insistence that one is of the opposite sex and persistent discomfort in one's biological sex.[4] Many ask to be treated medically and some request surgery to align their bodies to their transgender identities. According to the World Professional Association for Transgender Health (WPATH), adolescents assigned female at birth initiate transgender care 2.5 to 7.1 times more frequently than those assigned male at birth.[5] Peer groups and online media may be influencing many of these girls to turn to trans identification and to pursue medical transition, with potentially irreversible side effects. Trans identification can offer freedom from anxiety and satisfy the need for acceptance and belonging along with the thrill of transgressing the norm.[6]

Here too a closer look is needed regarding how boys and girls are socialized. Feelings of being accepted and belonging are important for a person's psychological well-being. These, however, ought to be managed in the context of preparing for a stable, committed, and fruitful marriage in the future. Though a girl may experience confusion about her sexual identity from influences in her environment, when she understands that her path is to prepare to be a good mother and a good wife, with a good husband who is a good father, she will not give in to internal and external pressures to pursue trans identification as a lifestyle, and much less seek to medically transition. In the past, the cases of gender dysphoria were few, mostly boys beginning in early childhood, and most were resolved as the child matured.[7] Data shows that persistence was very low before the nineties. The gay movement had little influence at the time. Children were socialized in the context of a culture where biological sex shaped sexual identity and marriage and the family constituted the foundation of society.

The reader at this point may be concerned that, so far, the negative side of purity has been emphasized. This is deliberate because it helps to look at what happens when chastity is lacking to appreciate the need for it and to foster interest in better understanding sex and sexuality. At the heart of Anthropology of Integration, however, is a positive outlook on sexual intimacy. The core principle is that the natural inclinations are given to us to lead us to the fullness of human life. The sexual inclination is not an exception. The framework developed in this text thus adopts a radically positive outlook on the sexual drive and the emotions related to it. When the sexual inclination on the biological and emotional dimensions are integrated into the spiritual, then it works to bring about the happiness of the human person in a profound and lasting way. The practice of chastity helps to bring this about.

The virtue of Chastity requires a more in-depth consideration because there are several factors that impact on how it should be lived in a given situation. Firstly, sex cannot be separated from sexuality. Sexuality refers to the fact that human beings are male and female and that they are complementary in nature. Sexuality, in fact, is prior to sex, both ontologically and existentially. In other words, one must be male or female before sexual attraction is felt and one is also aware of being male or female before the sexual drive is fully awakened. In this text we propose that the context for the integration of the sexual drive, is the anthropological principle of the complementarity of the sexes. This was discussed earlier. It is useful here to recall its three fundamental features:

> 1. The radical equality between men and women. Sharing the same nature, they have the same dignity, origin and destiny. They are called to adhere to the same fundamental goods of human nature, though in different ways. Their goal is the same fullness of happiness in union with God.
> 2. Natural differences. Men and women have different physiological and psychological makeups that give them aptitudes for certain functions in the relationship of marriage.
> 3. Harmonic collaboration with a unitary purpose. While affirming the differences, it is also understood that they work together to empower a man and a woman to have a family, committed to form a stable union via the bond of marriage.

In the light of the complementarity of the sexes, sexual union has meaning when a man and a woman are united in marriage. It is in view of marriage and forming a family that we can articulate the integration of this drive and, consequently, elaborate on the virtue of Chastity.

9.1.1 Chastity at different stages of development

Recently, in a school in England, there was uproar by parents about an activity that was sent out to their children ages 11 to 14, asking them to identify types of pornography. It was supposedly part of the Health and Family Life Curriculum. Parents were outraged to the point where the story reached the BBC and the school apologized publicly. How the school plans to repair the harm done has not received the same coverage, but we can suppose that the parents would demand some sort of counselling for the children who have experienced this abuse from persons whom they trusted. Common sense tells us that this is bad sex education, and especially so when dealing with innocent children. Proper sex education never includes pornographic material, as its aim is to integrate the sexual drive into sound spiritual values based on the dignity of every human being who can never be considered as an object of sexual pleasure.

While there are principles governing sex education that apply at every age, the form education in chastity takes should be adapted to the age of the audience in question. Important changes take place at different stages in the physiological and psychological development of boys and girls that shape their sexual awareness, interest and potential. Parents and educators need to monitor these changes and adopt strategies for sex education that are best suited to the child in question. The task of sex education could be defined as follows:

> Education in chastity is all an individual needs to know and the habits and attitudes that he or she needs to cultivate in order to properly manage feelings and emotions in relationships of friendship with both sexes and to be prepared for a lasting, happy and fruitful relationship in marriage, even though marriage is not meant for everyone.

a. The childhood years

Research shows that between 1 and 5 years, small children are very curious about the body. They enjoy their nakedness and are generally exhibitionists. As they enter the age of reason, this curiosity wanes and the period of latency begins. It is defined as the seemingly carefree attitude of children at this stage on issues related to sexuality. Melvin Anchell, psychiatrist, expert, and author, says: "The dormant sexual energies in the child do not disappear during latency, but are redirected by the mind and are used to serve other purposes. For example, during latency, some redirected sexual energy is used for acquiring knowledge. This is why the 6- to 12-year-old child is most educable."[8]

The minds of children in later childhood are particularly attuned to the development of ideals, dreams, romanticism, and faithful love. This stage is a window of opportunity for transmitting values and virtues to children. Ideals and good habits cemented at this stage impacts deeply on the personality of a developing child, giving the boy or girl a head start on happiness. Parents and educators should take advantage of this period to form the consciences of young children with clear notions of good and evil. Parents should be aware that their child at this age sees them as heroes, all powerful and wise. Children have total confidence in their parents and feel comfortable telling them openly their sins and failures, knowing that they will never be judged, but rather helped with the utmost delicacy and refinement. This setting is part of the window of opportunity that parents have to transmit the ideals and ways of behaving that they wish to be engrained in the minds and hearts of their children.

The latency period between 7 and 12 is also the time when children internalize their identity as male or female. Boys and girls naturally turn away from play in mixed groups and prefer to interact with those of their own sex. Boys develop their male identity and girls their female identity in this way. It would be a mistake to oppose this natural dynamic that is taking place. As the sexual drive is dormant, children understand male and female differences on a deeper level than aspects related to sexual intimacy. When the sexual power awakens, this becomes the centre of attention. At the pre-teen stage, sexual identity is linked to ways of thinking and interacting with the environment that can be characterized as typically masculine or feminine. When identity formation is properly internalized, boys can have a richer more meaningful interaction with girls and vice versa later in life. This happens because they would have had the mental schema for understanding the many different gifts that men and women can bring to the table in forming a family.

To facilitate identity formation during latency, it is healthy for fathers to spend more time with their boys and mothers with their girls in this period. This was the normal course of events when life was simpler, and families lived and worked in the countryside on farms. The boys would go out to the fields with dad from late childhood and the girls would help mom. This way of life had the advantage of facilitating the healthy development of male and female awareness in boys and girls. Back home, brothers and sisters gathered together for family life, where each was loved and respected equally, independent of his or her sex. The children would see the love their parents had for each other and comprehend that the differences in the sexes were in fact complementary for building and caring for a family.

b. Changes and challenges in puberty

Latency is the stage that precedes puberty. The transition from latency to puberty takes place at a different age for boys and girls and also varies from one individual to the next. In general, it occurs between 12 and 16 years old. At puberty, the sexual organs begin to develop accompanied by changes in how the brain works. A complex and yet at the same time simple process is set in motion that demands a new approach to education in chastity. It is complex from the point of view of the biological and neurological systems that are engaged in an aggressive way. The changes are at the same time simple because they have a clear direction, which is to prepare the bodies of the boys and girls for procreation in marriage. At this stage, the interest in the body reawakens and also an interest in the body of the opposite sex. For girls, the initial stages can be confusing as they begin to experience bodily changes associated with cycles of fertility. Boys experience strong drives for sexual stimulation as their sexual organs develop. Both boys and girls seem to be more rebellious at this time. This is due, in part, to the fact that they are emotionally driven during puberty, to bond affectionately with others outside of the home. The sexual energy that erupts at this stage drives them in this direction. It stands to reason that they become more interested in being cool with their friends and learning how to deal with the opposite sex, than trying to please their parents.

The factors outlined above necessitate a radically new approach to education in chastity during puberty. In the first place, parents need to have a new way of communicating with their offspring. When they are small, children look up to their parents for everything, and parents tend to communicate with them from a position of authority and power. During puberty, children look rather to their peers for affirmation and may appear to be rebellious and wayward. To connect with their children, it is important to communicate more like a friend than an authoritative figure. This means reasoning with one's offspring about their decisions while giving them space to find their own path. They will certainly make mistakes, but parents should remember that they too made mistakes at that age, and that those errors are part of the process of finding the right path. If parents and educators did a good job in inculcating values and virtues during latency, then they would find the task of educating in chastity—and for life in general—much easier during puberty. The groundwork would have been done to now reason with their older children based on principles they hold in common.

To illustrate the importance of a new strategy for communication during puberty, compare the following two dialogues:

A father finds pornographic material in the room of his son and confronts him in the following manner:

> (Barging into his son's room) Son, I found this in your room earlier today. What on earth are you doing with this? How could it possibly occur to you to bring such trash into our house! I am very disappointed in you. Watching porn is a mortal sin and I'm going to destroy this right away. Go and change because I am taking you to get confession right now and I hope you wise up to never do that again!

The virtues for integration related to relationships

Here is another approach:

(The Father knocks on the door and waits for his son to say come in). Son, do you have some time? I would like to discuss something with you. (They both sit comfortably). Son, I was trying to find the manual for the TV yesterday and I found this stuff under some papers in your room. I was confused why you would have something like this among your things. (Pause to give the son a chance to explain).

I remember the first time I saw pornography. I was your age as well. Some boys in school were looking at it and I was curious and joined in. That image is stuck in my mind even now 30 years later. I am married to the most beautiful woman in the world who is your mother, and it pains me to feel drawn in by sexual acts in pornography where she does not have and can never have any place. Your mother and I thank God for the intimacy we share and it is a sacred thing. You are fruit of that love. Imagine if your dad were hooked on pornography, how hurtful that would be for your mom? Porn is very addictive so stay far from it. I will send you a link about that later.

So what do you plan to do with that material? What helped me a lot to be chaste was going to confession frequently, praying to Mary and keeping busy. The most important thing is not to get discouraged. At your age, controlling the sexual drive is like taming a wild horse. You will find yourself thrown off from time to time, but the most important thing is to get back on and fight. You may think you are not getting anywhere, but your muscles are getting stronger from having to resist. OK Son. Back on the horse! (He gives his son a big hug and leaves)

A third approach that one finds is not to speak to one's son at all but to sweep the whole thing under the carpet. This is negligence and so can hardly be good parenting. Unfortunately, it is more of the norm than one would hope.

One finds that parents often leave education in chastity to the school or the Church. In this aspect of upbringing, it is of paramount importance that parents assume their role as primary educators. An atmosphere of trust and intimacy is the proper environment for speaking about very personal and intimate things such as bodily changes and challenges in living purity. Children look to the example of their parents to assimilate the criteria they give them on living purity. In the home, there is unconditional trust and love. Because of this, parents can be open with their children about their own experiences and vice versa. It is understandable that parents may be reluctant to talk to their children about chastity. They may feel they are invading their privacy or that they do not know how to explain things well. There are resources available to help parents with this task and, in any case, it does not matter too much if they make mistakes because they can revisit those points later on. The children are always at hand and see the good intention of their parents. Given the current breakdown in family life, there is a widespread lack of proper parental guidance for children during puberty. Character building programmes can help to make up for this deficiency, but it ought to be done in the context of clear guidelines to ensure that the privacy and intimacy of the students are respected. A further challenge is that students from broken homes may feel judged and insecure when family life is taught as a fundamental good. The *Alive to the World* series offers a useful approach. Values are virtues are transmitted using stories that are just that—stories. Thus no one in particular is implicated. The parents in the story fill in for parents who may be absent in the lives of some of the students. The message gets through correctly to the reader and he or she will have an idea of how to speak with his or her children, in the case that he or she becomes a parent in the future. It is very effective.

As parents learn the new way of dealing with their children during puberty, respecting their space and speaking to them as friends, they can give them useful advice for living chastity. As mentioned, in boys, the sexual drive erupts strongly in early adolescence. In this period a young man tends to be distracted and self-conscious as he begins to seek the approval of his friends and to relate more with the opposite sex. At the same time, this stage is also a time for ideals. Looking out onto the world, a twelve-year-old has a world of possibilities before him and is bursting with energy to go after his dreams. A boy at this age is starting an exciting journey, but without knowing exactly where it would lead. There has to be a bit of trial and error before a young person settles on a definitive path.

The lack of determination that characterizes early adolescence suggests that it is not prudent to stress on the dignity of the marriage vocation or of apostolic celibacy in conversations about chastity with boys in this stage of life. During childhood, they already understood that men and women are complementary. They know that Mom and Dad are different, and that those differences work together for having a family. In puberty, parents can explain in a simple way that this complementariness also applies to the procreation of new life through the sexual union of the bodies of a husband and wife. A father can tell his son in a straightforward way that this is how he and his brothers and sisters came into the world. By means of an explanation such as this, an 11 or 12-year-old boy will see intimacy as something beautiful that a husband and wife who love and respect each other share. With this backdrop, a father can proceed to chat with his son about the particular challenges for living holy purity that a 12-year-old faces. The conversation can be like this, for example:

> (The father is dropping his son to swimming) Andre, I wanted to share something with you. Can we chat about it now? I remember when I was your age, a friend in school showed me some pornographic magazines and told me that he would get sexual relief by playing with his private parts, pretending he was having sex. You know that the technical word for that is masturbation. That stuck in my head and has been a temptation for me all my life. I realize now that at your age, it is natural to have a great curiosity about sex and to seek sexual relief. It is as though you suddenly find yourself on a wild horse that has not been tamed. Son, you can't just give in. If you don't struggle to control the beast, it will end up controlling you and all your dreams in life will be shattered. Do you want that? Of course not! So you need to know that you have to fight to keep pure. Here are a few pointers:
> Guard your senses. When you catch yourself looking at a woman in an inappropriate way, turn away immediately. If something pops up on the Internet or TV that is vulgar and/or

The virtues for integration related to relationships

explicit, navigate away from that without delay. Be strong to tell your friends that you are not interested in pornography or in participating in conversations that are disrespectful to women. Keep in mind that your mom and sisters are women, and we love them very much.

Try to pray to our Lady in the moment of temptation. I say, for example, "Mother of fair love, pray for me". I know some people who pray to their guardian angel. Someone the other day told me that he thinks of Jesus on the Cross who died to save us from sin and he says: "Heart on the Cross, Heart on the Cross". It's up to you to find an aspiration that works for you. Keep busy with good and noble things. If you are focused on doing lots of good things for love of God, it's harder for temptations to come. The most important thing I wanted to share with you, though, is that you should not be surprised if you find that you are thrown off the horse from time to time and find yourself flat on your face on the ground. The thing to do is to pick up yourself, get back on the horse and struggle with it even harder. At times you may think you are not getting anywhere, but that is not true. The struggle itself gets you stronger, just like the resistance of the water when you swim is getting you fit. One day, the sexual drive of puberty wanes a bit and you will find that you have pretty good control of the animal. That will make you very happy.

(They arrive to the pool) What do you think about this son? Does it make sense? We can continue chatting about this another time. See you after training. Try not to stare too much at the pretty girls! (laugh).

The bodily and psychological changes in puberty are different for boys and girls. The timing of these changes is different as well. Because of this, the approach to educating in chastity during puberty is different for boys and girls. On the physiological level, a girl's body develops the mechanisms for fertility, pregnancy and nurturing a child. When the first signs of these bodily changes appear, the mother can have an open conversation with her daughter to explain what is happening and the meaning of it. Part two of this conversation can touch on sexual intimacy and the ways to safeguard holy purity. Louise Kirk, in her book *Sexuality Explained*, brings alive how these conversations can take place. It is always in the context of a confident trusting dialogue between a mother and her daughter, dealing with the topic in a refined and positive way.[9]

Regarding the different approaches to sex education in boys and girls in puberty, it is hard to put it better than Dr. Anchell does in an article on the stages of sexual development. He writes:

> The erotic feelings and behaviour of adolescent girls follow a much different course. Because her genital structures are biologically unready and remain anesthetic to sexual intercourse until much later in life, and because a girl's feminine psychology is not completed until late adolescence, the adolescent female has a natural aversion to sexual intercourse. Engaging in the sex act causes her unpleasant tensions, and these tensions reinforce the adolescent girl's normal sexual inhibitions.

A teenage girl's eroticism may be as intense as the boy's, but her desires are not for sexual intercourse, but involve fantasies and dreams, kisses and caresses, the wish to love and to be loved and sometimes thoughts of having a child. Her sensual feelings, however, are not inseparably entwined with the sex act, such as they are in the male.

Today's "sexually educated" and misled teenage female, who fails to abide by her natural feminine inhibitions and regularly engages in sex, reacts with feelings of coldness and emptiness. Her feminine psychology fails to develop. Her feminine emotions become dry and sterile. A lifelong conflict develops between herself and her inner femininity and motherhood feeling.

The dichotomy between the adolescent boy's readiness for sex and the girl's natural sexual inhibitions serves a vital purpose. Nature always has a reason for what it does. The girl's reluctance serves to strengthen the affectionate and spiritual nature of sex. Adolescent chastity is essential for the spiritualization of sex. Through sexual spiritualization, the adolescent learns to feel esteem for members of the opposite sex. In boys this esteem is especially felt for girls who are chaste.[10]

c. Cultivating chastity in middle adolescence

Both boys and girls in puberty benefit a great deal from having clear criteria in their early teens for struggling to safeguard purity. As they approach 14 and 15 it is hoped that they would have internalized this battle and be in a good position for developing friendships with the opposite sex. Up to this point in their lives, the friends that boys have are mostly with other boys and the friends that girls have are mostly with other girls. It helps a lot for a father to have a trusting conversation with his sons when they are approaching 15 years old about how to treat girls. Similarly, it helps for mothers to have conversations with their daughters about how to treat guys. A father can explain to his son that he would be on the wrong track if he goes along treating women like he deals with his boy friends. Girls do not appreciate rough treatment. Their bodies and psychology are oriented towards having children and caring for them. Women are very vulnerable and needy when they get pregnant and when they are nurturing their new-born babies. Because of this, a girl is drawn to a guy who makes her feel safe, who can provide and assure stability. It helps a great deal for fathers to give their young boys the good example of helping around the house, doing menial chores, cooking when needed, and doing simple repairs. Sensible women look for guys who will be good fathers and so a young boy should try to develop his personality to be engaging and responsible in dealing with children. In schools, it is useful for the older boys to have tasks of responsibility in dealing with the younger ones, such as being leaders in the recreational activities, clubs, and other school activities.

In a conversation that can take place in a casual, informal way, a father can remind his son that chivalrous gestures such as opening the door for a lady or offering your arm to help her down steps are never out of date. Women like being complimented and receiving tokens of affection. Beginning with his own example, a father has the role of teaching his sons to be gentlemen. It helps to be clear about boundaries. A boy should be careful in his conversations with the opposite sex to avoid comments or gestures that can even hint at being suggestive. This makes girls feel unsafe and disrespected for who they are and should never be entertained.

Fathers would do well also, to explain to their sons in early teens that women are more intuitive in their way of thinking. This means that they perceive the danger or the good in situations as a strong immediate emotional reaction, before they can articulate the reasons for this danger or benefit. There is an unfortunate stereotype that twists this into the idea that girls are not logical. While it is true that intuition cannot always be trusted, women are perfectly capable of analysing their emotional reactions in order to logically articulate the true danger in what provokes aversion or the true benefit in what attracts them powerfully. When this is explained to a young boy, he will understand that he would be misguided to go along with the stereotype that women are not reasonable. Rather he should cultivate the skill of trying to understand things from a woman's perspective, making an effort to see the good sense that is often enveloped in their intuitive reactions.

Boys are very grateful to their parents when they talk to them about dealing with the opposite sex. It saves them a lot of embarrassment and boosts their self-confidence as well. With these conversations, boys feel that they can be very open with Dad and Mom and can run to them any time with the challenges they face in puberty. The same occurs with girls. A young girl approaching fifteen greatly appreciates tips from her parents about dealing with the opposite sex. A mother can explain to her daughter that sexual arousal works differently in boys and girls. Unlike girls, visual stimuli can get boys sexually aroused very quickly. A girl may swoon and feel in love with a boy she sees, but men tend to feel an intense desire for sexual engagement when they see a woman who is dressed immodestly. In a calm and steady state, boys are inclined to do the manly thing of figuring things out and developing their talents and muscles so as to contribute to society in the present and later in life. Men are well-regarded by other men—and women too—when they are tough mentally and physically to get the job done, with or without the frills. In an aroused state, a man is not fully in control of himself and may say or do something inappropriate. He is just the opposite of the strong and clear-thinking creature that wins him approval from others and his own self. When he sees an immodestly dressed girl, the sexual drive in a man can be awakened suddenly, clouding his vision of things. A mother can explain to her daughter that a woman is meant to support a man and not to undermine his dignity and strength. Because of this she should be modest in her dress and actions. This does not mean that she should not be attractive. Physical attraction is often the first point of connection in bringing a boy and a girl together. The good boys, however, will be turned off when they perceive that a girl is using sexual appeal to have the upper hand.

When mothers explain to their daughters the need for modesty, further conversation may be needed to help them to overcome an excess of modesty that can lead them to be overly shy around men, and to give the impression that they are not interested and reject them. Mothers at times are the cause of this when they give their daughters the impression that guys are just out to get them to take advantage of them sexually. This is simply not true. Good guys pride themselves on being reasonable and in control. Because peer approval is important for boys, they do not handle rejection very well.

A mother can orient her daughter in her teens to understand that men can be a bit clumsy at the outset in approaching a girl and, thinking it cool, he may say something silly. A girl should try to be patient and friendly to help persons of the opposite sex to be more relaxed around them. It is not wrong even for a girl to take the initiative to talk to a boy she finds interesting. A tricky situation arises when a young man may say something clearly inappropriate or suggestive. At times things like these need to be reported. Sometimes they are done jokingly but in poor taste. A girl can talk these things over with her parents to see how best to understand such a situation and to address it. If it's not too serious, situations like these can be easily remedied by letting the young man know that the comment was not appreciated. Men don't mind this feedback. They will apologize, and things can return to normal without any big fuss.

The period from 14 to 17can be likened to learning to cycle or to swim. There is a bit of trial and error in the acquisition of new skills in order to be comfortable in a new sport. For a young person in middle adolescence, the new situation is interacting with the opposite sex. In sport, the mediation of a coach to give encouragement, tips and feedback is an important element for reaching proficiency. Similarly, the mediation of adults who the young people can trust and speak with openly is an important ingredient for socialization at this age. With the socialization of boys and girls in their teenage years, there needs to be opportunities for them to interact such as in outings, school functions, parish activities, and dances. As previously discussed, girls and boys becoming "girlfriend" and "boyfriend" is pretending to be somewhere that does not correspond to reality. We can liken it to someone saying that he or she deserves a prize for cycling when they do not even know how to keep their balance on the bike! Our society today needs to revisit urgently the task of socialization of boys and girls in middle adolescence. It helps to have clear principles, guidelines and norms that act as points of reference. It is also useful for parents to interact with each other so as to be on the same page in guiding their children through these challenging years.

d. Entering adult life

By the time boys and girls reach the ages of 17 or 18, one hopes that they would have properly assimilated the importance of living purity. It does not mean that it would no longer be a challenge, but rather that they would understand where the dangers and pitfalls lay, and how to avoid them. Furthermore, if properly socialized in their teens, a boy or a girl entering adulthood would know how to deal with the opposite sex in an educated and refined way. This being the case, a new dynamic sets in at the outset of adult life as young people become more tuned to what we can call a vocational sense of life. This is the time in life when one chooses a career path and perhaps moves out of home to study in a different state or country. Young people entering adulthood want to experience greater independence and are interested in preparing for a life-long committed relationship. This may be in marriage or in apostolic celibacy.

It is important for parents and educators to keep up a friendly dialogue with their children at this stage about relationships with the opposite sex. A young woman may be tempted to become sexually active with a young man she is infatuated with and who she perceives as being marriage potential. It should be recognized that this is not a good strategy for preparing for a happy marriage. She may be correct about many of the good traits she sees in the person she feels she loves. Nevertheless, there may be other important issues that need to be taken into account which she is not aware of or which she does not give sufficient importance to, being emotionally captivated by the young man in question. He may go along because of the good feeling of sexual intimacy and the fear of hurting the other person. Breaking off the relationship may also damage his reputation, impacting negatively on his friendships.

An important factor to consider is the scientific discovery that sexual intimacy is connected with increased levels of a hormone called *oxytocin* in the bloodstream.[11] This hormone is linked to long-term emotional bonding in women. In other words, it produces a desire to want to have the other person nearby as a physical necessity. When a boy and a girl are sexually intimate or engage in prolonged and frequent caressing, these chemicals are released making them feel that they want to be together forever, even though they may be far from ready for a serious commitment. When young people enter adulthood, they are in a time of remote preparation for marriage. It would be advisable for them to dedicate their energies to settling in their careers, deepening their spiritual lives, acquiring a broader culture, and fostering deeper conversations with their friends, men and women alike. A young man who is interested in a female friend or vice versa, having this idea in mind, will know that the first step in a relationship is communication, getting to know the other person. If they share ideals and are good for each other, they can begin to spend more time together and move towards commitment in marriage.

The following charts show how things unfold when there is order and when it is inverted.[12]

1 Virtuous relationship. Good sense prevails

1.	2	3	4	5
A young man and a young woman meet and feel **attraction** to each other.	They chat, exchange opinions and **get to know each other** well. They share ideals and goals.	**They decide that they are good for each other.**	They enter into a permanent **commitment** (marriage)	They begin physical contact that produces endorphins and oxytocin that unite them and make them feel that they "need" to be with each other.

Figure 9.1 Sequence of events in a chaste relationship

2 Disordered relationship. Irrationality easily prevails

1	2	3	4	5
A young man and a young woman meet and feel **attraction** to each other.	They begin physical contact that produces endorphins and oxytocin that unite them and make them feel that they "need" to be with each other.	**They are convinced** that they are made for each other and ready to commit long term.	They chat, exchange opinions and **get to know each other superficially.**	**They break up** or (rarely) enter into a stable commitment.

Figure 9.2 Sequence of events when couples choose to be sexually active before marriage.

The virtues for integration related to relationships

It is important for young people to understand that the second scenario presented above is on the opposite end of the spectrum to proper preparation for a true commitment in marriage. Married love is authentic when it is not motivated by a need to be with someone, but rather by a well-thought-out decision on both sides in a relationship, to mutually belong to each other as fruit of a completely free exchange. A person who feels either internally or externally coerced to be in a relationship out of a fear of loss or of hurting another, lacks the freedom to enter a true love relationship. A difficult but important truth to transmit to young people is that love is not a feeling, but a firm decision of the Will to seek the good of the other. This does not mean that emotions are not important. A core thesis of this handbook is that emotions are linked to natural inclinations, which point the human person to his authentic end. Furthermore, human beings are vulnerable, and so there can hardly be true love if the parties do not take into consideration the emotions that the other may be experiencing. Feelings, however, as was explained previously, need to be purified of selfishness, because they are self-referential in their desire to be satisfied. Reason is the proper guide for emotions, at times recognizing the need to subdue or control them for the sake of a greater, more spiritual good. It makes sense for persons entering adulthood to cultivate emotional maturity and a spirit of sacrifice in service of others and the common good.

An effective strategy that parents can adopt at this stage of development of their children, is to try to get them involved in clubs, groups, associations etc., where they could receive encouragement and formation in chastity adapted to their age. The ideal would be a more in-depth formation with a structured programme. The course does not have to focus on sex and sexuality alone, but it should include such a component. The explanations should elaborate on the complementarity of the sexes, the greatness of marriage as a vocation, and the dignity of sexual intimacy. It is important that many young people receive such a formation so that they, in turn, can explain to their friends the importance of saving sex for marriage and of living chastely. One can recommend here the programmes and materials developed by initiatives such as Alive to the World[13] and Canvox[14] and also by communicators such as Jason Evert[15] and Christopher West.[16]

e. Courtship and Engagement

The period of remote preparation does not have a clear time span but includes all of what is learnt in childhood. Proximate preparation depends on finding the right person and on being ready to settle down. The importance of good values and emotional maturity has been stressed in this section so far. There are also practical issues such as being able to provide for a family and attaining career goals. A young woman or a young man who is comfortable with the idea of getting married in the near future, while occupied with her or his career and other obligations, will begin to be more on the lookout for a person with the qualities and traits to be a future spouse for them. When they go on friendly dates, it will be with the idea of meeting someone they could marry. As they get to know someone of the opposite sex who they think is good for them, the topic of marriage arises and the two begin to have deeper conversations about their ideals and aspirations as a spouse. As they spend more time together, the parties have the opportunity to meet their respective families and to get feedback from them. If the two persons have been well brought up, it is rare that there will be any issue here. It makes sense, nevertheless, to take seriously the comments of parents, as it is not unusual that one may lack objectivity about some aspects of a person one is growing in love with. The two persons are not yet committed to each other, but the seriousness of the relationship merits its own description as courtship. Aware of the commitment that marriage entails, they should objectively consider whether the other partner will be a good husband or wife and a good father or mother to their children. Again, it helps count on the advice of their parents, close friends and their respective spiritual advisors.

It is natural that a couple who are courting each other would feel drawn to a level of physical intimacy that is proper to marriage. If they have received and assimilated a good formation in chastity throughout their lives, they would take care to ensure that such intimacy does not occur. Both parties would understand that saving sex for marriage is part of how they prove their love for each other and for God who has led them along this path. They know that they will never regret abstaining, whereas giving in on this point opens up a zone of corruption in their relationship, and can lead to deep regrets in the future, especially if the wedding does not take place for some reason. A good criterion is to keep gestures of affection such as kissing and embracing romantically, brief and sparing, and to avoid occasions of being alone in a lonely place together.

As the couple grows even closer, the day comes when they decide to marry. The young man asks the parents (customarily the father) of the woman he wishes to marry for the hand of their daughter in marriage. Traditionally, this is done to have their blessing and support. Couples married at a much younger age in the past, and the father of the bride was expected to be involved in helping the couple to get on their own two feet. Following this step, he proposes in the nicest way he can think of, a ring is given, and the period of engagement begins. Engaged couples have a deeper commitment than courtship. They are at the point of immediate preparation for marriage. It continues to be a time of getting to know each other better and so each party should feel free to break off the relationship if they so desire. To respect this freedom, they should be careful not to commit each other financially or emotionally in the long term. In this period the two can enjoy a greater physical contact than courtship, but never that which is exclusive for married couples. The criterion mentioned for courtship continues to apply.

Many people choose to get married in a religious ceremony where part of their preparation would be attending a marriage preparation course. These courses have proven to be very helpful for couples when they are open to learn. As part of this preparation, engaged persons will learn about chastity in marriage, which has new elements as it is lived in a different way compared to the other stages leading up to it.

A core principle that guides education in sexuality is that sexual intimacy has its proper expression only in marriage. Outside of marriage it contaminates relationships with the selfish desires that it fosters and can lead to hurts, regrets, and very big mistakes. In marriage, couples now have the task of ensuring that the sexual act always has its proper expression. In ethical language we say that they are called to safeguard the integrity of the sexual act. The sex act can be considered as a coin with two faces. For a token to be valid, both sides, the head and the tail, ought to have the required engravings. In the case of marriage, the head and the tail correspond to the unitive and procreative dimensions of the sexual act. The unitive dimension means that the couple is validly married. The procreative means that that sex act is open to life. When both are present, the conjugal act has integrity. If one is missing the integrity is destroyed. As part of marriage preparation, couples should study carefully the methods of natural family planning that are available. This will help them to respect the procreative logic in each conjugal act, while at the same time using the science of fertility cycles to space having children. Sometimes this responsibility is left entirely up to the woman. Husbands, however, should follow the fertility charts of their spouses so that they can discuss and plan together their conjugal life. It is clear that being married is far from a licence to have sex. Within marriage there needs to be, more than ever, the proper sensitivity and generosity towards the other person, taking into account their particular way of being, of manifesting affection and of experiencing sexual pleasure.

The virtue of chastity can be studied in much greater depth than is presented here. It is not the scope of this book to present a thorough study of the subject. The objective of the discussion was to elaborate on the practice of chastity from the perspective of integrating the drives related to sex on the bodily and emotional levels into the values of friendship and family. Chastity is an important virtue of integration and merits its own consideration as a virtue that impacts directly on human dignity and the attainment of true happiness.

9.2 The virtue of loyalty

The sexual urge and the emotional desire for company and appreciation is good and useful when purified of selfish self-seeking. Along with chastity, the virtue of loyalty can be identified as an essential habit for the proper integration of these desires into the spiritual values of family and friendship. Not infrequently, the easiest way to see the importance of a virtue is to consider scenarios from one's personal experience where that virtue has been lacking. A person who is not loyal is one who is inconsistent and superficial in what would ordinarily be considered a serious commitment to another person or institution. Think of a person who abandons his or her job on a whim, leaving the others to have to pick up the slack without a proper handover. It is also hurtful and saddening to get news that someone you trust and confide in has been spreading rumours about you and criticizing you with others. There is the classic case of a spouse who cheats on the other, covering it over with lies and deception. Without loyalty, friendship and family life are eventually destroyed.

Turning to the positive side, the image of a dog with its owner is often used to understand this virtue. A pet dog is always there to welcome its owner, regardless of whether its master has behaved well or badly that day. It will defend its owner and stay at his or her side when invited. While the pet is healthy and alive, this conduct does not vary. *Mutatis mutandis* (changing what needs to be changed), the imagery applies on the human level as well. A person who is loyal will not judge his or her friends but is always welcoming and open towards them. A loyal friend will defend those he or she loves and who love him or her in return. Figuratively, loyal persons stand by the side of their loved ones, supporting, sharing, and encouraging them in their endeavours. When a person has committed to a vocational path in life such as marriage or apostolic celibacy, loyalty is equivalent to being faithful or fidelity.

When this virtue is practised authentically, the parties who are connected feel assured that they can be open and sincere with each other. They are not afraid to show vulnerability, because the support of the other does not depend on how wise their decision-making has been. They know that they will always find support and encouragement in a loyal friend. This being the case, neither is it loyalty to give support to activities that undermine the dignity of the human person. A true friend will correct his or her companion, leaning on the trust and openness they have acquired. One who fails to do so is lacking the courage and detachment to live this virtue properly.

This well-known passage from the book of Sirach sums it up:

> A faithful friend is a sturdy shelter; he who finds one finds a treasure.
> A faithful friend is beyond price, no sum can balance his worth.
> A faithful friend is a life-saving remedy, such as he who fears God finds.
> For he who fears God behaves accordingly, and his friend will be like himself.[17]

9.3 The virtue of charity

Under the virtues for relationships, we find the most important of all virtues, which is charity. The word "Charity" is generally associated with generosity and helpfulness especially toward the needy or suffering. Here it is used in the biblical sense. In the New Testament, charity is the highest form of love, signifying the reciprocal love between God and man that is made manifest in unselfish love of one's fellow men.[18] Understood in this way, love is the fundamental interior calling of every human being. God is love and as the image of God, man is created for love. Love gives meaning to true freedom and self-control and orients them towards self-giving in communion and friendship with God and with others.

Charity or self-giving love ranks first among the virtues because it concerns union with God and flowing from this, union with others. In as much as it involves a certain art and training for relationships, it requires practice like the other virtues. It is important to briefly consider charity as it applies to God. The task of integration that is elaborated in this document begins and ends here. The ultimate goal of integration is to bring us into harmony with what we intuit as the origin and end of every tendency and inclination in us. We can call this the creator or God. When I feel at one with this creative power, in tune with his design, I have a deep sense of self-worth and identity. I feel worthy to continue existing and of being affirmed in the human nature I have received. If I live at odds with the design of the creator, I experience a deep sense of loss and confusion. I must now seek worthiness and affirmation in my human nature elsewhere, in created things. In this condition a person ends up alienated from himself or herself because all that one can possess outside of the supreme being is transient and limited. The life of St. Augustine brings this out in a powerful way. Looking back on the long and winding road that eventually led him to completely surrender to God, he wrote with deep conviction: "You have made us for yourself, and our heart is restless until it rests in you!"[19]

Love is such a broad and multifaceted theme that volumes could be written, and they would only begin to do it justice. St. John in his gospel says, "God is love", and from this truth proceeds the origin, unfolding and consummation of all things.[20] Here we can only highlight a few points and elaborate on them briefly.

Considered in its fullest meaning, charity gives shape or form to the other virtues. If we think of the virtues as balls on a billiards table, charity would be like the rack that gathers them together in a certain shape at the beginning of the game. When the game begins, the first player hits the white ball into the formation and the balls scatter. Without charity, the other virtues are a bit like this, scattered around the board of life. This example has obvious limitations because the virtues are dynamic and many-sided whereas billiard balls are static and uniform. The shape that charity provides helps the virtues to work together for a unitary purpose, which is ultimately self-possession and true happiness in union with God and others.

Looked at side by side with the other virtues of relationships, true self-giving love implies the cultivation of certain attitudes and habits. These come to light when we look at scenarios where charity is lacking or absent. The opposite of charity is often thought to be hate. This attitude towards another, however, means that some recognition is given to the other, if only it be that the person is causing me distress. Somewhere in our heart we want that person to change and so there is a chance for reconciliation. On the other end of the spectrum to charity, we find, rather, complete indifference. It is taking another person for dead in one's heart. It's heart breaking, for example, to hear of stories where two persons living under the same roof have no concern at all for each other. It happens that one person may be seriously ill and the other does not lift a finger, not even to offer a bit of water. The experience of many persons who have suffered indifference is that it is more painful than insults and humiliations.

True love, as a virtue, is misconstrued and distorted when it is equated with the emotion of feeling in love or infatuation. A young woman, for example, can feel a strong attraction to a man she hardly knows, with a longing to be often in his company. She may readily say, "I love so and so", as well. It is important to examine carefully such feelings to see if they may be motivated by disordered desires for affirmation, appreciation and belonging. These emotions are not bad in themselves, as it has been repeatedly affirmed, but they must be properly integrated into values. A young boy, for example, may join a gang to satisfy his longing to belong. Gang leaders know how to prey on this emotion in boys by giving them attention and gifts and making promises to them. Most of the times these boys do not have a father figure at home and the gang leaders come to fill that emotional gap. Among the gang members they may speak of a "brotherhood" and "love" but there cannot be any true brotherhood or love if the activity that unites the persons is degrading to the human being. We can also mention the case of women who stay in abusive relationships for attention, company, and affection. There is no

The virtues for integration related to relationships

justification for this and the word "love" that is touted about in these situations is not genuine charity but a caricature of it.

Related to the points above, a sign that charity is lacking is that there is division and conflict. Persons who feel they have been mistreated often react by responding in kind. There is a well-known story about two cowboys that illustrates this point. A cowboy rides into a town and goes into the first saloon he finds. Approaching the bartender, he asks: "What are the people like in this town?" The bartender answers asking in return, "What were the people like in the last town you were in?" The cowboy says, "They were kind people, gently disposed, agreeable and generally pleasant to be with." The bartender replies, "I suspect you will find the people here to be the same way." A little while later another cowboy rides into town and stops at the saloon. He sits down at the bar and says to the bartender, "I have just arrived here. What are the people like?" And the bartender asks, "What were the people like in the last town you were in?" Then the cowboy answers, "They were sour, difficult, disagreeable folk. In fact, I almost got into a fight there." To which the bartender says, "I suspect you will find the people here to be the same way." In other words, we tend to relate to others in the way we perceive that they treat us. The cycle needs to break somewhere, and this can only happen if one party decides to forgive and to seek reconciliation, willing to overlook the mistreatment he or she has received for the sake of unity and peace. The other person may respond to that gesture allowing the issues between them to be discussed and hopefully resolved, in a mature and reasonable way.

9.3.1 Charity and human dignity

The darkness in several of the scenarios discussed above brings to light the fact that charity is rooted in respect for the dignity of each person. From an existential perspective, it means seeing in each person "another me", no matter who they are. This is called the principle of solidarity. When an individual adheres to this truth, he or she recognizes others as equal in dignity and fundamental rights. This radical equality is the ground on which an authentic friendship or a deeper relationship can develop. This being the case, the building up of a relationship is not automatic. Every person is a gift and so worthy of love. Yet love and friendship must be freely given and freely received. Even after a commitment is made, a refined respect for the freedom of the other will always be required for a healthy relationship.

Grounded in solidarity, an essential feature of charity is to effectively desire the good of the other. Thus, a friendship that is based on a common activity that is degrading to the human person is not a true friendship. C. S. Lewis highlighted that friends stand side by side in some common endeavour.[21] This shared concern or interest can serve to foster a friendship once it affirms and bolters human dignity in some way. The nobler the ideal or activity, the surer and deeper the friendship can be.

When love is given it desires to be repaid with love. The result is the union of two persons in heart and mind in some way. Without union, charity is incomplete. A young man may be interested in marrying someone he likes, but if she marries someone else, it no longer makes sense for him to love her as one

The virtues for integration related to relationships

who could be his spouse. Love seeks union and it is a constitutive element of a fruitful and fulfilling love. In the example given, it may be that the young man continues to feel a desire to marry a married person. This is now a disordered desire, and the will must intervene, engaging the braking and navigating system—to use the example of the boat—to control and redirect that longing, orienting its energy to the real possibilities of union in marriage that he may have. To further illustrate the importance of union for love, one can consider the situation of the souls in hell. They have freely chosen to separate themselves from God forever. The Supreme Being who is Love itself can never be united with these creatures and so God does not love the souls is hell. He may "feel" sad because of how they suffer, but he knows that it could not be any other way.

In his book *Four Loves*, C. S. Lewis presents four types of unions related to love. These are: the love of affection, the love of friendship, erotic or spousal love and finally *agape* love. Love of affection is the good feeling that one may have for the person who happens to be sitting next to you in the airport when a flight is delayed. Love of friendship is one that is based on a shared interest that leads you to be side by side with someone in a stable way. You desire to have that person next to you and the feeling is mutual. Erotic love is spousal love where a man and a woman commit to bind together in a marriage alliance characterized by a special intimacy. Their union is expressed in the conjugal act by which new life is engendered. As spouses, their married love overflows onto their children, giving rise to new relationships of fatherhood and motherhood.

The fourth type of love is *agape* love. It is the creative and redemptive complete self-giving love of God. It is on a higher level than the other loves, but this does not mean that the other loves are lacking in some way. Agape love has an integrative function with respect to the others. It orders all other loves to love of God and helps an individual to detect and correct disordered desires that can easily infiltrate and undermine the noble loves of affection, friendship, and spousal love. It expresses the experience of a love which involves a real discovery of the other, where the affections are purified of selfish pleasure seeking. Concern and care for the other prevails. There is no self-seeking, instead the lover seeks the good of the beloved: it becomes renunciation, and it is ready, and even desirous, for sacrifice.[22]

Wherever there is true love, there is a community of will, thought and sentiment that is established, which makes the persons similar to each other in some way. From antiquity we have the expression: *Idem Velle atque idem nolle*, which means to want the same thing and to reject the same thing.[23] The way this is articulated depends of the type of union that is established. Part of the virtue of charity is to orient the sentiments in a way that corresponds to the type of union in question. Together with this, it is important to understand the other person. When two people make the effort to come out of themselves and to see things through the eyes of the other, they find that they can communicate better and help each other in the best way for strengthening the bond between them. In a letter on friendship, Fernando Ocariz highlighted this aspect of charity as follows: "True friendship also means making a heartfelt effort to understand the convictions of our friends, even though we may never come to share them or accept them. Thus, our friends help us to understand ways of viewing life that are different from our own, that enrich our inner world, and, when the friendship is deep, that enable us to experience the world in a different way. This is, in the end, a true sharing in other's sentiments, which is sharing in their life and in their experiences."[24]

9.3.2 Cultivating true love

St. Augustine has famously said: "Love, and do what you will!"[25] This is not equivalent to that other popular exhortation: "Follow your heart". No doubt sentiments are part of love. Two persons must move towards each other for a union to take place. The forces for this drawing closer are the sentiments. It is important to cultivate in persons from a young age the capacity to empathize and sympathize with others. Empathy means the ability to understand and share the feelings of another. Film directors, for example, try to make their audience feel empathy with their characters using the different tools of cinematography available to them. This emotion is important for moving the intellect and will to show greater understanding in practical ways. It helps for winning others over and for quickly establishing confidence in relationships. Sympathy means feelings of pity and sorrow for someone else's misfortune. When properly ordered, these emotions aid a person to be compassionate and thoughtful.

When we say a person is compassionate, we tend to mean sympathy shown with deeds. There are extraordinary stories of compassion that inspire one to cultivate this attitude. At one time, for example, when hospitals were overwhelmed with Covid 19 patients in New York, the authorities made a general request for volunteers to help. Hundreds came forward, knowing that their lives would be at risk from contamination. This happened in other cities as well, all around the world. The compassion and generosity of these people generated a wave on social media with people and institutions coming out to show their appreciation and to recognize these persons. In ordinary life, compassion is shown in a myriad of ways, such as opening the door for someone whose hands are full, cheering up others when they seem down, visiting the aged and infirm, consoling persons who have lost loved ones, helping the poor and disadvantaged and so on.

It is clear that it is important to "have a heart" as the colloquial expression goes. At the same time, it needs to be stressed that the spiritual powers must be in charge. Right reason must be like the gardener in the field of our heart. He plants and cultivates, but also weeds and prunes and may even have to cut down a tree that is stifling and invading the other shrubs. True love demands careful attention to ensure that love is never contaminated by selfish desires and pursuits. To truly love, I must forget myself and give of myself, seeking what is in the best interest of the other in the kindest of ways. In this way, my love flows from noble ideals and will seek to show itself through a genuine balanced affection.

Genuine love is shown in the ability to correct a loved one when needed. A credible source once told an inspiring story of a young girl who stopped talking to one of her friends because that friend pointed out to her that she was making a bad decision to get involved with a crowd who was heavy into partying and were not serious students. At the end of the term, the girl came back and apologized. She confessed that she had come to appreciate the correction she received, and that it proved to her that, more than all the others she partied with, the truer and more valuable friend was she who showed "tough love" and had the courage to confront her about what she was doing.

To this we can also add the well-known maxim that true love is ordered. This means that we ought to be more available for and more attentive to those who are closest to us. Naturally this means that family comes first. A person may spend a large amount of time helping others, but if their family is neglected, then their love is disordered in some way. There is some self-seeking or dominating fear that is warping their decision-making.

When we consider all that is enshrined in the word "love" or "charity", it certainly holds true St. Augustine's adage: "Love and do what you will". One who loves puts himself or herself out for the other in a myriad of ways. Small gestures such as a smile, a glance and a look can be immensely meaningful and important. It is impossible to make a list of "things to do" to prove love. There is an anecdote of a husband who wanted to prove his love for his wife and asked her to tell him what to do. She was pleased but explained that she wanted him to notice and be thoughtful concerning her needs. True charity leads one to be attuned to other people's joys, sorrows, and desires and to support them in creative ways without them having to ask every time. This reinforces the need for empathy and understanding that was discussed above. There is also what can be called the "good manners of charity". In different places there are customs for what is called good manners. These have been handed down from generation to generation as concrete ways to show charity. They normally consist of little things such as not keeping others waiting, keeping up a good appearance, details of hospitality when a guest arrives, proper table manners and ways of carrying oneself and so forth. Practicing these customs may seem stifling or lacking spontaneity at times so they need to be balanced with a healthy naturalness in our way of being. The goal of these customs, however, are not the mores themselves, but the charity that we show through them. One can safely suggest that it is better to err on the side of consistently using them than to make many exceptions.

Notes

1. R. m N, "Watching Pornography Rewires the Brain to a More Juvenile State," The Conversation, November 27, 2019, http://theconversation.com/watching-pornography-rewires-the-brain-to-a-more-juvenile-state-127306.
2. Mary Eberstadt, *Adam and Eve After the Pill: Paradoxes of the Sexual Revolution* (San Francisco: Ignatius Press, 2012), chap. 2.
3. Abigail Favale, *The Genesis of Gender: A Christian Theory* (San Francisco California: Ignatius Press, 2022), 74.
4. *Diagnostic and Statistical Manual of Mental Disorders: DSM-IV-TR*, 4th ed. (Washington, D.C.: American Psychiatric Association, 2000), 576.
5. Michelle Conlin, Robin Respaut, and Chad Terhune, "A Gender Imbalance Emerges among Trans Teens Seeking Treatment," Reuters, November 18, 2022, https://www.reuters.com/investigates/special-report/usa-transyouth-topsurgery/.
6. Abigail Shrier, *Irreversible Damage: The Transgender Craze Seducing Our Daughters* (Washington, DC: Regnery Publishing, 2020), 19.
7. Kenneth J. Zucker, "The Myth of Persistence," *International Journal of Transgenderism* 19, no. 2 (2018): 2.
8. Melvin Anchell, "A Psychoanalytic Look at Today's Sex Education," American Life League (ALL), July 13, 2010, https://www.all.org/guest-commentary/a-psychoanalytic-look-at-todays-sex-education.

9. Louise Kirk, *Sexuality Explained: A Guide for Parents and Children* (Leominster, U.K.: Gracewing Publishing, 2013).
10. Anchell, "A Psychoanalytic Look at Today's Sex Education."
11. Kerstin Uvnas Moberg, *The Hormone of Closeness: The Role of Oxytocin in Relationships*, Reprint edition (London: Pinter & Martin Ltd, 2013), chap. 6.
12. © Alianza Latinoamericana para la Familia (ALAFA) 2021. Reproduced with permission.
13. *Alive to the World* (www.alivetotheworld.org) Alive to the world is an educational tool that is designed to help students at each age level from 6 to 18 years old to discover, appreciate and assimilate universal values, incorporating them into positive attitudes and behaviour, so that they may lead healthy, happy and stable lives, both in the family and within their communities. It employs up to date pedagogical methods, in particular the use of a continuous story to create discussion and dialogue to bring about personal growth.
14. *Canavox* (www.canavox.com) is a movement that hosts reading groups to study and discuss the beauty of marriage as a lifelong commitment between a man and a woman.
15. Jason Evert is an author and chastity speaker. With his wife Crystalina, he founded *Chastity Project* (www.chastity.com), an organization that promotes the virtue of chastity through seminars, resources, clubs, and social media.
16. Christopher West is a renowned educator, best-selling author, cultural commentator, and popular theologian who specializes in making the dense scholarship of the late Pope John Paul II's Theology of the Body accessible to a wide audience.
17. Sirach 6:14-16 (New American Bible Revised Edition)
18. 1 Jn. 3:11-23 (New American Bible Revised Edition)
19. Saint Augustine, *Confessions*, trans. Henry Chadwick (Oxford: Oxford University Press, 2009), bk. I ch. 1.
20. 1 Jn. 4:8 (New American Bible Revised Edition)
21. Clive S. Lewis, *The Four Loves* (San Francisco: HarperOne, 2017), chap. 4.
22. Benedict XVI, *Deus Caritas Est*, 2005, para. 5.

23. Sallust, *Catiline's Conspiracy, The Jugurthine War, Histories*, trans. William W. Batstone, Illustrated edition (Oxford; New York: Oxford University Press, 2010), para. 20.
24. Fernando Ocáriz, "Letter," January 11, 2019, para. 8.
25. Saint Augustine, *Homilies on the First Epistle of John*, ed. Martin Thomas, trans. Boniface Ramsey (Hyde Park, NY: New City Press, 2008), VII, 8.

10 THE VIRTUES FOR INTEGRATION RELATED TO SOCIETY

Earlier we saw that starting from the drive of curiosity and the natural desire to be valued for our role in society, we can come to embrace the value of society. This ideal must then inform and guide the actions of an individual through the practice of virtue. Certain virtues can be identified that are directly related to the value of society. These are: Justice, Generosity and Prudence. Two of these are cardinal virtues. As a test, I leave it to the reader to identify them. In this section, these virtues will be discussed, highlighting the aspect of their connection with life in society.

10.1 The social dimension of the human person

Before elaborating on the virtues for society, it is worth stepping back a bit to review the anthropological underpinnings of human society. In the first place, we can consider that man is a social being by nature. "No man is an island", says a popular adage. To begin with, everyone needs his or her parents to come into the world. And then comes the patient effort that others must make to care for our nourishment and education. Turning to everyday life, the simplest things require the intervention of many people at different stages to be a reality. Even to type out these words on a computer, many people had to contribute to producing the gadget being used at this moment, the furniture employed and the electricity that is consumed. On a deeper level, without socialization, a person literally cannot survive. Human beings need interaction in order to know themselves and to find meaning in their lives. Relationships have been shown to be the main factor in happiness and even longevity, as was mentioned earlier.

The principal end of the social whole is to bring about what the just man wants to accomplish for those he loves but cannot because of his limits. The ideal he seeks is the well-being of every member of society. This is what is referred to as *the common good*. As all members pursue it together, the goals and aspirations that make up the common good have the effect of uniting the citizens of a nation together in bonds of affection and friendship. The coordinated effort of everyone to establish the common good enriches the lives of all within that community to a far greater degree than would otherwise be possible for individuals working independently.

As a consequence of man's social nature, there needs to be individuals or groups of persons who have the task to coordinate the processes of production, interchange of goods and ideas, movement of persons etc. on the different levels that they occur. In order to carry out their responsibilities, these persons or bodies must be invested with the authority to formulate guidelines, procedures and rules that ought to be followed. In this way there is order and peace.

The need for authority applies to any community and is a demand of the common good. It is not due to any original state of conflict as Hobbes would have us believe, appealing to the famous Latin proverb: *Homo Homini Lupus*, man is a wolf to another man. Neither is it a necessary evil, restricting spontaneous expressions of freedom for the

The virtues for integration related to society

sake of order, as Jean Jacques Rousseau suggested. The most basic society, which is the family, naturally has an authority, which are the parents. Associations such as schools, businesses and clubs have directors and boards to organize their activities. On the societal level, a governing body ought to be established to coordinate the different associations and communities on lower levels. This body has three fundamental aspects:

1. The legislative, which is the body that formulates laws and policies.
2. The executive, which is charged with the execution and implementation of these directives.
3. The judicial, where appointed judges arbitrate disputes regarding the application of the law.

In every country, there is an established procedure by which individuals are elected to carry out these functions. When the procedure has been correctly followed, then those elected are legitimate and those under their authority have a duty to abide by their directives and decisions, once they do not contravene the natural moral law.

By its very nature, an authority is established to seek the common good. The first common good that unites persons together is our shared nature and dignity. To form a human society, one must first be human. The first task of any authority is to reaffirm the equal and intrinsic dignity of every human being and the fundamental values by which the true good of the human person can be achieved. Without this, a group cannot claim to be an authentic society. The members, likewise, ought to adhere to these values and live by them.

Given this disposition, it helps to distinguish between external common goods and a common good that is immanent or internal.

Concerning the external forum, the common good are those material and cultural benefits or privileges that are reasonably sought after by many, within which the individual exercises a role with the performance of certain duties.[1]

Among them are included all economic products, transport, recreational and cultural activities, social institutions such as hospitals, educational and research establishments, the army, the police, and so forth.

The internal common good consists of the moral, cultural and material benefits to be achieved through the reciprocal help of men, where the individual understands his or her contribution as integrated into, or part of a whole and, as such, sought for the sake of a common goal.[2] For example, if a goalkeeper is happy about his performance in a game, his joy is only individual so far. His social action or internal common good is activated on considering himself as an integral part of a team and valuing the game as a whole. He thus seeks the success and joy of the entire team.

In virtue of the internal common good, the rules and guidelines established by authority are not received as an imposition or constraint. Citizens who are properly educated to internalize the common good, will adhere to these guidelines and put them into practice as a way to pursue their own happiness as an integral part of a society. As an analogy, suppose someone is in the business of processing cocoa. There are many stages involved from planting and pruning, picking, and gathering, fermenting and drying to the final stage where the beans are roasted and processed to make bars of premium chocolate. This end product is the external common good. If one person has to do everything, the process will be very slow and the output small. When different groups focus on different stages, then there can be more cocoa readily available for more people. A worker on the field may be proud because he is skilled at what he does, but the greater satisfaction lies in internalizing the bigger picture. He is contributing to improve the standard of living for many people, including his own, by providing quality cocoa in a large quantity. The managers of the enterprise need to ensure that the rights and dignity of workers are respected, so that they receive a fair compensation for their labour, which they need to provide for their families. As production becomes more efficient, the compensation to all employees can be greater. Managers and workers alike have in mind the same goal, which they seek in the context of having the right relationships with each other. Taken to the level of the state, there is a similar dynamic where the external and internal common good work together to bring about the greater well-being and happiness of all.

It was stated that authority is a function of the social nature of the human person. As a consequence of this principle, it is a false notion that authority goes from God directly to the ruler and, after the fashion of "divine right", he or she or a small group dictates and enforces laws. Authority goes from God to the social nature of the human person that he created, and as a function of this nature, an entity ought to be established to coordinate the common activity of all. When an individual obeys a legitimate authority, he or she is obeying God indirectly by exercising a demand of his or her nature as a social being.

If we emphasize the importance of the internal common good for social cohesion and the proper functioning of authority, then it is of great advantage that the individuals in a society be educated about the different systems of coordination that exist in society, and the varying roles that persons, including themselves, can have for its proper and efficient operation. Individuals should be aware of the rights and privileges accorded to them, and of their duties as well in view of the common good.

It is outside the scope of this book to discuss the different ways that authority can be established, exercised, and changed. Whatever the form that this may take, supposing that it is in keeping with human dignity, an activity that corresponds to a legitimate authority is to design and enact laws. These decrees have the true nature of law to the extent that they are in accord with and foster the common good. A classical definition of a law, which is useful for everyone to know, is as follows: a law is an ordinance of reason, promulgated by a legitimate authority, with a view to the common good, and enacted coercively.[3] This follows from the discussion we have had up to now. A law must be reasonable as it is meant to establish order. The authority that promulgates it ought to be legitimately in power, and it must seek a goal or aim that is good for all, which is the common good. Finally, some sort of penalty or punishment ought to be attached to a law, beyond the guilt that subjects should feel from transgressing a rule. In this way, citizens will take the laws seriously and not as mere wishful words.

10.2 Justice

The discussion above provides the context for delving into the virtue of justice. When justice is represented artistically, it is linked to a figure with a scale. The personification of justice balancing the scales dates back to the Egyptian Goddess of Justice, Maat, who stood for harmony, truth and fairness. In the *Duat*, the Egyptian underworld, the hearts of the dead were said to be weighed against her single "Feather of Maat", symbolically representing the concept of Maat. If the heart was found to be lighter or equal in weight to the feather of Maat, the deceased had led a virtuous life and would go on to paradise. A heart that was unworthy was devoured by the goddess *Ammit* and its owner condemned to remain in the Duat.

The imagery from Egyptian mythology is very rich and gives a broad notion of justice. The just man is the one who lived in harmony with the gods, nature and others with an upright intention. His heart was always in the right place.

This personalized perspective on justice is important because the concept of integration includes the integration of every decision into a life project. When a person reaches late adolescence, he or she begins to think about their definitive career, having a family, committing more seriously to his or her faith and so on. A young person at this age is a seeker for the meaning of life and, concretely, his or her place in the universe. From a personal or subjective perspective, justice means being true to self and to one's purpose in life. In the Hebraic tradition, the just man is a holy man, one who seeks the will of God and puts it into practice. Following this path is perceived as a calling or vocation

Introduction to Anthropology of Integration

from the one who created and sustains my soul. Hence justice is first to God, and to doing his will. Part of this, of course means being a good citizen because society is part of God's plan for man. Personal calling and civic duties should never be opposed one against the other. In fact, they both acquire their true meaning when they harmoniously affirm each other.

Considered in relation to the ordering of society, the virtue of justice is articulated along the lines of three basic relationships:

    1. Between individuals—commutative justice
    2. Individuals and society—general or legal justice
    3. Society and the individual—distributive justice

THE RELATIONSHIPS OF JUSTICE

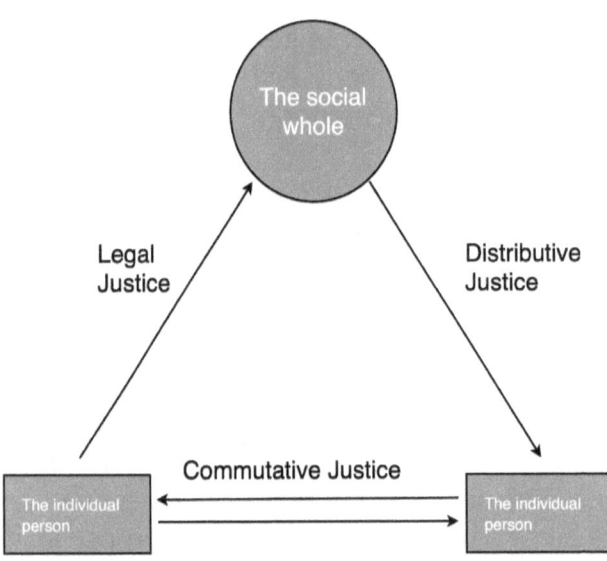

Figure 10.1 The three relationships in society and the corresponding types of justice.

10.2.1 Commutative justice

Commutative justice flows from the radical equality of each human being. As a virtue it means having the habitual disposition to see in others "another me" and to treat them according to the golden rule: "Do unto others as you would have them do unto you". The classical definition of justice in general is *the constant and perpetual will to give each person his or her due.*[4] In the relationship between individuals, the first thing that is due is respect for the dignity of every person. The just man wills that the natural rights of every person on the planet be universally acknowledged and guaranteed. Everyone, for example, has a natural right to life, to form a family and to be fairly treated before the law.

The notion of equality can be used to further understand justice between individuals or commutative justice. When a just person receives something from others not due to him, an inequality exists, and he or she should make an effort to return it. An important application of justice concerns the telling of truth in relationships where the parties entailed have a reasonable claim to that knowledge. A just individual recognizes that lying establishes an unfair relation of inequality between equals. As a result, he or she has a moral duty to communicate truthfully. If I lie, for example, about my qualifications and experience in order to get a job, I put myself in a relation of inequality with others who tell the truth. I do not have a special claim on that job in terms of qualifications and experience beyond those that I actually possess. An inequality with the employer arises as well, because I suppose that I have a special privilege to be hired for what I may not be qualified to do. If I were to put myself in the place of the employer, I would not accept that such a privilege exists. Honesty, then, is an important aspect of the virtue of justice. A person who lacks this transparency ends up separated from others and very unhappy. There is an adage that says, "It takes a forest to hide a leaf". In other words, one lie leads to another in order to hide it and those two to many more, leading eventually to a forest of lies just to hide the first small one. Persons in this state are cut off from meaningful relationships with others, as they must keep their distance to prevent being "found out". Without true friendships and closed off from being helped, they feel isolated, alone, and depressed. Interiorly, a person living a lie will also feel torn, divided by the truth in his or her mind and what is portrayed externally. This is a sad state of affairs that can only be broken by speaking the truth clearly, and then working to reestablish both the inner and external order that was broken.

10.2.2 Legal justice

When we turn to the relationship between the individual and society as a whole, the virtue of justice applies in a different way and is termed legal justice. It is distinguished from commutative justice, because, in this relation, the common good is the principal point of reference. The organized effort of many reaches further than the sum of single individuals who must carry out different processes. Legal justice concerns the role of the individual in bringing about the result of the coordinated activity through work and the systems for ordering society. It coincides with the internal common good that is a demand of man's social nature. Put simply, legal justice *is the habitual and persistent* will of the individual to have the common good realized in the fulfillment of his or her role or function in society.[5]

10.2.3 Social justice

In the social whole, there is a relationship in the other direction of legal justice. That is, from those in authority to the individual. Those who govern have the mandate and power to establish and enforce laws and policies to safeguard and foster the common good. Their responsibility is to seek a just order where the conditions are provided which allow people, either as groups or as individuals, to reach their fulfillment more completely and easily.[6] The habit of acting in this way is called *Distributive Justice* or *Social Justice*. It is worth reiterating that the first common good is the dignity of each and every person. This principle is at the core of any just social order. If the dignity of a person or a group is not respected, then that society is not a truly human one. There would be a dehumanizing element that undermines the whole community. Connected to recognition of the radical equality of every individual, is the protection of all fundamental human rights. The most important laws of a country are those that acknowledge and protect these natural rights. A significant step on the journey towards the full recognition of the demands of human dignity, was the Universal Declaration of Human Rights adopted by the United Nations in 1948. These rights were recognized as "universal, inviolable and inalienable."[7] *Universal* because they are present in all human beings, without exception of time, place or subject. *Inviolable* insofar as "they are inherent in the human person and in human dignity" and because "it would be vain to proclaim rights, if at the same time everything was not done to ensure the duty of respecting them by all people, everywhere, and for all people". These rights are *inalienable* insofar as "no one can legitimately deprive another person ... of these rights, since this would be to do violence to their nature."[8] This understanding of the source, nature and scope of natural human rights provides us with a powerful criterion with which to critique the actions of individuals and society. It also provides a vision or worldview that should inspire people of good will, to promote and defend natural human rights across the globe.

Some basic natural human rights are: the right to life, the right to private property, the right to security and a basic education, the right to basic health care, work and legitimate leisure, the right to marry and establish a family, the right to migrate, the right to religious freedom and to educate one's children in that religious tradition, the right to free speech, to a fair trial, to the truth and to seek the truth....

An important principle that ought to guide leaders is the principle of the universal destination of created goods. It is the reasonable conviction that the earth and all it contains was originally destined for all humankind and all peoples. A just order demands that we should all work toward assuring that the goods of the earth should be fairly distributed and that all should work to ensure a reasonable standard of living for everyone.

An important question that can be raised is how the principle of the universal destination of the world's goods can be reconciled with the right to private property. Human beings need stability to progress. In a factory, for example, raw materials are processed in stages and many things have to come together in an organized way to obtain the final product. It is paramount that the systems in place do not change from one day to the next. Once private initiative in industry is allowed, which it always should be, private property needs to be guaranteed. The logic applies to families as well. Parents need to count on a home where their children can be safe and provided for and where they can help their offspring to develop their talents and to mature. While this is very clear, it ought to be emphasised, nevertheless, that private property has a social function. Individual persons should not use their resources without considering the effects that this use will have on the wider community. They should act in a way that benefits not only themselves and their family, but also the common good. The right to private property is subordinate to the principle of the universal destination of goods. As a lesser right, it stands to reason that it should give way before the proper expression of the more fundamental principle, in the service of the common good.

In every society, there is an organ of government that is entrusted with the task of elaborating on the rights that ought to be guaranteed for every citizen and at the same time outlining concrete ways that this framework is to be applied. Laws and procedures aim to achieve a just and humane society that bolsters the freedom of each individual and enables him or her to have a richer experience of life. It happens, however, that the persons who govern can abuse their power, usurping the rights and privileges due to citizens for their personal gain. Sadly, in the twenty-first century, there has been a progressive decline in the liberty enjoyed by citizens in many countries compared to places where liberties have been gained.[9] Regimes that impose themselves by force, seeking to make the populace subservient and dependent on them, are not friends of freedom and treat it like a threat.

Freedom is a basic human good that ought to be protected and fostered. It does not mean the ability to follow one's whims but, rather to know and to adhere to what is true and worthwhile. It can be used to do good or to do evil. Leaders, however, must take this risk. By cultivating virtue in the citizens of their country, those in authority can have a reasonable assurance that good will prevail in the coming together of the innumerable decisions that each person makes on a daily basis. Every person, family and group has something original to offer to the community, and this can only be materialized in an atmosphere of freedom. When freedom is stifled, authentic progress and development are undermined. In this context, an important principle of social justice is the principle of subsidiarity. This principle states that the State should not take to itself functions and roles that the individual person and organisations can do for themselves. It recognises that families, groups and associations - sports, cultural, political, social—make a necessary and invaluable contribution to the life of society. In this they should be encouraged and supported.[10] Families should be encouraged, for example, to take initiative in education and sport. Leaders in government should not feel threatened by the formation of groups that seek social reform or to create awareness of injustices that may exist. At the same time, these groups on a lower level should be coordinated by the legitimate authority in a way that fosters the common good. Governing bodies, for example, can set standards for education and guidelines for public manifestations.

A glance at the world in recent times and over the last century in particular, can make one wonder if justice is a fairy tale or wishful thinking. Consider, for example, the large number of countries that are still ruled by dictatorships and where there is no freedom of expression to propose alternatives. Freedom House reports that 2019 was the 14th consecutive year of decline in global freedom. Added to this are the alarming statistics of abject poverty and material inequality on a world scale and within some nations as well.[11] Large numbers of people are displaced because of wars and strife, and they are often mistreated or taken advantage of. Human trafficking takes place on a large scale and drug cartels in many places are very powerful and influential. There is also the rising discontent surrounding racial discrimination worldwide that has led to riots and deepened political strife. Corruption continues to be widespread in numerous countries and the list of woes goes on. There is a growing hunger for justice, but it seems more and more elusive. Men and women with big hearts and a great spirit of sacrifice are needed to bring about a new world view where individuals and groups do not see themselves in competition with each other, but rather called to work together to bring about a better world for all.

Justice is a broad topic, and what is written here hardly does it justice. The objective was to introduce the different elements of this virtue, so as to give the reader a gist of the role of justice in the proper integration of the natural inclinations on the biological and emotional levels that are related to the value of society.

10.3 Social love

The deepest calling in the heart of every person is to true self-giving love. In the light of this, it is clear that human relations cannot be governed solely by the measure of justice. Justice must be complemented to a considerable extent by love. If someone is grateful, he or she recognizes that a great deal of what one benefits from in society, came about through the establishment of social conditions by persons who made great sacrifices for love of their country and of their fellow men. Social love is not a virtue just for the leaders or for persons in positions of influence. It is a virtue that all the members of a society should seek to cultivate in order to have a more complete and fulfilling life, and to contribute to the happiness of all. It is interesting to recall at this point, that charity is shown in deeds and not in nice words only. It is easy to give a long discourse about the ills that are present in modern society or a given society or community. One can propose many initiatives that can remedy the issues affecting that group. If one does not lift a finger, however, to remedy the situation, this can hardly be called charity. Persons who are long on talk and short on deeds are not really seeking the good of others, but rather to look good in the eyes of others as having good ideas. A woman who is inspired by true social love, will study, discuss, and share opinions with others about how society can be improved, but with a view to do more, to take initiative, to reach out and to reach further in her sphere of influence for the benefit of others.

In every country, there are a myriad of charitable initiatives that play an indispensable role in helping the less fortunate. The importance of social love challenges us to ask ourselves sincerely, what have I done? What am I doing? Do I go beyond the call of duty to make the world a better place for all, for love?

In her book *Mujeres Brújulas*, Isabel Sanchez tells the stories of women who have gone beyond the call of duty to make a difference in broken societies in the world today, and especially in the lives of the poor and marginalized in many places. The main theme connecting these stories is a clear affirmation of the dignity of every human being, and a call to women to help transform social structures with love—especially with the peculiar style of caring and nurturing love that characterizes feminine affection.

She tells the impactful story, for example, of the first case of a premature baby that arrived at the Monkole Hospital in Congo. The founders of this initiative have mobilized donors and health care professionals from around the world to provide quality health care services to persons of all social classes in and around Kinshasa. The baby was not in good shape and needed urgent attention. The clinic was outfitted with the equipment and personnel needed to provide incubation and the care that the child needed at the moment. They were lacking oxygen but could hold out until the following day when new tanks would be delivered. The following morning the hospital staff received the terrifying news that, due to setbacks at the plant, oxygen could not be delivered that day, but on the following day. The baby could not be kept alive without oxygen. What could they do? As the oxygen supply began to fail, the nurses devised a system where, by blowing into balloons, they could provide a supply of air to the tubes connected to the nostrils of the infant. But how long could they keep this up? There won't be oxygen for 24 hours. The nursing staff felt defeated. Reaching deep into their caring drive, unlocking heroic love, they resolved to keep the child alive. With the parents and relatives of the baby, they took turns for over twenty-four hours to blow air into the nostrils of the child with the breath from their own lungs. These women went way beyond the call of duty to save the life of a poor baby in Kinshasa.[12]

There are many moving stories about persons going the extra mile to serve for love. A case in the Caribbean was featured some time ago of a couple who took in numerous abandoned children into their home over the course of their lives and raised them like their own offspring. Many of these children have gone on to have solid careers and good families of their own.[13]

The examples given above of ordinary people making a big impact on the lives of others are ones we can all relate to. It is fair to say, at the same time, that those who have a greater possibility to do more, should also do more. Large profitable businesses can do a great deal to make quality education and health care more widely available, for example, by being more generous in their contributions, financial or otherwise, towards institutions who struggle to provide these services.

Turning to a more specific application, an important role of social love is to mitigate punishment due to crimes and to seek the reform of the wrong doer over his or her chastisement. There is always the danger that the will to punish can be contaminated by a desire for revenge. The meaning of punishment is to correct an unfair inequality and restore order. When there is love, the true meaning of punishment is preserved. The injustice committed and restoration needed is clearly identified. A failure to state the truth of an injustice is a lack of social love. This virtue will also be lacking if revenge and resentment are allowed to prevail, giving rise to an excessive punishment. Love is a difficult virtue to live because it also challenges us to forgive and to help those who have done wrong to definitively change their lives and, given this reform, to return to participate in society. Penalties may even be diminished when the person who perpetrated the crime shows regret, a desire to amend his or her life and shows consistent behaviour change.

A person who gives of himself or herself in social action for love finds great fulfillment in doing so. That person will feel the affection and appreciation of many people and will experience the joy of having many close friends. Working in a social project with other people creates deep bonds of friendship that endure the test of time. Social love brings personal growth as well as making society more humane. This is needed in every age, but in our times, it is clearly urgent.

Notes

1. *Catechism of the Catholic Church*, no. 1924.
2. Arthur Fridolin Utz, *Etica social*, vol. I (Barcelona: Herder, 1964), 200.
3. St Thomas Aquinas, *Summa Theologiae*, I-II, q. 90, a. 4.
4. *Ibid.*, II-II, q. 58, a.1.
5. *Ibid.*, II-II, q. 58, a.5.
6. *Catechism of the Catholic Church*, no. 1906.
7. Pontifical Council for Justice and Peace, *Compendium of the Social Doctrine of the Church*, para. 153.
8. *Ibid.*.
9. www.freedomhouse.org.

10. *Compendium of the Social Doctrine of the Church*, para. 185.
11. "World Poverty Clock," World Data Lab, accessed November 15, 2023, https://worldpoverty.io/headline.
12. Isabel Sánchez, *Mujeres brújula en un bosque de retos* (Barcelona: Espasa, 2020), 171.
13. Kavarly Arnold, "Queen of Foster Care - Supermom Mama Sweetie Opens Big Heart to More than 40 Children," The Gleaner, May 10, 2020, http://jamaica-gleaner.com/article/lead-stories/20200510/queen-foster-care-supermom-mama-sweetie-opens-big-heart-more-40.

11 CHARACTER FORMATION AS INTEGRAL DEVELOPMENT

"Look at the choices you are making now in your work, your family life, your relationships, and your faith. Now envision yourself ten, twenty, thirty years from now, looking back at what you have done with your life. Which choices do you think you will be happy with, and which ones do you think that you may regret?" The above exercise is an interesting one that a mother spoke about in a parenting forum. It helped her to get her children to see the importance of acquiring good habits and not just giving into their whims. Parents and educators have the hard job of cultivating proper habits in their children, so that they will be protected from harm and be truly happy, not just now, but in their future lives, their marriages, their careers, and their souls. This task is what is referred to as character formation.

Traditionally, character formation is identified with the acquisition of a series of virtues. For Aristotle, these would be virtues such as justice, courage, temperance, magnificence, magnanimity, liberality, gentleness, prudence, and wisdom, as already stated in an earlier section. These attributes characterize the good man or women who is truly happy and, at the same time, most beneficial to society. Following St Thomas Aquinas, many educators use the cardinal virtues of prudence, justice, fortitude, and temperance to elaborate on the habits that are needed for good character. In the Thomistic tradition, character formation also includes and is connected to an understanding of the moral law.

In the United States, up to the turn of the century, character education built upon the rich heritage of classical anthropology. It was widely accepted that the human person was body and soul and that there was a common set of beliefs and values about which consensus can be reached, and that these could be taught. Character formation, understood in this way, was part of the educational mission of schools and other institutions that trained or formed young people in skills for work and life. The work of social scientist Thomas Likona and other persons from a wide range of specialities and positions of influences, gave prominence to character education in the nineties as a common task of all stakeholders in education.[1]

Coming out of the intellectual and cultural trends from the sixties and seventies, however, the notions of character and virtue began to have a negative connotation, which came to the fore in the millennial generation. Character and virtue are perceived in many sectors as the imposition of moral norms from a past generation that is disconnected from the sensibilities and aspiration of the present generation. The cause of this change is complex and multifaceted, beyond the scope of this book. Perhaps there have been deficiencies in how values and virtues have been transmitted in some places. Researcher Eleanor Smith found that at the end of the eighties decade, character educators focused more on how students acted on a daily basis as opposed to their ability to reason through a moral problem. The strategies used centred around direct instruction in positive social values, coherent school policies, a recognition system for students and schools that demonstrate good citizenship, and a consistent and firmly enforced system of discipline. Stakeholders in education began to use new strategies in order to adapt to the cultural changes that were taking place.[2]

While it ought to be admitted that new strategies are needed, it is also important to retain the anthropological richness of the notions of virtue and character as they have been traditionally understood. The impression that virtue can be imposed, for example, is contrary to its very nature as fruit of free choice. Anthropology of integration seeks to retain the original richness of these terms, while offering a new perspective. In this new framework, character formation takes place in the context of the upward and downward integration of the three dimensions of the human person. The virtues are not presented as a list of good habits from the outset. Through stories and life experiences, children need to be guided to discover the fundamental values for themselves, expressing them and formulating them in their own ways. This is the upward dimension. It is what we have termed cognitive integration in this book. As the children assimilate the values that constitute human dignity, they can be led to see for themselves how certain good habits are needed to live by these principles. Their parents and educators facilitate the process, teaching them more precise ways to express what they naturally grasp. It is here that they are introduced to the virtues. This is the downward side or formative integration. In this new approach *character building is a process of ongoing formation aimed at leading a progressively more integrated life*. It includes the acquisition of virtue, but in a framework that keeps in view and actively engages the core anthropological principle of the dignity of the human person as a unity of body and soul. The dynamic interplay of upward and downward integration bolsters human dignity and brings personal growth, along with deeper and richer relationships. Framed in this way, character education aims to bring about the integral development of the human person.

When the perception or teaching of character formation is reduced to the practice of a list of good habits, the important side of cognitive integration is lost. In this scenario, children and young people see character as a list of habits that they need to acquire when they are not sure that they connect with them or are interested in them. They can come to see character formation as something that is imposed and forced on them against their free will. This gives rise to a distorted concept of virtue. Cognitive integrations grounds the discourse on virtue in the natural uptake of fundamental values that are constitutive of human dignity. When the upward aspect of character formation is ignored or neglected, the unifying connection of virtue to human dignity can be lost.

An integrative approach to character formation demands a great deal of attention to the proper assimilation of the fundamental values and their connection to the virtues. Programmes such as *Alive to the World* do this very well. Students are initially introduced to a story. A discussion ensues where the class participants are guided to discover the moral principles that are at stake, expressing them in their own words. It is then a natural step for them to grasp the habits that are needed to live by these principles.

In this way, character formation takes place but it does not seem forced or imposed in any fashion.

An integrated approach to character formation has the added advantage of providing a framework for the proper application of virtue. In this framework virtue is always understood in the context of human dignity, concretely the fundamental values. This is important, because without this proper context, it is not hard for a virtue to be confused with its excess or defect. In other words, it is the reference to human dignity that helps the practice of virtue to have its authentic expression as a middle ground between excesses, in accord with the reality at hand. A violent act in a protest, for example, can be seen as courageous. The person, however, may be acting recklessly, putting others at risk unfairly. Such an act may be motivated by anger that is not properly oriented by the values of life, friendship and of society. A more integrated approach, for example, would be that proposed by Martin Luther King. He intellectually articulated and put into practice the way of non-violent resistance. King eventually decided not to use armed bodyguards despite threats on his life, and reacted to violent experiences, such as the bombing of his home, with compassion. In part VI of his first book, *Strides towards freedom*, he articulated six principles of non-violence where fundamental values such as life, friendship, and love, supported by faith, orient protest action.[3] He saw non-violence as being more courageous because it overcomes the internal violence of the spirit. "The nonviolent resister not only refuses to shoot his opponent, but he also refuses to hate him".[4]

When character formation is misunderstood as a list of correct and incorrect behaviours to practise, it follows that it could lead persons to be scrupulous. Take the case of the virtue of temperance. If this is internalized as a list of actions to do and not to do, a young girl, for example, can come to regard temperance in a strict way as not snacking between meals. When her work is particularly draining and her regular meals are wanting in some way for whatever reason, a nourishing snack can help her to perform her duties better. Out of her rigid outlook she may regard this as a lack of temperance when clearly it is not. Her body simply needs a little extra to perform her duties to others. This is scrupulosity. It is contrary to the true meaning of virtue which seeks an appropriate middle ground and is directed to the overall good of the person. An integrative approach avoids this pitfall. She would bear in mind that work is an important value and will have the self-confidence to eat a snack when the demands of work require it.

Misinterpreted as a checklist, the practice of virtue can appear to lead to scruples as discussed above, but it can also appear to make persons proud and judgemental. "I don't see you doing X so you are not virtuous." "I am doing X and you are not, so I am more virtuous than you." It is not hard to see how this kind of thinking can be associated with virtue when it is misapprehended as a long checklist of concrete actions.

While the usefulness of having some practical guidelines ought to be recognized, an integrative approach to character building does not place the emphasis here. Before going to concrete action, I need to understand and adhere to the fundamental values at the heart of human dignity. Actions must be motivated by the golden rule, which is to say that they must be done for love.

Together with this, the virtues that are more directly connected to human dignity are the ones that are more important. These are habits such as diligence, industriousness, charity, loyalty, justice, and social love, which were discussed in a previous section. One finds that programmes for character development sometimes present a list of virtues to be lived without saying clearly which are the more important ones. At times the cardinal virtues are given the highest places. It was explained earlier that the cardinal virtues were conceived in antiquity as habits linked to the appetites. The dignity of the human person is implicit but not immediate in this list. As a result, they are useful for classifying virtues, but not for being the most important ones. To respond to the challenges and positive sensibilities of our times, a shift is needed in character formation to stress the virtues where the link to human dignity is more immediate.

Integration is a task. I am on a journey to live a more integrated life. I know my true potential and I try to put into practice the virtues, especially the more important ones. Right now, I know that some virtues are more important for me to work on than others as a demand of charity towards others in the specific circumstances of my life. For others who are in a different context to mine, other virtues need to be focused on. In the context of a life project of integration, virtue can never be the pretext for being judgemental or a motive for pride. The point of arrival is not conceived as possessing or lacking a list of virtues but having an integrated life in the specific context of one's life, limitations, obligations, opportunities, and talents.

Together with this clear point of arrival, that is always work in progress, it helps to recall that the three dimensions of the human person is an underlying factor that ought to guide character formation. The acquisition of good habits goes through the stages of knowing, feeling, and doing. This model is very important. The bodily and emotional dimensions each have a dynamism of their own that need to be understood and integrated. There may be obstacles on these levels that resist proper integration. I would be wrong to hold someone up to the standard of a list of what I may consider virtuous deeds without knowing if such obstacles are present. I would need to understand the extent to which they render integration difficult and how they are being addressed. There may even be medical illnesses. Many challenges are not of this sort and can be addressed through the effective collaboration between the family, the school and one-on-one mentoring.

11.1 The Pedagogy of the integration of the human person (PIHP)

The Pedagogy of the Integration of the Human Person (PIHP. In Spanish PIPH) was developed during the practical development of *Alive to the World*. Carlos Beltramo of the University of Navarra described this process in his doctoral thesis and it has been adopted as a guiding pedagogical method in *Alive to the World* for character formation in students. PIHP is based on the anthropological truth developed in this book that the human person cannot be happy and at peace if the three levels of the person are not fully aligned. In order to be consistent with our purpose and dignity, actions (corporal level), must be aligned with what we know (spiritual level) and what we desire (emotional level).

The approach used in this methodology establishes a process of teaching and learning whereby the students at each age are offered a carefully crafted narrative containing age-appropriate adventures, situations and relationships where they can discover for themselves the just and positive attitudes and options appropriate to these.

Beltramo summarizes the pedagogical proposal of PIHP as follows:

1. Lead the student to understand in what way he or she is an integrated person, and thus living out what the human person is: an integrated being, a unit with parts that acts according to different dynamisms.
2. Show that there is path to follow that has a purpose: to become an integrated person. Achieving greater unity is a task that involves harmonizing the internal parts that constitute it.
3. Give clues about how to concretely follow the path to integration, pointing out the way that allows the person to:
• become aware that he or she is made up of parts
• to develop a desire for unity (intrinsic motivation)
• to recognize the disordered pull to internal disintegration ("non-integration"), and to know what concrete strategies make it possible to obtain unity through human action.[5]

The strategy of PIHP is to use scenarios related to the common experience of students at each stage of development in the sessions and allow them to recognise positive options of behaviour that lead to an integrated way of being. In framing the pattern of behaviour that is in focus, it is important to give attention to the three levels of action—corporeal, emotional and spiritual. An example could be whether or not to follow the 'popular' group in an outing where it appears that a little shoplifting is the sport of the day. Alicia's impulse is to agree to taking something, to prove she is not a sissy and willing to fit in with the leader of this 'group'. Her intelligence meanwhile is telling her it is wrong to shoplift. The realistic narrative of Alive to the World leads the reader to understand, not only the emotions and thinking of a person in this position, but the outcome of this situation confirms that the intelligence should be the leading level, and not the feelings of wanting to belong.

An important strength of Alive to the World is that values and virtuous behaviour are not "taught" as such. The narrative trusts the synderesis of each student to discover for themselves the implications of the golden rule in a situation as they observe the unfolding of each part of the story. They naturally grasp what is the logically correct option. This invariably turns out to be effective because children are totally open to learning how life works, and adolescents are in the stage where they question many things and do not like to be told, but to discover.

11.2 Alive to the World. A model PIHP programme

PIHP has been applied as a comprehensive programme for character building called *Alive to the World*. There have been many references to this programme in this book. In a nutshell, it is an educational tool that is designed to help students at each age level to discover, appreciate and assimilate universal values, incorporating them into positive attitudes and behaviour, so that they may lead healthy, happy and stable lives, both in the family and within their communities. *Alive to the World* also provides for the older students the principles for interacting fairly and positively with others and for taking decisions. In this way they are equipped to make good choices as they build a unitary life project.

The founder of *Alive to the World*. Christine de Marcellus Volmer, saw the need for a programme of this sort in the face of the social challenges that many countries in the world were facing, and still now face in the aftermath of the social and political revolutions of the sixties and seventies. Around the globe, societies struggle with broken families, absentee fathers, spiralling crime and gang violence, and teenage pregnancy. She saw that the transmission of values that had kept humanity relatively stable over the millennia had been broken by the new trends of the twentieth century, including the two World Wars and the appearance of Marxism. Important commercial and ideological interests exploited this void with reductionist Sex Education programmes which exacerbated the sexualization of youth, leading to epidemics of STI's and STDs. Since this time, other programmes under the banner of Personal, Social, Health and Economic education or PSHE have arisen, but none have been able to detain the tragedies of teenage pregnancy, drug addiction and other symptoms of youthful insecurity. Often the strategies that were being adopted consisted of quick fix courses with a negative tone which can sometimes exacerbate the problems they seek to solve from the curiosity they generate in the disordered behaviour that is being addressed. In addition, these strategies are often framed in terms of perpetrators and victims, which does not favour social cohesion.

While avoiding ills is important, Ms. Vollmer sought to elaborate a programme aimed at developing strong rounded characters in children and adolescents built up on virtue and confidence in their unique contribution. A Fundamental thread throughout *Alive to the World* is The Golden Rule: "Do unto others as you would have them do to you!" It is a practical expression of recognition and respect for the dignity of every human being which is at the core of integral human development. Applying the golden rule, students are helped to harmonize their thinking, feeling and behaviour enabling:

- Empathy and objective analysis
- Understanding options and their consequences
- Forming a life plan in accord with human dignity

Alive to the world adopts a holistic or integral approach to character formation, always having in mind the dignity of the human person. It progressively and systematically cultivates:

- Love of life
- Healthy relationships with family and friends
- Willing involvement in community
- Positive Leadership and development of teamwork
- Critical Thinking and Decision-making

The founder developed *Alive to the World* with the strong friendship of Viktor Frankl and with Carlos

Beltramo and found a great deal of support for this approach in renowned authors such as James Coleman, Robert Putman and Gary Becker. It is widely understood that the economic and social development of a nation hinges on what may be termed the "social capital" of a country. It is the sum of shared values and standards of behaviour that sustain economic life and peaceful democratic relations. They are intangible yet very real goods such as respect, humility, diligence, loyalty, justice/order, honesty, reciprocity, and generosity, which are the underlying fabric of progress.

The application of values to ordinary life requires use of proper reasoning. *Alive to the World* gives great importance to the cultivation of intellectual skills such as analytical thinking, language and communication skills, and logical thinking. The programme stresses discussion among the students that is simply moderated by an adult. In these exchanges, the facilitator can point out the logical errors and strengths in the statements put forward, and with leading questions can help them to develop analytical thinking. The programme also includes activities that are structured to develop these skills.

In the elaboration of the *Alive to the World* series, the founder chose an anthropology that is built around three distinct levels of action in the human person: the biological, the psychological or emotional level, and the spiritual level. At the same time, a key feature is to show that everything about the human person is connected with everything else, and the goal is unitary or integrated behaviour that advances the good of the whole person. In this book we have sought to elaborate on the philosophical side of this anthropology in a way that teachers, educators and parents would find helpful in their task of forming the next generation.

Connected with the anthropology adopted, *Alive to the World* uses the new pedagogical strategy described above, called the Pedagogy of the Integration of the Human Person (PIHP). Implemented in the classroom, the educational process goes through three fundamental moments:

> **1. Knowing:** A cognitive objective in which the narrative helps the student to understand the objective good in a given reality, situation or relationship. The students are asked to explain the initial elements of the story, discussing the emotions that are felt and the thoughts and actions that result. In a second stage they are invited to consider how the golden rule applies (do unto others as you would have them do unto you) in the story to lead to a moment of knowing more fully.
> **2. Accepting**: Leaning on the narrative, the teacher helps the students to connect personally with the concept known in order to motivate an understanding and acceptance of the values and virtues that are at stake.
> **3. Doing**: With the help of class discussion, the students consider actions in their own lives that are consistent with the concepts and values from the story. Knowledge and acceptance organize feelings and illuminate actions leading to a more integrated way of being.[6]

Alongside PIHP, the series created by Christine Vollmer and her team incorporates other proven and up to date pedagogical strategies. An important method that has greatly contributed to the success of the series, is the use of narrative in a carefully articulated way. It may be clear to adults what is good for young people but how does one impart it to them without sounding preachy? How does one encourage them to put into practice behaviour which demands discipline and is often counter-cultural? It dawned on Christine Vollmer and Carlos Beltramo that an effective way would be to just give the students vicarious situations and relationships which would gradually unfold over twelve school years. The stories capture common experiences of persons all over the world as they grow up so that anyone can relate to them. They tell the tale of some friends who grow up as all children do, with their normal points, good and bad. Little by little they open their eyes to the world about them, to what they can achieve if they try, and to the values of life, family and friendship, which bring true peace and happiness.

The use of a narrative in *Alive to the World* is not merely to illustrate values, but ought to be accompanied by a pedagogical approach that facilitates the natural uptake of values and virtues on the part of the students. The first module of the text for teacher training explains:

> It is important to emphasize that values cannot be imposed. The teacher has instead the continuous task of helping students to discover these values within themselves as well as in external and objective situations.
> When teaching values, it is important to lead students to see the importance of developing their own reasoning. This is in contrast to applications of certain sciences where formu-

lations are more functional and external, and students need to use more memory.[7]

To this end the proper use of the programme is based on the important concept of fostering an atmosphere of freedom in the classroom. This means making the students feel comfortable with openly expressing what they feel and asking questions, leading to logical conclusions, always respectfully. The teacher should conduct the class in such a way as to foster active participation from all the students, helping them to articulate values and their points of view using sound reasoning in an impassioned way. This demands the creation of an atmosphere of trust as the teacher training notes explain: "This will be possible if students feel they will not be judged on the "right" or "wrong" answer, but on their effort to analyze, to develop logical reasoning, and on their openness and respect for others. They also need to feel safe from peer ridicule. Peers often tend to censor those who they feel are not 'in tune', through disapproving gestures and hurtful comments. As teachers we must try to discourage this."[8]

In *Alive to the World*, the students are exposed to stories of "others", not their own. The teacher will be able to lead the students to think in an objective way, thus fostering the development of a detached and fair vision that will lead them to have a magnanimous attitude when dealing with others, seeing themselves 'in the shoes' of the other. They are helped to keep in mind and to think using the golden rule of treating others as you would want to be treated by them. In dialogue they are encouraged to achieve a literal analysis of the situation presented. This literal analysis (of facts, characters, and events) will be the basis for a later analytical evaluation where the students can identify their own emotions and ideas and bring them to bear on similar situations in their lives to those presented in the story.

The manner in which stories are used in *Alive to the World*, as well as encouraging the love of reading, facilitates the important process of what we have described as *cognitive integration* in this book. The training materials stress that imitative thinking should be avoided because the use of borrowed formulations on the part of an individual leads to a lack of understanding of the underlying principles that apply in a given situation. This gives rise to a false sense of autonomy that weakens his or her real autonomy. The result is that the person is vulnerable to peer pressure and manipulation by the media. Instead, students should be allowed to see and feel for themselves in the stories and be guided to grasp the fundamental values that are at stake. Using logical analysis, they can confidently apply these values in creative ways. This produces a true autonomy where the individual is able to think originally and so resist peer pressure and manipulation by the media.[9]

An important reason for the success of *Alive to the World* was the use of backward planning. With this method, the objectives for each chapter are set before the chapters are written, assuring that the progression of learning is solidly based upon logical steps as it unfolds. The narrative is focused on age-relevant, real-world situations that can spur critical thinking and constructive dialogue in order to achieve the desired goals. Another basic technique employed was that of scaffolding, by which the teacher becomes a facilitator and mentor as students take an active role in their learning.

In the elaboration of the *Alive to the World* series, the founder drew on the work of researchers such as David Isaacs and Dr. Thomas Likona who proposed models for character building that are linked to what can be termed windows of opportunity in the psychological development of a child.[10] The work of Dr. Melvin Anchell confirmed the authors in the conviction that no explicit or genital information should be given prematurely. Tying this in with the abundance of research that is available on the development of the brain and of mental functions, the books in the series are oriented as follows:

- 0-5 years: Motor skills, affective stability and self-control
- 6-12 year: Ideals and virtues of sport and family
- 13-18 years: Self-mastery again and virtues related to freedom and responsibility
- 19-25 Virtues of knowledge and participation in society

While windows of opportunity provide a framework for character building, educators and parents are encouraged to evaluate the specific circumstances and needs of each child and group of children and to adapt the use of the materials accordingly.

To help teachers to maximize the impact of the programme, *Alive to the World* offers a training course for teachers and volunteers consisting of several modules:

1. Introduction to the *Alive to the World* programme and pedagogy

2. Anthropological foundations
3. Psychological foundations
4. Ethical foundations
5. Family
6. Values of sport
7. Values of social order and harmony
8. Values of diversity and complementarity
9. Values of Integration
10. Values of Friendship
11. Affectivity and sexuality

The course covers a broad range of topics in depth in order to equip education providers with tools to effectively implement the programme.

To close this section, mention should be made of the teacher and student books that are provided. There is a teacher's guide and a student book for 14 levels as follows:

Level 1: Getting to Know Myself (5-6 years old)
Level 2: Happy and Healthy (6-7 years old)
Level 3: Growing Together (7-8 years old)
Level 4: We are a Great Team (8-9 years old)
Level 5: Mine, Yours, Ours (9-10 years old)
Level 6: Different and Complementary (10-11 years old)
Level 7: Friends! (11-12 years old)
Level 8: Changes and Challenges (12-13 years old)
Level 9: Personality Plus (13-14 years old)
Level 10: Worth Waiting For (14-15 years old)
Level 11: Feelings and Ambitions (15-16 years old)
Level 12: The Future Begins Now (16-17 years old)
Level 13: Major Decisions (17-18 years old)
Level 14: Ready for Take-Off (18—19 years old)[11]

Notes

1. Stacey L. Edmonson, Robert Tatman, and John R. Slate, "Character Education: A Critical Analysis.," *International Journal of Educational Leadership Preparation* 4, no. 4 (2009).
2. Eleanor Smith, "The New Moral Classroom: All over the Country, Schools Are Using New Methods to Teach Kids Old Values," *Psychology Today* 23, no. 5 (1989): 33.
3. Martin Luther King, *Stride Toward Freedom: The Montgomery Story*, ed. Clayborne Carson (Boston: Beacon Press, 2010), pt. VI.
4. *Ibid.*, pt. VI.
5. Beltramo, "Marco Teórico Del Proyecto Educación de La Afectividad y La Sexualidad Humana," 58.
6. Carlos Beltramo and Christine de Marcellus Vollmer, *Alive to the World*, Teacher's Guide (Gracewing, 2009), 12.
7. © Alianza Latinoamericana para la Familia (ALAFA), "Teacher Training Course, Module 1– Introduction," 2009 Reproduced with permission.
8. © Alianza Latinoamericana para la Familia (ALAFA) Reproduced with permission.
9. © Alianza Latinoamericana para la Familia (ALAFA) Reproduced with permission.
10. Isaacs, *Character Building*, 15–21.
11. See www.alivetotheworld.org for a synopsis of these texts.

12 EVIL, SIN, AND DISINTEGRATION

Virtue without freedom is not virtue. At the very beginning of this handbook, the case of aliens visiting earth was presented. There is a big difference between persons being forced to conform to a social order and persons who do so freely and who contribute to it through spontaneous and generous initiative. In the latter case, citizens are happy doing good because they are virtuous. It has been proven that this obeys a neurological reality: doing good and sacrificing for others produces endorphin-type chemicals which give a sense of well-being.[1] To use the term developed in this document, they have integrated lives.

Respecting freedom, however, has the risk that persons can choose to do evil. When someone habitually chooses disordered acts, this is the opposite of virtue. It is vice. It consists in an evil disposition of the will to "hijack" the intelligence, so that selfish motives prevail in decision-making as opposed to universal values. These can be, for example, excessive love of comfort, disordered pleasure, exaggerated desire for recognition, domination over others, etc. Following on the natural inclinations, it is natural for the intelligence to recognize the spiritual values and virtues as good and worthy of putting into practice. To do evil, the will does violence to the intelligence, directing it to side-line the consideration of transcendent goods, perhaps regarding them as unrealistic, over-idealistic or impractical.

Our habits forge our character. Thus, a young man who repeatedly makes selfish decisions will develop a selfish disposition at the core of his way of being. His recurring poor choices give rise to disordered habits or vice which cements his self-seeking orientation. In a quiet moment, the conscience awakens, and this person will see the ugliness and repulsiveness of this deep-rooted disposition. Given over to whims, he will see his lack of internal harmony, and, at the same time, his disconnect with others and a sense of meaninglessness to his life. This state of affairs is the opposite of integration. It is the disintegration of the human person.

The concept of disintegration can be illustrated in the context of the core natural tendencies. We will consider three scenarios that are highlighted in the teacher training notes of the Alive to the World programme.[2] Regarding the drive to feel safe, we can consider a healthy scenario to be that of a woman, for example, who has managed to cover her basic needs and has a healthy lifestyle. She feels free from imminent threats to her life and livelihood, has developed a good appreciation of her limits and is confidently able to evaluate and manage her fear of harm. In her routine, she works diligently, is hardworking and ordered, having in mind not just her own well-being, but those of others as well. All these elements, consistently lived, contribute to an integrated way of being.

It can occur, in a different case, that the drive to feel safe may be excessive and disordered. This happens when egoism dominates, leading to corrupt practices, deception and manipulation of others, and the disregard for the well-being of others. Work is not done diligently, but only for personal gain. A lady who lives in this way will find herself plagued with anxiety and low self-esteem. Her way of being is progressively disintegrated.

Turning to the sense of belonging or being valued for who one is, in a healthy situation, a boy, for example, feels loved and respected for who he is by his family and friends. In his dealings with them he is cared for and they are attentive to his concerns, treating him with wholesome affection and respect. All this he also reciprocates so that in his relationships there is mutual loyalty, caring, modesty and faithfulness. By developing relationships in this way, he has a strong and healthy sense of belonging to his family and community. When all these elements are present in a consistent way, they contribute to the forming of an integrated way of being.

In a different case, the desire for belonging may have an inappropriate expression. It may be the case that a boy is taken advantage of emotionally by a gang leader who provides the role of a father figure that the boy never had. Search for belonging in gangs or close-knit groups that are involved in destructive behaviour is not coherent with sound decision making based on values. The desire to be valued for who one is can also go awry, for example, when it becomes an emotional dependency in a relationship. Take the case of a woman who is emotionally dependent on a man she is seeing for company and romance and the man on the woman for physical pleasure. Such mutual dependencies lead to dysfunctional and abusive relationships and both parties suffer anxiety and low self-esteem. In situations such as these, integration is undermined, and the individuals involved experience disintegration in their nature as a human being.

Another powerful drive is that for significance or being valued for a role in a community. A wholesome case would be that of a man who, through honest hard work, understands and has developed his talents. In the working world and in his community, he is recognized by his colleagues, those in authority and friends for his contribution over many years of dedication in his field. He has thus acquired prestige and persons seek out and value his contribution in his area of expertise. This individual feels settled in his career and works to improve the standards of excellence and integrity that are upheld in his profession. In this and in other ways, he goes beyond the call of duty, seeing his profession as a way to serve and improve society. Having this attitude, the man in question does not seek recognition for personal affirmation but sees it as a reality he can lean on to influence policies, customs and culture in a way that advances justice, freedom, participation and the common good, bolstering respect for the dignity of every citizen. Reaching such a place and having a well-respected role in society, this person understands himself to be a protagonist in the betterment of society and is enthusiastic and confident in the contributions he makes. He is generous in doing so out of a sense of responsibility and love for his people and all mankind.

The scenario presented above may seem idealistic. Anthropology of Integration suggests that through appropriate character-building strategies, it is actually within the reach of the common man or woman. All that was included in the description of a wholesome state of affairs in having a healthy sense of significance is valid for all occupations, from those that are more intellectual such as architecture or engineering, to those that are more manual such as masonry, carpentry and domestic services. As the features described acquire a greater solidity and consistency, the subject under consideration has a more integrated life.

As with the other core emotions considered, the drive to be valued for one's role and contribution can be skewed and inappropriate. A case that is often encountered is that of a boy who fails to settle during his teenage years due to a lack of proper parenting and a rebellious attitude on his part. He drifts into the wrong crowd and just wants to have fun, often in disordered ways. A boy in this situation is unlikely to understand and develop his talents. Persons in authority and his more serious colleagues will have little regard for what he is able to contribute, seeing the bad decisions that he is making. If the situation is not remedied, he will acquire a bad reputation of being frivolous, incompetent and perhaps spoilt. The desire for recognition persists. If the teenager does not try to "pull up his socks" and seek to merit the esteem of adults and his more serious colleagues, he most likely will turn to his peers who are having a bad influence on him. The desire to stand out will make him try to impress them by doing silly and irrational things such as proving he can hold alcohol better than others, driving more recklessly, getting away with flouting the law, doing dangerous stunts and other immature things like these, thinking that it makes him "cool". To feel recognized, the individual in question may be loud in dress and appearance, get into fights, and try to impress impressionable girls in deceptive ways. Unabated it leads to delinquency. In a quiet moment, this subject will see that he is getting nowhere in life and is a burden to society. He experiences low-self-esteem and can easily fall into depression. Some teens in this situation commit suicide. Through poor choices and the absence of proper guidance, the way of being and the life of this teenager becomes progressively disintegrated.

To address disintegration, it is important to know that there is well founded hope that one can change. A single good deed where the three levels of action are engaged contributes to building and restoring integrity. Much more impactful are repeated good actions. Traditionally these are called good habits because they become integrated as dispositions to perform good deeds. Getting up a little earlier to exercise, for example, may be very difficult the first time you try. If you stick to it, it becomes easier over time and can even become second nature. This is an important reason why great attention should be given to individual actions, even though they have to do with little things.

Some individual actions, however, have an important impact beyond that of being habit forming. This occurs when the actions concern grave evils. These are actions that show open disregard for fundamental values such as life, family and fairness, values we know to be constitutive of human dignity. One thing is not to study today for an important exam, but another is to bribe someone for the answers or for a grade. The first can be the beginning of a bad habit or the falling away of a good one, but the second does greater internal damage. If not corrected, it is like a structural fault in the whole edifice of our being that makes us inhuman and antisocial in some way. It impacts directly and radically on one's sense of self and one's personal relationships with others and God. A girl in university, for example, who performs a gravely evil act like hacking the school system and falsifying her grades, if she is caught, will be regarded as a criminal, and will be immediately expelled from her programme. She will be ousted from the university community and kept apart until she can prove that she has changed and can behave in a dignified way. Most likely there will be criminal proceedings.

We all naturally agree that some acts are outright criminal and ought to be punished. We know it to be a demand of justice. When that person is our own self, it is natural that we apply the same judgment in a moment of clear thinking. I see myself as a subject unworthy of being valued by others. I have betrayed the dignity given to me by the creator. My sense of self-worth plummets for having disregarded a fundamental value. In the example above, it was the virtue of justice. If, out of pride, I do not repent for committing a gravely evil act, I can come to see myself as unworthy to belong in the community of human beings, because I have shown disregard for the dignity of others. How can I demand that my own dignity be now affirmed and respected? Furthermore, I am aware that I have turned my back on God, on Him who gave me my dignity as a gift. Only He can now restore it because my dignity did not come from myself. Failing reconciliation, persons who commit gravely evil acts can become entrenched in delinquent behaviour, become antisocial and join antisocial groups. Alternately, tormented by guilt, they can fall into depression and be driven to suicide.

Vice and gravely evil actions cause structural defects in one's being and leads to unhappiness. There is a positive side, however, in that there is almost always a remedy. If a young girl who has strayed is humble, for example, she will seek help, open herself to others and accept the counsel and support she receives to patiently mend her life. It is moving and edifying to hear, for example, the testimonies of persons who participate in support groups such as alcoholics anonymous or sexaholics anonymous, who have changed their outlook on life and have overcome their addictions. When a person seeks help quickly from someone they trust—a parent, sibling or friend, the damage can also be quickly averted. A case that is not unusual is that of a young woman working on her career who has an unplanned pregnancy. She realizes that this will set back her career goals significantly and add financial and psychological burdens that she is not prepared for at the moment. To make things worse, perhaps her boyfriend has abandoned her to flee the responsibility. In circumstances such as these, a girl may opt for an abortion without telling anyone, thinking that it will just erase everything, and life can get back to normal.

There is another side to having an abortion, however, to which she may fail to give due consideration. The child within her is her own child, which is a marvellous gift—the gift of human life. Mothers who have an abortion often suffer from tremendous guilt afterwards that requires years of support to adequately deal with. When the pregnancy was first discovered, the setbacks seemed insurmountable. Women who have chosen to have their child, however, never regret it and testify that things work out more easily than they would have imagined because of the avalanche of support that somehow appears. A young lady who gets pregnant when she is not ready to have a child sees the impact on her goals and may not have the full picture from a deeper anthropological perspective. The best thing that she can do in such a circumstance is to speak up and confide what has happened to someone who loves her and is ready to support her. Doing this, she can be helped to see the bigger picture and to make a wiser decision. Much damage, internal and external could be avoided in this way. Because of this, the virtue of sincerity is invaluable and almost indispensable for developing and maintaining an integrity.

Sin and evil constantly threaten integration. Evil can be prevented by the practice of virtue. In addition, it is important to be sincere and to seek counsel from wise persons who care for us and are there to guide, correct and encourage us. Often, however, the evil is already done, and part of the support needed is forgiveness for wrongdoing. When someone is taken to court, a sentence is given that the condemned must fulfil. That person may get a lesser sentence if he or she shows willingness to remedy the harm done and to reform his or her life. This, however, is not the forgiveness that a subject seeks in the depth of his or her being. An individual who acknowledges his or her sin, seeks to have his or her dignity as a human being restored. If I am that person, I will experience some restoration if I am reassured of acceptance and love by those close to me. On a deeper level, however, I know that no one but the creative power can forgive me for taking for granted the gift of my very self. Faith is needed to acknowledge one's sins before this supreme being in the depth of one's heart, and to trust in the infinite mercy and love of the ever-present, all-knowing Deity.

It is useful here to call to mind, for example, the many episodes and stories in the bible that assures one of the unfailing mercy of God. A parable that stands out is that of the prodigal son.[3] He squanders his inheritance on loose living. Then, in that state of alienation and hopelessness, he "comes to his senses" and acknowledges that his brokenness is a consequence of his selfish pursuits. A longing for his father's house, which he alienated himself from, wells up within him and he has a burning desire to be whole again and to belong again. He returns to the home of his father and asks for forgiveness. His father had been longing for his return. On seeing him, he runs out to meet him. The son confesses that he had foolishly gone after selfish pursuits, taking all he had for granted. His father embraces him, puts sandals on his feet and a robe around him—symbols of restored dignity. Then he has the fattened calf killed and the entire household is called to make merry for the return of the lost son. Through faith, forgiveness becomes an experience of joy, and an opportunity for a new commitment to be close to God and others. Part of this commitment will be a determined struggle to develop an integrated life through the practice of the virtues.

Notes

1. "Brain Imaging Reveals Joys of Giving," National Institutes of Health (NIH), May 26, 2015, https://www.nih.gov/news-events/nih-research-matters/brain-imaging-reveals-joys-giving.
2. © Alianza Latinoamericana para la Familia (ALAFA), "Teacher Training Course, Module 2—Anthropology," 2009. Reproduced with permission.
3. Luke 15:11–32.

13 INTEGRATION AND IDENTITY

This text has presented human action as occurring on three levels, the biological, the emotional and the spiritual. These distinctions are important because they help us to appreciate that there are many factors that influence how a person—including the writer and reader of this document—may react to a given situation. On the biological level, there are genetic and developmental conditions that impact on how the memory and imagination are engaged before an external stimulus. Stepping up to the emotional dimension, modern psychology has helped us to appreciate how dynamism here accounts for a great deal of human behaviour. Having a spiritual component, emotions have a far deeper and lasting impact on behaviour compared to the biological level. There are deep emotions that drive a subject powerfully to possess goods that are perceived to satisfy strong drives related to the sense of self. As these drives often regard goods that persist through time or that require consistent action to be obtained in the future, they influence action in a habitual way, having an important impact on a person's entire way of being. The effort to habitually have the right feelings and a fitting response in different circumstances that is in accord with human dignity is an important part of character formation. Then there is the spiritual level, where, along with self-awareness, which begins on the emotional level, personal freedom comes to the fore through the action of the intelligence and will.

Making these distinctions are important for many reasons. Regarding ordinary life, they prevent us from judging the actions of our own selves or others in a simplistic way. Teachers who work with children needing remedial work, for example, know that a child who is not performing in a regular classroom setting can easily be seen as badly behaved. It turns out that the bad behaviour is often not the cause but the effect of not being able to perform. Learning disabilities linked to genetic or emotional disadvantages can be the cause of this non-performance and with appropriate remedial attention, these deficiencies can be addressed. The disruptive behaviour then disappears. The reader may also be familiar with the example that Stephen Covey—may his soul rest in peace—liked to give to illustrate over-simplification at times. He tells the story of being in a bus where a mother seemed completely unable to control her three children who were being very disruptive. It reached a point where he felt he needed to do something and asked the mother to settle her children. She explained that they had just come back from the hospital where they had accompanied their father in his last moments. Their bouncing around was probably their way of handling it. Hearing this, Stephen Covey was completely disarmed and felt embarrassed for having judged the children as unruly and the mother as lacking control without thinking that something may have happened that upset them emotionally. Like this, there are of course many examples, and the reader can most probably think of a number of scenarios where he or she has personally experienced this sort of superficial appraisement or rash judgement taking place.

Making clear distinctions between the factors affecting human behaviour has been the first task of the presentation in this handbook. Throughout the exposition, however, it has been emphasized that, as distinctions are made, it is with the view of understanding how the different elements work together to bring about the overall well-being and happiness of the whole person. This led to the important notion of integration.

Integration takes place in two ways. There is upward or cognitive integration where powerful natural tendencies on the lower levels lead the intelligence to grasp fundamental universal goods of human nature on the spiritual level. Freedom intervenes when these goods are adhered to as fundamental values that are objective and personal at the same time. There is also downward or formative integration where objective goods that are understood on the spiritual level are accepted by the subject in such a way that they generate positive feelings and independent decision making, leading to attitudes and behaviour that reflect the internalization of that which is known and accepted. Cognitive and formative integration mutually reinforce each other. The values that are adhered to in cognitive integration are the integrative principles for orienting the emotions and guiding actions in formative integration. These in term dispose the intelligence to more readily grasp the values at stake in new scenarios that life brings.

Take the case of a girl or woman, for example, who normally tries to make decisions and cultivate habits that are rooted in fundamental values. When she is in any given situation, her patterns of thought from these past decisions and the habits that she would have cultivated will be automatically engaged. She would experience appropriate feelings that point her to consider the fundamental values that are at stake and how they apply in the given situation. In this way the fundamental values are reinforced. When a subject is faithful to the core values at the heart of human dignity, he or she acquires a progressively more integrated way of being. There is a greater actuality in body/soul unity which brings personal growth and true human fulfilment.

13.1 Identity

The notion of the human person as an integrated unity has a direct relationship to the concept of identity. Identity answers the question: *who am I?* It begs further questioning: *Why do I exist? What is my purpose?* On the metaphysical plane, there is an objective aspect to identity. My identity is my current state of actuality as an integrated being plus my real potential to attain a more fully and complete actualized state through integration. From this perspective, our truest identity is not linked to a present state of bodily, emotional, and spiritual activity, but rather in the full actuality that is possible by striving to live a more integrated life.

In the media and in contemporary culture, identity is often associated with emotions. This is so deep rooted that Mark Yarhouse speaks of a script that runs as follows:

> • The feelings that emerge when you imagine yourself free from oppressive societal norms from the past are natural.
> • These feelings, especially the sexual ones, tell you who you really are. They reveal your identity.

- If you supress these feelings, you will never be yourself and will never be happy.
- Look for a community that can help you to be yourself.[1]

This is very misleading and based on a faulty and dangerous anthropology. It reduces the essence of the human person to his or her emotions. This gravely undermines the true dignity of the human person as an integrated being with three dimensions: body, emotions, and spirit.

Sexual feelings are real, and a person may even feel attraction to persons of the same sex. The intellect can consider the nature of these feelings and come to understand that there is an inclination which is oriented toward procreation and marriage. The concrete expression of a feeling may be disordered, but the nature of it continues to hint at a good for the human person. This is because the nature of a thing does not hinge on a singular expression, but the end or purpose that emerges in when it is considered universally—as something belonging to human nature. A sexual feeling that may be excessive or misdirected does not determine identity but points, rather, to a lack of proper integration.

If we admit a wholistic approach to identity, then the body too is important. Consider the case of girl of 11 or 12 years old who feels attraction to other girls and displays some of the aggressive behaviour that is typical of boys her age. She may even feel a distaste for feminine ways of dressing and talking and feeling attractive. It is likely that her peers at school or in the neighbourhood would pick up on her boyish ways and tease her about it. Within herself she could be very confused and wonder if she was meant to be a boy as many things about how she feels are like boys. Now suppose we were to take this girl to a clinic to get a thorough biological profile. We would discover that she has a feminine brain, a feminine bone structure, a feminine immune system, a feminine liver, not to mention a feminine reproductive system. These things are much harder to change than feelings because feeling depend on thoughts and we have control of our thoughts. It would not be wrong to say that there are more stable things about this individual that is feminine than is masculine. The clinic may well discover that the testosterone and oestrogen levels of this girl are not in the usual ranges for a girl of that age. Treating her to normalize the levels of these hormones in her blood can significantly bring her emotional reactions to be more in line with a typical girl her age.

In common language, identity is associated with things that make us unique and/or which are constant in one's life. In terms of uniqueness, each person has a unique identity that is received as a free gift from the creative power at the origin of his or her coming into being. Part of the identity of every human being is the unique relationship of creator/creature which is established with the creation of each soul. God creates out of faithful love, and so part of the radical uniqueness of each person is that he or she is a child of God and called to love in a unique way to build up the family of God.

There is also a uniqueness that arises out of the relationship parent/child that is established in procreation. Every child is a gift entrusted to parents as a life that belongs to them. It works the other way too—parents belong to their children. This lifelong mutual belonging makes each individual in a family unique and unrepeatable. They are expected to love each other, help each other, and feel responsible for the lifelong happiness of each other. Family is an important part of one's identity.

Relationships of belonging can take place in different ways and to different degrees as people come together in communities. The people of the country where one grows up, for example, are felt to be extended family in some way. We are raised by our family, but also by the community around us. This is a relationship of mutual belonging that is weaker than that of the nuclear family, but nevertheless very real. A person feels that he owes it to his fellow countrymen to work hard, to care for them and to promote a better life and standard of living for all, in response to all that he or she has freely received. The society you grow up in is also part of your identity.

To flesh out the idea of identity, different levels of relationships of belonging have been considered. It is assumed that these relationships are healthy and lead to an integrated life. To a lesser degree, commodities as well can be part of identity when they are held as lasting personal belongings and as something one must care for and cultivate. Such commodities could be cultural goods such as language, education, rituals, health, various skills and competencies. They can be material goods as well. People feel a strong connection to the hills, mountains, and rivers of the places where they grew up. The produce of the fields and the local dishes freshly prepared are realities that are treasured as blessings and gifts that are part of a shared heritage that ought to be cherished and passed on to others. This too is part of identity.

While many aspects of identity can be identified, anthropology of integration suggests that the unifying principle is the progressive actualization of an integrated life. Only in this way can a person be said to be who he or she truly is.

Centring on the deepest aspect of identity, from a subjective perspective, identity is experienced as a sense of harmony, connection and identification with the origin and purpose of my unique existence as a unity of body and soul. The framework presented in this book suggests that this harmony and identification with one's origin and purpose cannot be separated from personal adherence to the fundamental goods of human nature. This occurs because the fundamental goods of human nature, when they are perceived, not only are they grasped as unchanging and universal, but also as obligatory in accordance with the principle of *synderesis* which says: "Do good and avoid evil". The fundamental goods of Life, Family and Society, when grasped, are understood to be benchmarks of right and wrong. The goal, purpose and meaning of human life is at stake. Acting in accord with these goods keeps us in "good standing", one might say, with our nature and with the entire race of human beings who share our nature. One feels a strong sense of belonging in the family of human beings, and harmony with the origin and purpose of one's life. Acting contrary to these goods places us as "outcasts", one might say, with regard to our nature and with the entire race of human beings. There is a loss of harmony and identification with the origin and purpose of one's life. A man who recognizes the fundamental goods and fails to adhere to them feels a deep sense of guilt and alienation from his creator, his purpose and his own true self. In a moment of clarity, his conscience will

Integration and identity

judge him unworthy of being valued by others. This deep lack of self-worth, if not addressed, can be the origin of harmful and destructive behaviour, leading the subject on a downward spiral of internal conflict, disconnect with others and despair.

The table below illustrates the relationship between knowledge of fundamental goods, personal adherence to these goods, and sense of dignity or self-worth and identity on the spiritual level.

Knowledge of a good that perfects human nature	Personal adherence to that good	Sense of dignity (self-worth) and identity
I know it as a fundamental good of human nature, worthy of adherence	I choose to adhere to this good as core to my belief system. It informs and guides the development of my way of being, excluding contrary elements.	Strong. I know myself to be united and in harmony with the Supreme Being at the origin of this good and my nature. He will help me to reach my full potential. I am secure and stable in who I am.
I know it as a fundamental good of human nature, worthy of adherence.	I do not adhere to it as core to my belief system. There are elements contrary to it that inform and guide the development of my way of being.	Weak. I am alienated from what I see as good and will never possess it. I do not seek unity and harmony with a Supreme Being at the origin of this good and my nature. I am internally divided. I will never attain my full potential. I am insecure and unstable in who I am.

Figure 13.1 The relationship between knowledge of fundamental goods, personal adherence and sense of self-worth and identity.

As a subjective reality, identity is not something static, but grows as the subject acquires a more integrated way of being. This happens because integration consists in grasping and adhering to fundamental goods, and bringing them into one's decisions, feelings and actions. A girl or woman who is progressing in living in an integrated way will experience a deepening connection and identification with her origin and purpose in life. This brings growth in a healthy sense of self-worth and self-confidence. She feels secure and stable in who she is.

The presentation above does not pretend to give a detailed discussion about identity, but mainly to show its connection to personal growth through integration. Looked at in a subjective way, one can find persons who connect their identity in realities that may even be at odds with the fundamental goods. The human person is free and so is capable of identifying himself or herself with whatever is capable of being idolized as a God. Money, power, and pleasure, for example, are the usual candidates. When the desire to be materially rich predominates and shapes the decisions, feelings, and actions of a young woman, for example, then the question of who I am becomes difficult to answer. One can say that she was born to consume and experience comfort and pleasure, but this belies the true dignity of the human person. She may have a feeling of fulfilment and accomplishment at some point when she is materially well off. This, however, must be recognized as superficial and vain, because material things do not endure. They are not capable of satisfying the deeper tendencies of the human spirit.

Notes

1. Mark A. Yarhouse, *Homosexuality and the Christian: A Guide for Parents, Pastors, and Friends* (Bloomington, MN: Baker Publishing Group, 2010), 48.

CONCLUSION

This handbook is an attempt to unpack for teachers and educators, the richness of the simple proposition that the human person is a unity of body and soul. It suggests that there are different dimensions of the human person that need to be carefully differentiated and articulated, and at the same time, there is a unity that must be understood and fostered for our behaviour to be truly human. This perspective where differences and unity are affirmed at the same time is what is meant in general by the notion of integration. The handbook seeks to give a new fresh perspective on the human person from this point of view, developing the notion of integration in the context of time-tested metaphysical principles and modern discoveries in psychology and neuroscience. There is upward or cognitive integration where biological and emotional tendencies lead to the comprehension and acceptance of fundamental goods of human nature in the spiritual faculties. There is also downward or formative integration where values imbue and orient the emotional and corporeal dimensions of the human person. In this way a philosophical framework is provided for the task of forming the characters of the children and young persons of today who will shape the future of society.

Persons involved in the moral education of young people today are aware that moral norms are no longer accepted for the fact of being established by an authority. The new generation has the view that leaders can be wrong or motivated by greed and self-interest. As a result, they can twist the norms to pressure or brainwash people into keeping them in power. These and other doubts make it expedient to move from a morality of obligation to a morality of integration. Everyone wants to be truly happy and young people are searching for something different from the status quo. A long list of qualifications is no longer the criteria for winning the ear of the new generation. Authenticity and friendship are just as much valued for getting their approval.

Anthropology of integration is just the opposite of the rigid morality of obligation. It does not begin with a meticulously elaborated logical system proposed as an ideal for morally upright behaviour or for a perfect society. Instead values are naturally grasped through cognitive integration and applied using logical reasoning and open discussion where freedom has an important role. Education has a function to play in facilitating the proper integration of values and virtues in the lives of each individual.

The framework presented also supersedes the utilitarian perspective prevalent today where the criteria for evaluating moral action are often based on a quality of life ethic, which loses sight of the transcendent dimension of the human person. Anthropology of integration develops the idea from classical philosophy that the human person is a unity of body and soul. The material aspects of the human person are fully affirmed but without losing sight of his or her spiritual or transcendent dimension.

The system of Marxism has become a tool for oppression in many places. It postulates the ideal of a classless society that is brought about by revolution

Conclusion

where the end justifies the means. The system may be well elaborated, but the premises are faulty. The perspective defended in this text does not propose an ideal scenario of a perfect world from which moral obligations are derived. Whatever that reality may be in the future, the path to building it begins with the clues in our nature, with the crude natural inclinations in the organic systems that make up the human body. These, however, must be integrated upward to the spiritual realm where the intelligence grasps the fundamental goods of human nature. It is up to each individual to adhere to these values and to integrate them into their lives with the help of others. The way individuals then associate to form communities and societies cannot be predetermined. Each person freely discovers and chooses his or her path in life. When the values and the virtues are widely adhered to and integrated, one can have faith that society will be united and strong and authentic progress will be assured.

It was mentioned that the youth today are attracted by authenticity and friendship. This is something generally to be praised. It can go awry, however, when being authentic is construed as giving way to one's feelings and emotions without critically evaluating them. The analogy of the boat is useful here again. It helps to have a powerful motor, but without an adequate braking and navigation system, the vessel may end up lost or shipwrecked. Similarly, emotions need to be guided and managed by reason and the cultivation of good habits. Added to this, contemporary marketing strategies are very sophisticated, where artificial intelligence is used to suggest products to individual users on the Internet in a way that is particularly suited to their preferences. One can have the sensation of giving free expression to one's uniqueness while actually being led along emotionally to favour certain products and even purchase them. At times the product one is led to can be addictive as in the case of pornography and gambling. The paradox appears where, beginning with a sense of exercising freedom, one ends up a slave to an addiction.

The study that has been presented can be considered a framework for a programme of character building understood as integral human development. It is meant for everyone, independent of the religious persuasion of the persons reached. Reading the text, some persons may be concerned about the scarcity of considerations related to God and faith. The handbook is meant to help teachers, educators and parents of all faiths in the transmission of values and virtues to the next generation. It uses arguments based on philosophical principles and science, which provide a convincing and self-contained body of knowledge for this task. We live in a pluralistic society, where citizens of different religious persuasions must come together to address social ills and formulate common policies. In this context it is important, if not necessary, to have a common ground for reflection and dialogue based on principles that can be argued and defended on the basis of our shared nature and dignity as human beings. Faith can and ought to inform this discussion. At the same time, it ought to be acknowledged that the basic tools for an effective dialogue between different cultures are those accessible by the natural light of reason.

Conclusion

While the text does not adopt arguments based on religious faith, the ideas and concepts presented in this book are not opposed in any way to religious beliefs but are rather in harmony with them. The framework presented uses metaphysical principles from the Aristotelian and Thomistic tradition. The notion of God as first and final cause underlies and sustains these principles. In the discussion on values and virtues, for example, the ultimate grounding for adhering to spiritual goods was shown to be a relationship with God.

On the question of harmony with religious belief, a particularly interesting aspect of virtue is the fact that the reward for virtue, if there is one, cannot be assigned to life on earth. By its very nature, a virtuous act is done because it is good, and not because there is a quantifiable reward or punishment attached on this earth. In fact, virtue can demand accepting suffering and death rather than doing evil. Nevertheless, it seems right that virtue should be rewarded, and this leads to faith in the afterlife where those who led good lives are rewarded and those who did evil without repenting are punished.

It is outside the scope of this handbook to discuss in detail how anthropology of integration connects with and can enrich religious belief. Further study will be needed to elaborate on this important topic.

A particular strength of the perspective presented in this work, is the connection with human dignity. This link is developed, not as an add-on, but intrinsic to the notion of integration. We are living a time in human history where the dignity of the human person, every human person, needs to be affirmed and respected anew. There is a lot of fanfare to equality, but in practice, there are deep-rooted prejudices and stereotypes that often govern a person's reactions in different situations and also his or her self-perception. In some places there are structural inequalities, where certain groups are unfairly privileged over others in the laws and customs of a society. Integration ties in with human dignity because at the spiritual level, the fundamental human values are adhered to from seeing and accepting others as "another me". They have the characteristic of being universal, immutable and obligatory. From this fundamental intuition and choice, an individual captures the validity of the golden rule to do unto others as one would have them do unto you. He or she will understand the need to cultivate the virtues of integration and will feel compelled to acknowledge, respect and bolster the dignity of every human person. Human dignity and the fundamental goods of human nature go hand in hand. This link is made at the heart of anthropology of integration.

To close, it is hoped that this text will provide new lights and encouragement for the reader in his or her task of forming the next generation. The work of a parent, teacher and educator can never be sufficiently recognized. It is a true vocation, and love is the only explanation for the many sacrifices they make for others every day. They are unsung heroes who spend themselves every day to nourish the bodies and minds of the little ones in their care. This book is meant to support them in this task, so that sound up-to-date philosophy may orient their love to effectively educate and guide their children.

www.ingramcontent.com/pod-product-compliance
Lightning Source LLC
Chambersburg PA
CBHW030333240426
43661CB00052B/1620